FORBIDDEN LAND

FORBIDDEN LAND

THE STRUGGLE FOR ACCESS TO MOUNTAIN AND MOORLAND

Tom Stephenson

with a personal memoir by Mike Harding

edited by Ann Holt

Manchester University Press

Manchester and New York

Distributed exclusively in the USA and Canada by St. Martin's Press

Copyright © The Ramblers' Association 1989

Published by Manchester University Press
Oxford Road, Manchester M13 9PL, UK
and Room 400, 175 Fifth Avenue,
New York, NY 10010, USA

Distributed exclusively in the USA and Canada
by St. Martin's Press, Inc.,
175 Fifth Avenue, New York, NY 10010, USA

British Library cataloguing in publication data
Stephenson, Tom, *1893–1987*
   Forbidden land: the struggle for access to
   mountain and moorland.
   1. Great Britain.   Rural regions.   Private
   land.   Access by public
   I. Title   II. Holt, Ann
   33.73'17

Library of Congress cataloging in publication data applied for

ISBN 0–7190–2891–4 *hardback*
     0–7190–2966–X *paperback*

Photoset in Linotron Plantin
by Northern Phototypesetting Co, Bolton

Printed in Great Britain
by Biddles Ltd, Guildford and King's Lynn

Contents

Illustrations

Unless otherwise indicated, the photographs are from the Ramblers' Association Collection

Front cover: High Cup Nick from the Pennine Way. Photograph by Tom Stephenson
Back cover: Tom Stephenson, 1986. Photograph by Mike Harding

Acknowledgements

Tom Stephenson called his book on the campaign for access to uncultivated land 'The Right to Roam', a slogan associated with the campaign. This is not a title which appeals to present-day publishers, so Tom's book comes into the world as 'Forbidden land'. This adapts the title of a pamphlet written by E. A. Baker, a writer much admired by Tom, and the Ramblers' Association's current campaign 'Forbidden Britain', which continues to highlight the denial of rights access to the walker.

Tom was helped in the writing of his book by Eileen Daley and Hilda Beaufoy, and also by Andrew Dalby of the Ramblers' Association National Office. I would like to thank them on his behalf and apologise to anyone whose contribution he would have wished to acknowledge but of which I am unaware. As editor I had much assistance from Alan Mattingly, Director of the RA, and from Stephen Morton, who, sadly, died while this book was in preparation. My thanks are also due to Lt.-Col. Gerald Haythornthwaite, Roger Sidaway, Ruby Irlam, Manchester Reference Library Local History and Archive sections, the House of Commons Library, and to the RA staff and Pedestrians' Association volunteers who were inconvenienced by my burrowing in the RA archives. The RA has supported publication of this book generously, but the opinions expressed in it are those of Tom Stephenson and the editor as individuals. Finally I am also grateful to my husband, David Rubinstein, who acted as resident social historian and general encourager to the project.

Ann Holt
1988

The publishers wish to acknowledge the material assistance of the Countryside Commission, made available through the Ramblers' Association, in enabling the book to be published in a popular format.

Part 1
Tom Stephenson

A personal memoir

Mike Harding

Tom always insisted that he wanted no memorial, plaque or hagiography after his death. He objected forcefully to the idea of a bronze statue at either end of the Pennine Way because, as he said, it would turn it into a mausoleum.

It was not that Tom was shy or self-effacing or even mock-humble. He just hadn't any time for all those things. He was more concerned that people should get on with living and fighting for the things that had been his own lifetime struggle; access to and the conservation of our national heritage – the open spaces of these islands.

To all but certain gamekeepers, politicians and military men Tom was an extremely likeable, even lovable man. He suffered fools not gladly at all and what hatred he did have within him he reserved for the spivs and crooks and warmongers that he saw running the world. He was uncompromising in his espousal of what he saw as the truth and he worked tirelessly for the cause he believed in.

I came to know him only towards the end of his life, when a walk of anything more than a few hundred yards was a major struggle. But during those half-dozen years we spent a good deal of time together. Friends would bring him from his home in Oxfordshire to our house in the Yorkshire Dales and we would spend days driving round the area in which he had spent so many of his younger rambling days, the Pennine Dales of Yorkshire, the Howgill Fells and the still inaccessible fells of Bowland.

I have a photograph of Tom taken on one of those trips when, altogether with my wife Pat and Eileen Daley, a lifetime friend and a great helpmeet of his latter years, we drove through the Trough of Bowland. All along the road, every hundred yards or so, were wooden signboards carrying the hated legend 'PRIVATE. KEEP OUT'.

After we had passed a couple of dozen or so of these signs Tom asked me to stop the car because he wanted to take a photograph of them. Then, in his ninety-third year, he was still as angry and concerned about the lack of access to the Bowland fells as he had been fifty years before. The photograph shows him with a grin on his face standing by the sign, both feet trespassing.

To the end of his long life, though this body failed him, Tom's mind was as keen as ever. His memory was quite amazing and he could quote verbatim sections of parliamentary acts, remember almost to the hour dates and times of meetings that took place thirty or forty years ago – who was there, what was said, and often how so and so had gone back on his word or such and such had been as good as his word years later. He was a good friend but he must have been a terrible enemy.

Yet a quality that many of us will remember him for was his sense of humour and love of a bit of fun. Unlike most politically committed people he could laugh at himself and see the funny side of most things. He never lost the soft burr of the North Lancashire accent and towards the end of his life it became even more pronounced. He would tell stories of meetings with keepers and landowners that would have people howling with laughter. He had an incredible memory for places and people too. He could tell you the name of every hill and beck and copse and stone outcrop, not just in the Pennines, but in Wales and Scotland too. He seemed to have complete visual recall of the whole of the landscape, almost as though the Ordnance Survey's complete output had been imprinted in his head. He knew the land so well, of course, because he had walked every corner of it. He also knew a tremendous amount about wild flowers and animals and, of course, geology, his first love, gave him an understanding of the landscape that I have found few other men possess.

People figured largely in Tom's life, too. He would remember with affection the farmer's wife who refused payment for a glass of milk when, as a young lad he was tramping the hills. Driving through the Bowland Fells one day, he pointed out a farm close to the roadside.

'I used to stay at that farm once,' he said. 'This road was just a rough track then and I used to stop here at the end of my first day's walking from Whalley on my way up the Dales or into the Lake District. The farmer used to like my staying there. He had thirteen daughters. I think he was looking to marry one of them off.' Then he paused and with a grin said, 'But I wasn't to be catched. I was more interested in walking.'

Tom was one of the last of a long line of northern autodidacts, men and women who worked sixty or more hours a week in the mills and factories yet still managed to educate themselves, often to a high level. It was a tradition that went back a long way and can be seen in such men as the shepherd Jemmy Dawson of Sedburgh, who taught himself Euclid while minding his flocks on the Howgill Fells and went on to become Professor of Mathematics at Cambridge University. It goes on through the characters described in Mrs Gaskell's *Mary Barton*, through the Mechanics' Institutes and Botanical Societies where men who had been in the mills all week tramped the hills on their day off studying and collecting plants, ferns and insects, scraping together what money they had to buy collectively a rare or expensive book on plants. The thirst for knowledge of such men and women was incredible. Billy Holt of Todmorden tells how he taught himself Latin, Greek and most of the European languages as he stood at his loom, writing the words down in the cotton dust on the bars. Billy went on to become a well-known writer, broadcaster and visionary painter.

Such a thirst for learning Tom had and though he was thwarted from taking his degree by his criminal record for pacifism, he never lost that love for learning. His vast reading gave him an understanding and an ability with words that produced a clear and direct prose style and a great command of the language. His submission to the court martial at Saltburn in 1918 published in this book is a wonderful example of English prose at its best. 'You, as much as I,' he told them, 'are but puppets in the play. We matter very little in the march of humanity. The significant fact is that there are twelve hundred men in gaol today and all the king's horses and all the king's men cannot make soldiers of them.'

Tom was an unforgettable man and it is a shame in a way that there will be no memorial for him, because future generations seeing such a memorial might ask who he was and seek to find out more about him. In a time when it looks as though market forces and the spiv philosophy are becoming the new credo, it would be nice to point to at least one man to whom such a philosophy was anathema. He was always a fighter and fought to the last. I think we all knew that he was weakening during the last twelve months of his life, yet he held on long enough to receive an honorary doctorate from Lancaster University for his contribution to our outdoor movement and in particular, as the public orator said, to partly right a wrong that had been perpetrated all those years before when he had been refused admission to London University because he had served time in prison.

He is missed by all who knew him. But Tom wouldn't want us to mourn. He'd want us to carry on fighting because he knew himself that there was always more to be done and that the forces of greed and privilege are always on the lookout for the main chance. Perhaps the greatest memorial to Tom is his work. The Pennine Way, the effort he put into the formation of the national parks (he personally saw to it that the southern end of the Howgill Fells were included in the Yorkshire Dales Park) and the fight for the North Pennines AONB (Area of Outstanding Natural Beauty). It would be nice if we could complete his work by gaining free access to the Bowland Fells. I think that would please Tom greatly. But I think I'd still hear him saying, 'What about Scotland? It's there next.'

I never had an argument with Tom in all the time that I knew him. But I do disagree with him on one thing; some people do matter a great deal in the march of humanity – and Tom was one of them.

Mike Harding
Dentdale, 1988

1 Tom's mother, Annie Stephenson, *née* Criddle

2 Tom Stephenson, 1931

3 Madge and Tom Stephenson in 1933

4 Madge Stephenson, 1942

5 Tom Stephenson, 1942

6 Tom Stephenson, 1960s, The Cheviot in the background

7 Autumn 1968. Tom Stephenson hands over as secretary of the RA to Christopher Hall

9 Tom Stephenson inspecting an artificial footpath surface (*Peak Park photograph*)

8 Madge Stephenson, aged over seventy, Shepherds Crag, Borrowdale

10 Alan Mattingly, RA Director, Peter Melchett, Vice-President, Mike Harding, President, and Tom Stephenson at the start, at Royal Holloway College, of a round Britain walk to celebrate fifty years of the RA

11 Tom Stephenson chatting with Princess Alexandra when he was awarded an Honorary Doctorate by Lancaster University in 1986 (*Lancaster University photograph*)

Tom . . . in his own words

Tom wrote constantly – journalism, polemic, pamphlets, proofs of evidence for inquiries – mostly on the issues about which he cared passionately. But he also wrote about himself and, as he was insistent that he wanted no biography, let Tom tell his own life story. A good deal about his later life is woven in his history of the campaign for access to mountains and moorlands; what follows therefore concentrates on his life before that time. It is drawn from articles he wrote himself and a verbatim account of an interview he gave in 1971.

Family and early childhood

'. . . I was . . . born on 12 February 1893 in Chorley, Lancashire, where my mother had gone to her parents' home for the event – the first of nine she was to bear in the next twenty years . . .

For the first three years of their married life my parents lived with my father's mother in Whittle-le-Woods, a village three miles north of Chorley. My father was an engraver in a calico printing works. My mother and grandmother were both four-loom weavers in a cotton mill. All three started work at 6 a.m.; so every morning at 5.30 my mother carried me, wrapped in a shawl, to spend the day with "Bertha at top o't' steps". My earliest memory is of peering between the iron railings framing the square flagged platform at the top of the flight of stone steps leading to Bertha's front door.

When my mother had her second child she sent me to my grandparents at Chorley, where I lived for the next four years. Theirs was a comparatively prosperous working-class home with grandfather, a blacksmith, and four unmarried daughters cotton-weaving. All handed over the whole of their earnings to the matriarch on Friday nights and were then allotted their spending money.

Although only three years old, I immediately started school and, with the added tuition of a fond grandmother and four aunts, soon learned to read and even to decode the railway timetables then published in the local paper . . .

While living at Chorley, and in later years, I spent occasional weekends and holidays with my grandmother at Whittle. Even to a child's eyes there were obvious contrasts between the two homes and the two grandmothers. The one at Chorley was stout, comfortable and cheerful, still retaining traces of the beauty for which she was noted in her younger days . . . Grandmother Whittle was gaunt, hollow-cheeked and work-worn; she was weaving on four looms until a few months before her death at the age of seventy-three. In addition she did all her housework: cleaning, washing, cooking, baking, and carrying the drinking water a quarter of a mile uphill. In broad dialect vigorously expressed she spoke of thee and thou and thine.

Often I sat with her on Sunday afternoons before the fire blazing in an old-fashioned range which shone with black-leaded iron and gleaming steel. There was a home-made hearth-rug, but the rest of the floor was of stone flags, well washed and sprinkled with sand. She had had no schooling but had somehow learned to read in middle age. We would tackle the *Chorley Guardian* together, stumbling over the long words and improvising the pronunciation; Egypt we once read as 'egg-pit'.

My pampered days ended shortly after my seventh birthday when I rejoined my parents, who then had two other children. For the next six years, during which three more babies arrived, much of my time was spent in household duties – as nursemaid, kitchenmaid and general runabout . . .

My father . . . was much more of a handy man than I have ever been. Indeed he was a man of many parts, of considerable ability. As an engraver he was regarded as specially skilled. Good at metalwork, he made for sale match, snuff and tobacco boxes, engraved them from original designs and then had them silver-plated. In the village orchestra he had played the clarinet, and he had also been in demand at local concerts as a baritone. He read widely, the books being mostly borrowed, though he had several Dickens novels and a copy of Dana's *Two Years before the Mast*, obtained by collecting Sunlight soap wrappers. Unfortunately he was a heavy drinker and in some weeks spent more money in the pub than on the family . . .

My mother had incredible vitality. At the age of nine she started work in a cotton mill. Despite her child-bearing, her years of penury and unhappiness, of struggling and scheming to run the home, she lived until she was eighty-nine; and up to the last few months she was remarkably vigorous. Throughout she maintained a surprising serenity. Although she would sacrifice anything for her children, she never made a show of her affection – no kisses or endearing words . . .

My father's habits led me, at the age of eight, to sign the pledge for him at a Band of Hope meeting. A year later, that having failed, I decided to stand outside the pubs at closing time and preach total abstinence. My mother killed that notion by insisting on my being in bed when the pubs closed. So, having heard that Parliament could do anything, my next idea (also unfulfilled) was to become an MP and pass a law closing all pubs.'

Starting work

'My working life began at thirteen, as a labourer in a calico printing works. That meant working (illegally) a sixty-six-hour week. The works ran from six in the morning to six at night, with half an hour for breakfast and an hour for dinner; women and lads under eighteen were not supposed to start until 6.30 a.m. By taking only ten minutes for breakfast and twenty for dinner one could earn overtime pay for an hour and a half each day. The wages for those long hours were nine shillings a week; and adult labourers were earning only twice that amount.

My parents were then settled in Whalley, a village in the Ribble valley. It was situated in a pleasant countryside (now an Area of Outstanding Natural Beauty), where the River Calder had breached a long spur of Pendle Hill, the dominant natural feature in the north-east of the county and traditional rendezvous of the Lancashire witches. On the first Saturday after starting work I climbed Pendle and from the summit, 1,831 feet above sea level, beheld a new world. Across the valley were the Bowland Fells; and away to the north Ingleborough. Pen-y-ghent and other Pennine heights, all snow-covered, stood out sharp and clear in the frosty air. That vision started me rambling, and in the next sixty years took me time and again up and down the Pennines and farther afield.

On the following Saturday I walked the four miles to Clitheroe and paid a shilling (my first two weeks' spending money) to join the public library, taking home as my first choice Darwin's *Origin of Species*. I spent a year struggling through that weighty work which, fortunately, was not in great demand. The glossary at the end of the book was not enough to supplement an elementary school education and, as there was no dictionary at home, I took lists of the incomprehensible words to the reference library. Often the dictionary did not take me far, but a friendly librarian was always willing to direct me to other sources of information.

At the age of fifteen I started a seven-year apprenticeship as a block printer: that is, a hand-printer as distinct from a machine textile printer. During that apprenticeship there were frequent periods of short-time working, perhaps only two or three days a week. This left me with little or no money but ample leisure for rambling. Passing rich with a few pence in my pocket and with a little food from the family larder, I would set out before sunrise and make a round trip of up to a hundred miles. Nights I spent rolled in a groundsheet in the lee of a drystone wall, or in a barn if one were handy. Sometimes there was a welcome at an out-of-the-way farm and an invitation to a meal. On other occasions a village policeman would question me closely as a suspected runaway.

From 1910 onwards an occasional guinea, earned by a published account of a walk, would enable me to . . . walk forty, and occasionally fifty, miles a day . . . The recurring sequence of limestone, shales and millstone grits in the local landscape led me to a study of geology and to dream of becoming another Darwin. Having heard of evening classes in geology and kindred subjects at Burnley Technical School, I scraped together thirty shillings to buy a second-hand bicycle and enrolled as a student. That meant, after a day's work, cycling eight miles to school and back again, four nights a week, thirty weeks in the year, for four consecutive years. I never got more than six hours' sleep in a night, often less.

In those days the Board of Education awarded annually two scholarships in geology, open to the whole of the British Isles, including Ireland. They were worth £60 per annum and free tuition for three years at the Royal College of Science, London, and that became my goal. Before sitting for the finals one had to pass qualifying examinations in eight subjects. In my second year I attended classes in four, studied another six at home and, by concentrated effort and much burning of midnight oil (and it was oil), passed the second stage geology and mineralogy and also scraped through the eight qualifying examinations.

My apprenticeship ended in March 1915. Six months later I left for London, thrilled as a scholarship winner and more than a little proud of my success, though not wholly confident about the future. The war which was to have been over by Christmas 1914 was still raging; conscription was in the offing, and I was a declared pacifist.'[1]

Conscientious objector

'From the very outbreak of the war I opposed it. I felt that the country was being bamboozled and I didn't accept that we were going to war for the defence of poor little Belgium . . . Very few people agreed with my stand on the war. There was one man who worked in the same works as myself; an older man, too old to be conscripted, but I was certainly the only man in the village to oppose the war. Of course I was the subject of a good deal of abuse, accused of cowardice and all the rest of it and threatened I should be run out of the village, but I never suffered any violence there . . .

I went before a local tribunal, whose chairman was a Catholic priest from Stoneyhurst College, Father Pennington, who, I suspect, was not very militaristic himself, because he congratulated me on the way I put my case and on having achieved so much. I was given absolute exemption, which was very unusual in those days. Very few people got absolute exemption as a conscientious objector, except on religious grounds, and I was an agnostic.

Twelve months later there was a great comb-out, as they called it. All the exemptions were reviewed. When my call-up came in 1917 I just ignored it. Eventually I was arrested by the village policeman, taken to Clitheroe Magistrates' Court and they fined me forty shillings [£2] and costs and remanded me to await an escort. I said, "Well you have deemed me to be a soldier, you can deem the fine paid", and that is all I have ever done about paying that. I was then taken to the Third East Lancashire Regiment and after three weeks in the guardroom I was court-martialled . . .'

Prison

'At the court martial I was sentenced to twelve months' hard labour and went to Wormwood Scrubs. There I was a neighbour of the late Sydney Silverman.* We were both working together in the brush shop.

The solitude of prison didn't bother me so much as some people, because I had been accustomed to wandering day after day by myself over the hills. I was quite accustomed to my own company. I didn't suffer from that. We worked in association, but we weren't allowed to talk . . . It was a punishable offence to be caught talking to another prisoner, and Sydney and I were arguing fiercely on a number of issues and I always got caught. He somehow managed to escape.

After about the first twelve months they brought in what they called the Churchill concessions, which Churchill made in the time of the suffragettes. Among other things you could have your own clothes if you wanted them. The most important thing was you could have your own books in. Now that was a great asset. They also had quite a good library in the Scrubs and I did a lot of serious reading I never would have done outside.

. . . I read a lot of heavy stuff, for instance Gibbon's *Decline and Fall*, which I couldn't read today, and Mill's *System of Logic*. I read all of Meredith's novels. So the time wasn't entirely wasted.'[2]

'A second court martial resulted in a two year sentence, and I was sent to Northallerton jail. There, from the cell windows on the top storey, we had a view on one side of the distant Pennines and on the other of the Cleveland Hills. That second sentence was never completed, for there was a general release of objectors in April 1919.

Free again, I found work with a lead-mining company on Grassington Moor in Upper Wharfedale and lived in a second-hand army bell tent pitched on the 1,000-foot contour. The job lasted for only a couple of months, but I stayed on for a time, finding my walking legs again on the fells.'[1]

'In October 1919 I returned for a short time to my early trade of block-printing, this time near London. From there, during the next ten years, I rambled over much of southern England; but the North Country still pulled. When, in the late twenties, I started to write again it was to describe walking days in the Pennines and the Bowland Fells.'[3]

*Sydney Silverman was Labour MP for Nelson and Colne 1935–68.

Politics

'Only a few weeks after beginning work in Kent I went to a reunion of conscientious objectors in London, where Philip Snowden* spoke and appealed to the conscientious objectors not to think that they had done their life's work. There was still a lot to be done in the campaign for socialism. I walked down from that meeting in Bishopsgate to Charing Cross with Emrys Hughes,† whom I had known in prison, when he was always lecturing me for continuing my academic studies instead of doing something useful. The outcome of it was I went back to Dartford and the next week set about starting a branch of the Independent Labour Party.

In this way I met many of the Labour leaders of those days . . . . I also ran a meeting with Bernard Shaw in Dartford. I had a typical letter from him, saying he couldn't understand why anyone wanted him to speak for them at an election, because he went and spoke for Philip Snowden at the 1918 election. They had large audiences who applauded most enthusiastically and then went and voted for the Tory candidate. But we had a packed audience with Shaw. We'd sold the seats and made I think about £40 profit, which was quite useful to a struggling ILP branch in those days. We were able to carry on more vigorous propaganda with that little windfall. I also ran a meeting with Bertrand Russell, who was very clear and logical, of course, and also had a packed audience. This would be in 1921 or 1922, I think, when he had just come back from China. He had a very clear, thin voice that kept the audience quite interested right to the end of his talk.

In 1920 I became part-time agent for the Labour Party, at a wage of fifty shillings [£2.50] a week. By that time I was earning about £6 a week, but this was a job I thought I would like to do and I could live on fifty shillings a week. So I offered my services and was taken on. They were only too glad to get a full-time man for a part-time salary. In 1922 the Labour Party offered me a post at their head office in Eccleston Square. I remained first at Eccleston Square, then at Transport House, for eleven years. When I took the job I never thought to see a Labour government. I thought we were working for some far-off

---

*Philip Snowden was MP for Blackburn 1906–18 and Colne Valley 1922–31 and was Labour Chancellor of the Exchequer in 1924 and 1929–31. In the crisis of 1931 he joined MacDonald's three-party 'national government' and campaigned on its behalf in the general election of the same year, though he did not stand himself.
†Emrys Hughes was a writer and Labour MP for the South Ayrshire Division of Ayrshire and Bute 1946–69.

Utopia, some idealistic state. I certainly was surprised, I think most of us were, when Labour scraped in in 1924.

Arthur Henderson* was the party secretary. We saw more than one side of him. One member of the staff once said that he could be uncle Arthur, but he could also be the bloody foreman. In fact I had a brush with him myself. In 1931 the Labour Party was in low water financially and they started an economy campaign and, like some other employers, the first thing they did was to start cutting down on staff and making various reductions on overtime pay and that sort of thing. We had a staff association of which I was chairman. The secretary was a married woman, who was dismissed with other married women on the staff as an economy measure. I had to go before Arthur Henderson and protest about this, and had a rather heated half-hour with him threatening me with the sack myself if I weren't less unruly.

At the time of the General Strike I was in the Labour Party directory department, as they call it, which kept all the records and addresses of the secretaries throughout the country. The Trades Union Congress and the Labour Party jointly were organising a system of couriers who were taking out bulletins all over the country, and one of my jobs was to get these bulletins despatched. It was really like a post office sorting office. I had to work all the parcels out every afternoon and have them all bundled up by midnight. I remember Willy Gillies, the international secretary, being very despondent; he thought it would be the end of the trade union movement if we had a general strike. When the strike was called off we thought there had been some sort of gentleman's agreement between the trade union leaders and Stanley Baldwin, but of course once the strike was over we felt that Baldwin hadn't lived up to the pledges we understood he had given to the trade union leaders.

The crisis of 1931 was heartbreaking, particularly as far as Philip Snowden was concerned . . . he was really my hero in the Labour movement in those early days. When the break came I remember him saying in the House of Commons that the electioneering pamphlet *Labour and the Nation* was Bolshevism run mad. A Labour member reminded him that he had had a hand in the writing of that pamphlet and he denied ever have seen it. I knew that at that time there were in

*Arthur Henderson was Labour MP for Barnard Castle 1903–18, Widnes 1919–20, Newcastle 1923, Burnley 1924–31 and Clay Cross from 1933 until his death in 1935, and Foreign Secretary 1929–31. His nickname was 'Uncle Arthur'.

fact proofs of that pamphlet in the Labour Party offices which
Snowden had checked. Here was a man who I felt would tell the truth
if the heavens fell. I don't know whether it was a slip-up; I felt at the
time that he was deliberately lying, something I never credited him as
being capable of, and that did shatter my faith in Philip Snowden.
After the fall of the Labour government in 1931 there was a general
feeling of despair at having been badly let down by MacDonald and
Snowden and the rest of them who went over. We felt that they had
panicked. There was a feeling of bafflement and despair, and the
feeling that we were going out into the wilderness again.'[1]

Countryside campaigner

'In 1933, on the invitation of Ernest Bevin, I left Transport House
and became a journalist, writing a weekly article for the *Daily Herald*
and editing a little magazine called the *Hiker and Camper*, which was
controlled by the TUC. From that point on, though *Hiker and
Camper* didn't last very long, all my journalism was concerned with
the countryside.'[2]

'As the newly appointed editor of *Hiker and Camper* and open-air
correspondent of the *Daily Herald* I was invited to attend the annual
meetings of the National Council of Ramblers' Federations at Ilkley
in 1933. T. Arthur Leonard, founder of the Co-operative Holidays
Association and the Holiday Fellowship, was in the chair. Edwin
Royce, eloquent champion of access to mountains, was there. So also
were G. R. Mitchell, first honorary secretary of the RA, Alfred
Embleton, honorary treasurer until 1961, and Stephen Morton, who,
with G. H. B. Ward of Sheffield, convened the first meeting of
National Council.

The next year I was a speaker at the access to mountains
demonstration in Winnats Pass at Castleton in the Peak District and
panicked at the thought of addressing 3,000 ramblers seemingly
glued to a perpendicular hillside. Phil Barnes and G. H. B. Ward
were also at this rally. Those two, plus Morton and myself, with
Royce as the mainspring, were among the chief campaigners for
access, united in a common cause but differing fiercely at times on
tactics.

The Monday after the demonstration I told the then editor of the
Daily Herald of the enthusiasm and dedication of these young folk
who were campaigning for the right to walk on their native hills, the

preservation of footpaths and the creation of national parks. There-after I was allowed free rein in boosting the aims and activities of the Ramblers' Association so long as I wrote nothing contradictory to Labour Party policy (the *Herald*, now defunct, was linked to the Labour Party) and did not hold any office in the association . . .

I was elected to the executive committee at National Council in April 1943. A week earlier I had left the *Herald* and joined the new Ministry of Town and Country Planning as press officer . . .

The Ministry of Town and Country Planning was a cheerless place permeated with a fear of publicity. John Dower was my only kindred spirit and publicising his famous national parks report in 1945 was one of the most satisfying tasks I ever had. The climate of the time came out clearly at the small monthly planning dinners, followed by a speech and discussion. When Dower spoke some planners could see no reason for barring motorways from national parks. When I spoke on access to the countryside it was clear that the rights of the rambler were a featherweight against the rights of property. A small Pennine Way exhibition in the entrance hall of the ministry attracted consider-able attention and some press comment. This led one assistant secre-tary to complain that all this publicity about a Pennine Way might lead to a demand for something actually to be done about it.

What a change there was in 1945 with the coming of Lewis Silkin as minister! He was surprised to find that an Independent Labour Party colleague of some twenty years before was now his press officer. We spent an afternoon in informal discussion on legislation the RA was seeking. He promised that he would, at the first opportunity, receive a deputation from the association, which he did in December 1945. With his authority I issued a press statement quoting the deputation as saying that some of the finest scenery in the country could only be enjoyed by trespassers. There must be facilities for access to the wild, uncultivated parts of Britain, drastic revision of footpath law and the creation of national parks and long-distance footpaths such as the Pennine Way. The minister said he was in full sympathy with almost everything that had been said. He hoped to introduce the necessary legislation and would be happy to seek the advice of the RA at a later date.'[3]

'When the honorary secretary of the Ramblers' Association resigned in 1948, I offered to fill the post temporarily, never imag-ining it was to be my job for nearly twenty-one years, for most of them full-time. Crowded years they have been, writing, lecturing, arguing, going on deputations to Ministers, giving evidence at public inquiries and spending innumerable hours on a multitude of committees.'[3]

'In the long campaign for RA ideals Parliament was the prime target and we attacked on many lines. It might be by personal approach, or by asking our members to write to their constituency MPs, or by persuading someone to ask a parliamentary question. From time to time we circulated all members of the House of Commons with memoranda or pamphlets. Most of them, no doubt, went straight into the wastepaper basket, but some fell on fertile ground . . .

I count myself lucky to have been associated with so many like-minded people. For myself, as secretary, and then for three years as president, I can recall twenty crowded years of glorious life. Beyond those years I can look back to the modest beginnings of the great association of today. For me it has been fifty years of fellowship with men and women who found beauty in the land and strove that others might enjoy that beauty.'[4]

References

1 'The way I have come', 1, *The Countryman*, Spring 1969, pp. 51–9.

2 D. Rubinstein, 'An interview with Tom Stephenson', *Bulletin of the Society for the Study of Labour History*, 22, 1971, pp. 27–32.

3 'The way I have come', 2, *The Countryman*, Summer 1969, pp. 239–49.

4 'Fifty years of fellowship', in Ann Holt (ed.), *Making Tracks: A celebration of fifty years of the Ramblers' Association* (London, 1985).

Madge Stephenson

It would be impossible to give an accurate impression of Tom Stephenson's life without mentioning his wife Madge, his companion for over fifty years. They met shortly after the 1914–18 war. She was a keen walker and climber but arthritis affected her from an early age and she became progressively disabled. She is remembered as a vivid personality and those who knew her tend to enthuse about her 'wonderful gravelly voice' and sometimes devastatingly direct conversation. 'Two things I really enjoy now', she is reported as saying at the age of seventy-four, 'are cigarettes and whisky.'[1] Another characteristic story illustrates her ironic acceptance of her status as an 'amenity widow'. She came round after a minor operation to find a neighbour waiting to take her home rather than Tom. 'If I were a national park', she said, 'Tom would be here.'[2] She died in 1982.

References

1 Helen McCarrick, 'Learning to live with it', *Nursing Times*, 11 July 1974.

2 James Atwater, 'Tom Stephenson – his long walk', *Reader's Digest*, Vol. 104, No. 624, April 1974

Tom as writer

Tom's writings and speeches span most of our century. A small
selection is included here. They were intended for many
different audiences – general readers, dedicated ramblers, public
inquiries, political opponents in both the labour and the outdoor
movements. The voice, however, is unmistakable.

He began writing journalism at a very early age, about the
rambles he took in the countryside near his home. This excerpt is
from an article published in a magazine called *Health and
Strength* in May 1911, when Tom was eighteen.

'I have never had an uninteresting ramble yet. I can always find
something to attract my attention and give me food for thought.
Nature has an inexhaustible store of wonders which all of you can
explore. "How?" some of you will say. By simply being observant
and using your brains.

I have seen youths come here from some of our large towns who
could not tell the trilling of a lark from the warbling of a thrush.

Two lads from Bradford accompanied me on a ramble last summer,
and the questions they asked me were innumerable. I remember
showing them some fossils in an outcrop of 'Mountain Limestone'.
"What are they made of? Who's put them there?" were some of the
queries they put to me. Then when I explained to them that the rock
was almost wholly composed of the remains of plants and animals that
lived thousands of years ago they looked at me in an incredulous
manner, evidently thinking I was mad.'

Pendle Hill has a special place in Tom's memories. It was the
scene of his first ramble, that of the Saturday afternoon following
his first week at work. What follows is part of a description of a
ramble over Pendle which dates from February 1912, and

appeared in the *Whalley Wheatsheaf*, a local Co-operative Society
journal, in February 1912.

'About an hour after leaving the Nick o' Pendle we came to Ogden
Clough, a deep gully cut right down into the very heart of the
mountain. At the bottom of the clough a small stream rushes and
splutters over its rocky bed, and as we stood there the faint mur-
murings of the falling waters were carried upwards to our ears. The
sound of the water made us thirsty, so we made our way to the stream.
This was no easy task, though, for the almost perpendicular sides of
the gully were covered with loose fragments of rock, and afforded but
scant foothold. The descent was safely accomplished, however, so
sitting down on the side of the stream we ate the lunch we had taken
with us, washing it down with copious draughts of the cold, sparkling
waters of the brook.

Having finished our meal, we walked slowly upstream for some
distance, along the side of the whimpering burn, then, climbing out of
the gully, we walked in a north-westerly direction.

No sounds whatever broke the almost eerie silence – not even the
faint whisperings of a gentle wind – whilst the rising moorland
completely cut off our view on every hand until we reached the edge of
the hill, where it slopes right down to the banks of the Ribble. Then,
what a superb scene we overlooked . . .

Some thirty miles northwards rise Ingleborough and Pen-y-ghent,
and to the east of them the hills above Malham meet the horizon.
Across the valley we have Grindleton Fells, and behind them the high
moorlands stretching to Clapham and Lancaster. Just peeping over
Browsholme Fells are the crests of the hills forming the Trough of
Bowland. More to the left the hills above Chipping bound the view.
Still further to the left is the blunt termination of Longridge Fell, with
its thickly wooded summit. Due south stands Whalley Nab.

These hills are but the frame, though, that surrounds a most
exquisite picture. With undepictable irregularity the meadows and
woodlands stretch from one hill to another, whilst here and there are
dotted tiny villages. Down in the bottom of the valley the Ribble
meanders gracefully through verdant meadows and golden woods, by
rocky cliffs and grassy knolls, as it makes its way to the sea, just
discernible, like a silver ribbon, behind the tops of proud Preston's
tallest chimneys.'

What follows was intended for a very small audience, the court
martial held at Saltburn-by-Sea on 16 March 1918 which sent
Tom to his second term of imprisonment as a conscientious
objector. His submission in his defence has survived and extracts
are reproduced here. It represents the pacifist credo for which
Tom was prepared to suffer loss of liberty and of his hopes for a
career as a geologist, for he knew that if he went to prison he
would lose his scholarship at the Royal College of Science.

'. . . Whilst admitting that in general it is necessary to good
citizenship for a man to obey the laws of the land, I hold that in
certain cases a man's first obligation is to the dictates of his own
convictions.

If I am convinced a certain action is right then I consider it my duty
to follow that course no matter what resistance I meet with and with
no thought of my own personal discomfort.

Therefore, believing as I do, that the only way to prevent war is by
abolishing the armies and all the machinery of war, my only course is
the one I have adopted and still adhere to after a year's imprisonment.

The militarist believes, or professes to believe that he is fighting to
prevent war in the future; that the only way to maintain peace is to
prepare for war. My reading of history refutes these notions. Instead
of preventing war, the battles of the past have only led to more strife
and dissension. We are told the German people have prepared for this
war during the past forty years. Such lengthy preparation has certainly not procured peace for them.

. . . Had every man of military age refused to bear arms when this
country declared war, then I believe the wholesale slaughter of the last
three and a half years would have been unknown.

On both sides the belligerents have been led to believe they were
fighting in self-defence; that the only way to avoid extermination was
to murder the men who by a similar delusion were led against them.

If the German people could have seen the entire English nation
refuse to fight, then they would have seen the emptiness and fallacy of
the arguments of their militarists.

I do not think I should wrong you, gentlemen, if I said that in your
minds conscience was synonymous with cowardice, but I would ask
you for a moment to imagine yourself divested of all those military
trappings, to rise above Army Regulations and to view the question
reasonably and philosophically. With you in such a frame of mind I
would submit that if men will enlist and die for a cause it is not feasible

that other men will submit to imprisonment, contempt and contumely for a cause they just as sincerely believe in.

To save one's skin, I assure you, is not the primary consideration of a pacifist. In my own case, I have had ample opportunity of evading the trenches. To have done so would have saved me from any stigma in the eyes of my fellow men, but in my own mind I should be aware that I was a traitor to my beliefs; that I had sold my principles rather than face a hostile public opinion.

In conclusion, I would say, that whilst you are supposed to be sitting to deliver justice, I entered this room certain that your decision would be 'Two Years Hard Labour'. For that I do not blame you. You, as much as I, are but puppets in the play. We matter very little in the march of humanity. The significant fact is that there are twelve hundred men in gaol today and all the king's horses and all the king's men cannot make soldiers of them. Those men stand for a mighty movement that will grow and flourish until eventually war becomes a thing abhorred and men and women throughout the world shall live in peace and brotherhood.

So, gentlemen, I bid you, proceed to your judgement. The present is yours, but the future is ours.'

> After his release from prison Tom became an Independent
> Labour Party activist in Kent and in 1921 engaged in a long
> correspondence in the *West Kent Advertiser* in which he articu-
> lated the political position of the ILP. The letter from which the
> following extract is taken was published on 4 November.

'It is suggested that the ILP is an opportunist organisation. This is not very explicit, but if the writer means the party is prepared to scrap its principles to take advantage of the occasion, he cannot be very well acquainted with the history of the ILP. Had the ILP been opportunist in this sense of the word, then during the late war instead of maintaining its stand for internationalism, instead of having its speakers mobbed, stoned and flung into goal, it would have devoted its energies to denouncing the atrocious Hun, to singing the glories of imperialism, and to convincing the working man this was a righteous war we were fighting in the interests of small nations, a war to end war, and so on, *ad nauseam*.

We are gravely warned of the extremist danger. Overthrowing a system is no remedy, quoth the oracle. Who says it is? The ILP certainly does not say so.

The ILP seeks to convince the people of this country that the collective ownership and use of land and capital in the interests of the workers is a vastly superior system to that of private capitalism. Let us assume we are successful in that part of our programme and that the great mass of the people desire such collective ownership and control . . . a believer in democracy will perhaps admit that the will of the majority should be complied with. If that is done where does the revolution come in? Any danger of revolution would arise from the minority in possession of the country's wealth being reluctant to part with it. I would suggest, therefore, that the revolution would be more likely to be forced not by the ILP, nor by any other Socialist body, but by the privileged few who control the nation's resources, and who are in the main represented by the Coalition.

Again, if the experiment in Russia was so certainly fore-doomed to failure why have the allies spent so many men, and so much money in endeavouring to crush the Bolsheviks? Would it not have been more diplomatic to allow the Soviet regime to fail of its own defects, rather than give the Bolsheviks the opportunity of saying in the future the Soviets failed not because of any inherent weakness, but owing to the intervention of capitalist enemies?'

> Tom was soon back writing about the joys of the open air. This piece on winter walking appeared in the Scottish edition of the *Daily Herald* on Boxing Day 1933.

'There is a notion prevalent among the uninitiated that tramping is a summer pastime, and that for the winter months rucksacks are stored in lavender and boots carefully wrapped in cotton wool until flowers bloom in the spring.

This may be true for the ukulele amblers, but the enthusiast is not deterred by weather. He knows the exhilaration of battling with a nor' easter on the hill-tops, the warm tingle on reaching shelter after facing stinging hail, the joy of achievement on attaining his goal when driving snow and obliterating mist have necessitated steering by compass . . .

At Glen Nevis and Loch Ossian there will be brave exploits. From Arrochar stalwarts will attack the grim old "Cobbler" and neighbouring Bens. For the less ambitious there will be New Year fraternising at Birnam.

Aviemore Hostel at the foot of the Cairngorms has its bookings for New Year and three venturesome spirits tell me they are tackling the

Larig Ghru.

Ten hours is the average summer time for the twenty-two miles of the "Gloomy Pass" that rises to 2,733 feet before descending by the head waters of the Dee. Except for the primitive shelter of the Corrour Bothy there is no intermediate resting place for the storm-beaten tramper.

Though they make an early start and however good their journey, nightfall will overtake these stawarts in Glen Lui Beg, and by the Linn of Dee they will hear the rush and swirl of unseen water . . .

If travelling alone, do not venture on dangerous ground.

Many years ago, as an inexperienced youth, I attempted the crossing of a lonely stretch of snowbound country.

At the last house I was likely to see for a dozen miles the farmer's wife sought to dissuade me from the venture. After she had described the difficulties and dangers, I jauntily assured her that there was no need to worry on my behalf.

In withering tones which I still remember, she replied, "Worry aboot ye? I'm no likely to bother my heid about ye. It's my husband I'm thinking on. I'm no wanting him trailing thae hills a' nicht seeking the likes of ye."

> Politics and love of the outdoors came together for Tom, as can be seen from this article published in the *Daily Herald* on 30 June 1934 about one of the rallies organised to press for access to mountains, the subject matter of the second part of this book.

'On Saturday last I met, in the Derbyshire hamlet of Edale, an official of the Manchester Ramblers' Federation. We had planned to make the circuit of the Peak, that southernmost upward fling of the Pennines; the tailpiece of that long line of moor and fell the school geographies termed "the backbone of England".

It was grey morning with rain in the offing, but there was sufficient wind to bring the tang of peat and the freshness of the moors into the dale. By an old packhorse trail we crossed a thrusting spur of the Peak, to the head of the valley round which curved the dark gritstone fells.

. . . The route was carefully marked by the signs of the Footpaths Preservation Society, more as an indication of a right of way than from any necessity to direct the stranger.

Only by unceasing vigilance and determined effort have these few remaining paths been retained for public enjoyment, and alternating with the direction posts were those provocative wooden liars,

"Trespassers Will be Prosecuted".

Every week-end, like sheep passing through a narrow defile, crowds of ramblers file along this track. Across on the right rise the tempting slopes of Kinder, and the long line of "The Edge" with its castellated escarpment of millstone grits.

Let any traveller deviate from the narrow way, in the innocent hope of scaling those alluring heights and apparently from nowhere, arises the forbidding keeper . . .

Sunday was Demonstration Day, and into Castleton there poured lads and lasses, middle-aged and elderly folk, all keen, enthusiastic trampers, eager to reiterate their demand for the passing into law of the Access to Mountains Bill.

With splendid faith and admirable determination these stalwarts press their claims, confident of ultimate victory. They are convinced that the day will come when a few selfish grouse-butchers will no longer be allowed to close vast stretches of moorland, and deprive the people of the rightful enjoyment of their common heritage.'

> When war came (again) into Tom's life, he found a platform for his love of the outdoors and a chance to promote its politics in the left-wing journal *Tribune*. This extract appeared on 20 February 1942.

'Those who have long been advocating town and country planning on a national scale doubtless felt that some progress had been made when it was announced last week that a Ministry of Works and Planning is to be established. The cautious ones, however, are not likely to sing Hallelujah until satisfactory plans have been produced, together with some guarantee that they will be adopted.

Any schemes concerning the countryside will be of particular interest to ramblers, of whom there were many thousands before the war, and whose numbers are likely to be considerably increased when peace returns.

They in their wanderings were only too familiar with the havoc and senseless desecration that was being wrought in rural Britain. They had long known the need for national planning to overcome the sorry consequences of the indifference, the neglect and the short-sighted policy of local planning authorities.

In many parts of the country the hideousness of the towns from which they sought relief was becoming almost inescapable, completely so, in fact, for those without the means to travel beyond the sprawling suburbs and the spreading tentacles of ribbon development.

When they did reach unspoiled country it was likely to be well sprinkled with forbidding notices – PRIVATE: TRESPASSERS WILL BE PROSECUTED: NO RIGHT OF WAY. According to the cynical author of a Scottish guidebook the making and erecting of such signs was "One of the few staple industries of the Highlands".

There were, then, for the rambler, and all lovers of the countryside, two main problems: the preservation of the remaining natural beauty of Britain and the obtaining of a general right of access to that beauty. It is of this question of access that I wish to write, for it is the less widely recognised of the two problems . . .

To begin with there is an area of something like 2,500 square miles of common land in England and Wales. Contrary to the prevalent idea, the public have no general right of access to all common land. Section 193 of the Law of Property Act 1925 provides for public access to common land, any part of which is in the Metropolitan Police District or in any borough or urban district, and to any common where the owner has requested the application of the section. This section should be applied to all common land, irrespective of its location. A large amount of wild and attractive country would thus be opened to the people.

Another step would be the creation of National Parks whereby large areas of beautiful country would be preserved for the enjoyment of the people and protected from the ravages of unplanned buildings, and the devastation of uncontrolled industrial development whereby the national heritage is sacrificed to private gain.

Another urgent need is revision of the law relating to the establishing of proof of a right of way. This is based on the legal fiction that at some time some owner of the land must have dedicated such a right. The absurdity of this is apparent when it is remembered that some of our rights of way go back to Roman and perhaps pre-Roman days.

We would not tolerate an attempt by a landowner to close a part of the Great North Road. A footpath in law is just as much a highway as an arterial road and should be equally protected.'

Tom was a climber as well as a rambler. This extract, from an article in *Out of Doors* of November–December 1949 reflects his great love of mountains.

'Most mountaineers have said at the end of a day, on more occasions that they can remember, that it was the best day they had ever spent on the hills . . . after a day on Glyder Fawr, seven of us were unanimously of the opinion that we had shared an unsurpassable day . . .

Overhead was a soft blue, cloudless sky, below a billowing expanse of sunlit mist contracting and falling to lower levels. Soon the whole range of the Carnedds was uncovered down to about the 2,500 foot contour. On the left, across the cloud-filed Cwm Idwal, the pyramid of Y Garn was cleared. Next the three peaks of Tryfan, across Cwm Bochlwyd, were revealed, and a few minutes later the upper mass of Glyder Fach from the skyline of the Bristly Ridge to the piled rocks of the Castle of the Winds was uncovered.

So clear was the air above the cloud level that we could pick out a surprising amount of detail of Pen yr Oleu Wen and Tryfan, and the Bristly Ridge was sharp etched against the blue sky and people climbing the ridge were plainly discernible.

It was unthinkable that we should hasten from the heights while surrounded with such magic transformations. So on a rocky perch we sat and watched the dissolving views and constantly changing scenes.

For some time after the summits had cleared the mist still seethed and spumed below us, sending up tongues and pillars of mist to brush us with a damp caress and wreath the crags before vanishing completely. Away in the distance were piled cumulus clouds rearing like sunlit alpine peaks.

Presently there was a sudden commotion and a swirling in the clouds beneath, then a rift rapidly widening to reveal the dark waters of Llyn Ogwen. Wider and wider the gap became, drawing away to disclose more and more of the Nant Ffancon, then a silver streak of the Menai Straits and finally the Isle of Anglesey.

After that the clouds began to break up into isolated masses leaving for a time narrow girdles round Tryfan and the Carnedds. Those in turn contracted and dissolved. So by the time we reached Ogwen there was not a vestige of cloud anywhere visible. The whole valley, the long slopes of the Carnedds and the west face of Tryfan were gilded with the mellow sunshine of a warm autumn afternoon.

Yes, I would certainly place it among the best of the hill days I have known.'

As secretary of the RA Tom continued to write about the joys of the open air, but inevitably his time was much taken up with 'official' writing – designed to sway politicians or inspectors of

public inquiries. This example, from towards the end of Tom's
life, is from his Proof of Evidence, presented to the Public
Inquiry on whether the North Pennines should become an Area
of Outstanding Natural Beauty, in October 1985. It brings
together the story of his professional involvement with the outdoors and his personal passion for the wild northern fells.

'For twenty-one years I was secretary of the Ramblers' Association.
Then followed a three-year spell as president, and since then I have
been vice-president. I am also vice-president of the Northern Area of
the Association. I was the originator of the Pennine Way and am
president of the Pennine Way Council and wrote the guidebook to the
Pennine Way published by Her Majesty's Stationery Office. I am
vice-president of the Open Spaces Society . . . vice-president of the
Council for National Parks . . . For more than forty years I served on
the executive committees of these two bodies. I have also served on the
executive committee of the Youth Hostels Association and the
Council for the Protection of Rural England. I was a member of the
Hobhouse Committee on Footpaths and Access to the Countryside,
which reported in 1947. From 1949 to 1953 I was a member of the
National Parks Commission, the forerunner of the Countryside Commission, and in that capacity was involved in many of the negotiations
for the Pennine Way. I was a member of the Gosling Committee on
Footpaths which reported in 1968 . . . For more than seventy years I
have rambled in the Pennines, having started at the age of thirteen and
when turned eighty-three I stood on the summit of Cross Fell, 2,930
feet above sea level. During the same period I have walked and
climbed in most of the moorland and mountain areas of Great Britain.

With that background I believe there is no area in England better
qualified to rank as an Area of Outstanding Natural Beauty than this
region in the Northern Pennines.

It includes the most extensive area of wild moorland in the Pennines; the nearest approach in England to what might be termed a
wilderness; mile after mile of uninhabited moorland. Eyes accustomed to softer scenes may see in these landscapes only a grim
desolation. There are, however, many people today who may find a
great satisfaction in these places of silence and solitude, places where
they can feel they are in a world of their own.'

Finally, an extract from a speech Tom made in June 1986, at a
rally held in Cavedale, near Castleton in the Peak District, as part
of the National Parks Awareness Campaign.

'By use of its power under the 1949 National Parks Act, the Peak District National Park Planning Board has gained access to nearly eighty square miles of open moorland. They have given the rambler the right to walk on the once jealously guarded moors of Kinder Scout and Bleaklow . . .

In other parts of the country such freedom is not to be found.

In Lancashire in the Forest of Bowland there are sixty-two square miles of beautiful moorland country where access is strictly limited and Lancashire County Council has only been able to gain minor concessions from the landowners.

On the banks of the stripling River Wyre almost every tree is plastered with a notice forbidding trespass. On the roadside are stark notices saying "Private", with a background of several thousand acres of rural land.

By persistent pressure Lancashire County Council persuaded the Sefton Estates to grant an access strip seven and a half miles long and about forty feet wide between Clougha and over Ward's Stone to Tarnbrook. Here, with far reaching moorland on every hand, one is expected to walk along a line marked by a double row of pegs. Step outside those pegs and one immediately becomes a trespasser.

The land with the same limitations now belongs to the Duke of Westminster.

We would suggest to his grace that for one year at least he throws the whole area open to ramblers. We are confident that at the end of the year he will find the area had in no way been damaged or depreciated . . .

However that may be, the Ramblers' Association will continue to press for the right to roam, for access to the Forbidden Lands.

One way of achieving that end would be to adapt James Bryce's Access to Mountains (Scotland) Bill of 1884 which would then read: "No owner or occupier of uncultivated mountain or moorland shall be entitled to exclude any person from walking or being on such land for the purposes of recreation or scientific or artistic study, or to molest him in so walking".'

Part 2

The right to roam

Introduction

Ann Holt

When Tom Stephenson died in 1987 at the age of ninety-four, he left unfinished the book he had been writing on the history of the movement for access to open country – uncultivated land or, in the usual slogan, mountains and moorlands. My job as editor was to get the book into publishable form, following his intentions as closely as possible. Only Chapter 2, 'The origins of the Ramblers' Association', cannot be said to be Tom's work, and even this has been written using his partial drafts and materials collected by him for use in it. However, no work had been done on drawing the material together into a whole. In this introductory chapter I have tried to do this, making use of what guidance Tom left, but it represents my interpretation of his material and of my own research.

There are many strands which could be, and have been, written about in the history of walking as a recreation. Those which interested Tom Stephenson most were those which were woven into his own life story. He was a working-class rambler who became involved in the organised rambling movement. Eventually he became secretary of the Ramblers' Association, deeply involved in representing, at the national level, ramblers' interests to government, public authorities and landowners.

Thus he wrote about ordinary ramblers, describing their lives in the industrial cities of the North, the foundation of organisations to further the interests of ramblers as a group, of their struggles against entrenched interests, whether they were individuals assaulted by farmers or gamekeepers, mass trespassers, or volunteers arguing against bureaucrats at public inquiries. He wrote about the rambling movement, coming together, organising, demonstrating, publicising, lobbying the legislators. And he wrote about the long history of attempts in parliament to gain the legal right to wander over mountain and moorland. He traced the campaign's roots in the enclosure of common land and the policy of excluding people, native and tourist, from open country which intensified after shooting became a source of profit as well as an upper-class recreation. He went on to examine the repeated attempts to remedy the situation with legislation and the role of the organised rambling movement in agitating for such legislation. This culminated, in Tom's narrative, in the flawed victory of the 1949 National Parks and Access to the Countryside Act. Finally, he looked at the objections to access in the light of modern research and found them wanting.

What ramblers were asking for under the shorthand of 'access to mountains and moorlands' is best defined by referring to the Bill which the Liberal MP James Bryce first introduced in 1884. Clause 2 stated that no owner of uncultivated mountain or moorland should be entitled to exclude any person from walking on such lands for the purposes of recreation or scientific or artistic study.[1] The original Bill referred only to Scotland, but the principle that the public should have the right to walk on uncultivated land was the vision which sustained the access to mountains campaign through innumerable setbacks.

It is an apparently simple idea with revolutionary implications. This may seem a large claim for something which concerns people's leisure activities. Embedded deep in our culture is the puritanical notion that work is what is really important so leisure must be trivial, but this simple equation underestimates its importance in people's lives, at all levels of income and social aspiration. Recreation is what makes life worth living for many people. In addition, the way people spend their leisure is not only a matter of personal choice; the ideas and attitudes underlying the way we think about sports and pastimes are part of our culture and society. We do not subscribe to all these ideas – in fact most of the time we are not even aware of them – but they are there as part of the social background to our lives. They inevitably, therefore, affect our views of particular leisure activities and their practitioners. For instance, there are unspoken hierarchies attached to different ways of spending leisure time; for example, 'art' is serious, 'sport' is frivolous. Pastimes are also loaded with connotations of social prestige. From the point of view of the present book this is most obviously the case in the contrast between rambling and shooting game, but it also exists in much more subtle distinctions, such as that between Rugby League and Rugby Union. Leisure is not, therefore, either marginal to the serious business of society or a matter simply of personal avocation. For all sorts of reasons, personal and sociological, people care passionately about what they do in their spare time.

This is part of what underlies the controversy over access to uncultivated land. It is not, however, the whole story, for being able to walk on land which belongs to someone else, as a matter of right, touches on other cultural, economic and political factors which lie at the heart of the way our society works. These centre on the idea of private ownership and whether the ownership of land gives the owner an exclusive right to determine its use. James Bryce stated during a debate on his access bill in March 1892:

land is not property for our unlimited and unqualified use. Land is necessary so that we may live upon it and from it, and that people may enjoy it in a variety of ways; and I deny therefore, that there exists or is recognised by our law or in natural justice, such a thing as an unlimited power of exclusion.[2]

This is a fair summary of what has been the attitude of the pro-access lobby throughout, and it has been bitterly contested by those opposed to access.

The struggle for access has been couched from its earliest beginnings in terms of the 'rights of the people' and the 'rights of property'. Our society places a high value on respect for private property, of whatever sort, and we are all prone to believe that what we are used to is the natural way of doing things. But if we look at land in other countries and how other societies regard the privileges attached to private ownership of land, we find considerable variation. In 1980 the Ramblers' Association undertook research into what rights of access to countryside exist in some other European countries. The data collected shows that in some places the situation with regard to privately-owned land in the countryside is very similar to that in Britain. In Portugal, for instance, the general public only has the right to walk along public footpaths and over land which is subject to an access agreement with the landowner.[3]

However, land is not always privately owned; areas such as mountain and moorland are often communal property, or not owned at all. The Swiss Civil Code grants the right to walk through forests and pastures to everyone and enclosure of wooded land is not permitted. However, 'such lands are seldom private but usually communal property and therefore anyway accessible as public ground. Mountain areas above the cultivated zone are invariably public ground, and so are lakes and rivers.'[4] Similarly, in Spain, access to privately-owned land is only allowed under certain types of right of way, but 'needless to say, everybody has the right to walk on uncultivated hill and mountain country if it has no owner or is in the public domain, always provided it is not part of a military or defence zone . . . There are vast areas which qualify.'[5]

A third situation exists where land is in private ownership but the public has rights of access. In The Netherlands, for instance, access to uncultivated land is permitted unless the contrary is clearly indicated.

It would appear that the situation in The Netherlands is somewhat opposite to that in the United Kingdom. Whereas in this country there seems to be no access unless otherwise indicated (for instance the public footpaths in the countryside), in The Netherlands the fact that access is not permitted must be clearly indicated (either by signs stating this fact, or by the fencing in of land or property).[6]

The country with the approach to access to uncultivated land which appeals most to ramblers, however, is Sweden. The Swedish *allemansrät* is not a law in the sense of a statute but it is a recognised customary right. This means that precision in explaining what it entails in a short summary is difficult, but briefly it gives people the right to cross and stay for a short time on land owned by someone else, without permission having been granted, subject only to the proviso that the domestic peace of anyone living on the property is not disturbed and economic interests are not harmed. Now these concepts are clearly a matter of interpretation and landowners, and others who wish to defend the total exclusion of members of the public from privately-owned land could say that they heartily concur. They would simply argue that their economic interest and privacy will be damaged by the public impinging to any degree at all on such land.

The Swedes, however, take a rather more robust view of the rights of the general public. One writer on the subject suggests that privacy could be protected if a house is shielded by trees, bushes and rocky outcrops by not venturing closer than 10 to 15 metres. If the house is overlooked he suggests the rambler should not go closer than about 60 to 70 metres. As to damaging economic interests, this is a matter of observing certain traditional rules about which berries and so on can be collected in addition to not, of course, damaging crops in any way and leaving litter.[7] A similar attitude pertains in Norway, where the traditional right to move over land was given legal authority in the Open-Air Recreation Act of 1957, and in Finland.

Thus land, particularly uncultivated land, is not always owned privately, can be owned communally or not owned at all, and private ownership is not always taken to confer exclusion rights on the owner. The situation in which almost all land, including mountain, moorland and rough grazing, is in private ownership and subject to only limited and specified rights of access by the general public is only one possible variant. It is, however, the one which underlies the story of the struggle for access to uncultivated land told in this book.

Attitudes to land ownership therefore differ from place to place. They also change over time. Tom traces the history of the movement for access to the countryside back into the social and economic changes in agriculture and industry which have shaped our present society. He records some of the early protests about the loss of the right to use uncultivated land as an economic resource by the poor. In Sheffield in 1812 a writer recorded that the poor used to be able to gather 'a few nuts in season'.[8] Later in the century the writer of a guide to Hayfield and Kinder Scout reported how, when the moor was enclosed, it was allotted to the owners of adjoining land. No allotment was made to the poor and they had lost their unrestricted right of access.[9] For people living their lives on the borders of starvation, the right to forage for nuts, berries and firewood would have made a considerable difference to their standard of living. Such people rarely speak for themselves in historical records. One who did was Murdoch Macrae, the protagonist of the 'Pet Lamb Case' discussed later in this book, whose evidence before a Royal Commission set up to investigate the lot of highland crofters is full of a sense of outrage at the waste of fertile land within sight of the poverty of his own family and community.

While the cottars can scarcely get a bit of land in which to grow food, there are many acres of excellent arable land at Morvich, which are admirably adapted for the use of crofters and which might have been given to them without damage to the deer forest. Of this land no use whatever is being made at present. Some of it is covered with weeds, and many acres (about 30) are under a most luxuriant crop of clover and grasses, which has been allowed to rot on the ground.'[10]

However, it was not only the right of access to land as a resource in the battle for survival which was lost and which was perceived as an important loss by the dispossessed. Tom Stephenson's examples of the artisans of the northern industrial cities whose leisure was spent searching the neighbouring moors for botanical specimens[11] disposes effectively of the notion that seeking recreation in the outdoors is either a modern development or something which was until recently restricted to the wealthy. A trade unionists' protest of 1833 at the enclosure of 'the commons of our fathers' is couched in terms of lost opportunities for relaxation, of 'the green grass and the healthful hayfield' being shut off from them.[12]

A wide social spectrum of people were prepared to protest at the high-handedness of landowners in taking away public rights. A fight through the courts after some paths in Flixton, near Manchester, had been closed by one Ralph Wright, who had built himself a house and wanted a completely private park around it, was begun in 1826 by a local farmer. When Wright blocked a footpath the farmer, 'assisted by his neighbours, broke down three several times the obstructions that had been put up, and restored the original road to the public by treading down the oats' which had been planted. The incident provided the impetus for the formation of a Society for the Preservation of Ancient Footpaths in Manchester, which supported the fight for the Flixton footpaths. This organisation had among its members a journalist, Archibald Prentice, and Richard Potter, a Manchester businessman who later became an MP.[13] A broader alliance against a footpath closure is described by Paul Salveson.[14] When a Bolton landowner closed a right of way over his grouse moor in 1896 a local journalist again played an important part in attempting to get it reopened, but the Labour movement was also heavily involved and there were 'mass trespasses' involving thousands of people.

Such assertions that land cannot be regarded as private property in the same way as any other are not only found, however, in the long history of resistance to closures of rights of way or of customary rights of access to, for instance, common land. It is expressed in the idea that responding to the beauty of landscape put people in a special relationship to it, and this was not the prerogative of poets and their leisured audience. The Mechanics' Institutes were expected to deal in severely practical knowledge, but in 1840 a speaker on the history of the Sheffield Mechanics' Institution saw fit to draw attention to the beautiful scenery surrounding the city and observe that 'there is no teacher like nature'.[15] The more extravagant G. S. Phillips, secretary of the Huddersfield Institute, went a stage further in saying, 'whoever may own the land, no man may own the beauty of the landscape'. Anyone who could see its beauty was 'the legitimate lord of the landscape'.[16]

It is not a coincidence that Phillips was an unapologetic trespasser.

There is a house in the next field and you must be prepared to trespass, under the lea of that house, if you would go along with me. You need have no qualms of conscience about it; for there is no sin in a question of this kind; and if the owner of the field should come to you, as he once came to me, with a great hedgestake in his hand, and hard words in his mouth, there is a kind of 'blarney' which he cannot withstand . . . indeed, the journey I am now taking you on is a perpetual trespass; so either make up your mind to the iniquity of the thing or go back.[17]

In some sections of the rambling movement there has always been a mystique surrounding trespass, and attitudes very similar to those of Phillips crop up regularly in rambling literature. The *Handbook* of the Sheffield Clarion Ramblers for 1916–17 contains a story of two ramblers outwitting a gamekeeper by 'blarney'. 'It is a truism', it begins, 'that the finest scenery, the best views, and the most exhilarating walks are to be found only by the intelligent and discriminate trespasser.'[18] In writing the trespasser tends to triumph, but trespass is a theme which Tom treats in a much more down-to-earth way; the often sordid details of personal violence and vindictiveness experienced by ramblers, trespassing or not, at the hands of gamekeepers and farmers.

Some ramblers used trespass more explicitly as a political statement of their refusal to accept that private ownership could exclude all members of the public from uncultivated land. This was the case, for instance, with the publication of *Trespassers Will be Prosecuted*, the work of Phil Barnes, a dedicated Sheffield rambler and persistent trespasser who plays no small part in the narrative which follows. It was also the case with mass trespasses, the most famous of which was on Kinder Scout in 1932, discussed by Tom Stephenson. Howard Hill,[19] who wrote about the subject from a different perspective, describes a second mass trespass, undertaken by Sheffield ramblers in September 1932 at Abbey Brook, and one planned for Froggatt Edge, also from Sheffield. These events suggest that the Kinder Scout mass trespass might have struck more of a chord among ramblers than Tom thought.

This is disputed, however, by Stephen Morton, veteran Sheffield rambler and a key figure in rambling federation circles at the time. He contends that both the mass trespasses which did take place were 'entirely political' and that the Froggatt Edge plan 'died from apathy'. Writing recently, he summed up the episode as follows:

today it is useful, almost valuable; at the time it didn't matter at all and if it hadn't been for the obvious viciousness of the courts and the sentences, I seriously doubt whether any one would ever have heard any more of them. That is not to say that they weren't right and, with hindsight, that it might have been better if we had taken it up and organised it.

But, he goes on, the Manchester Federation of Rambling Clubs and G.H.B. Ward, leader of the Sheffield Federation, 'wouldn't have stood for it'.[20]

Whatever the truth about the significance of this much-discussed incident, it was certainly outside the mainstream of the organised ramblers' movement of the time and the organisations which mattered in the access struggle at the time were the Manchester and Sheffield Federations.[21] In the view of many contemporary ramblers, the Kinder Scout mass trespassers were more concerned with the class struggle than with the struggle for access to mountains and moorlands. This does not mean that ramblers did not recognise the political nature of their cause. The discussion following the débâcle of the 1939 Access to Mountains Act shows that they did. However there was a strong disinclination to see their cause subordinated to more general political aims. On one level people knew that they were engaged in a political struggle; on another, rambling and the countryside were about freedom, beauty and a relief from everyday life and its problems. There was an understandable desire to keep the two apart.

Access was a political issue not only in the sense that it involved action in Parliament, but also in that it brought into conflict opposed groups in society with fundamentally differing interests. Although generalisations about working-class ramblers versus artistocratic landowners are too crude, failing to do justice to the heterogeneity of both sides, there is an element of truth in this view. Access to Mountains Bills were brought before Parliament by Liberal and Labour MPs, not Conservatives. Many of the ramblers' side of the contest held, like Tom Stephenson, radical views on politics.

It is also clear that the long series of Access to Mountains Bills brought forward by James Bryce did not fail through lack of interest on the part of other politicians. Speaking in the debate in 1892 Bryce commented that there had never been a debate before, even though the Bill had once passed its second reading, 'because on that occasion those hon. Gentlemen who did not agree with the principle of the measure were endeavouring to prevent you, Mr Speaker, from finding 40 Members present'.[21] In other words, parliamentary tactics were used to try to sabotage the Bill – on this occasion with the opposite effect to that intended. To those opposed to the idea of access to mountain and moorland, it was deeply political, because it was perceived as an attack on the private ownership of a very special sort of property – land.

The importance of land to the power holders in British society is difficult to overestimate. In a country with a strong aristocratic tradition, in which the aristocracy never lost its grip on power and in which the ownership of land, even when not particularly profitable, was a source of prestige and power, land is invested with a symbolic significance. In addition, the particular areas to which ramblers wanted access were those used for shooting, particularly grouse and deer. As Harry Hopkins's book *The Long Affray*[22] so vividly demonstrates, there was more to the landowners' obsession with the preservation of game than shooting as a way of passing the time. It was deeply bound up with the way the country gentleman defined himself as superior to the rest of the population. Land and shooting are part of the attributes of the powerful. To allow any diminution of the exclusive right to them – through poaching, for instance, or by allowing access to ramblers – calls into question the whole notion of land and shooting as the marks of superior beings particularly suited to the exercise of power.

The objections to public access to uncultivated land put forward during parliamentary debates centred on three points. The first was associated with the sporting lobby and was economic – the loss of income from letting sporting rights; the second, associated with the suppliers of drinking water, concerned maintaining unpolluted reservoirs; the third concerned the principle of private ownership of, and control over, land. The first two, as Tom Stephenson shows, were based less on a dispassionate analysis of the situation than on the assumption that they must be true. From time to time the attitudes which underlay these assumptions emerge into the open, perhaps most clearly expressed in a memorandum prepared by the British Waterworks Association to argue against the 1939 Access to Mountains Bill. It referred to 'the tendency of such areas (i.e. mountains and moorlands) to become a resort for undesirable characters among whom immorality and licentiousness are rife'.[23] Speaking in 1888 an MP opposed a similar bill for Wales on the grounds that people would overrun the country, doing as much damage as they could, and only lodging-house keepers would benefit.[24]

What lies behind such statements is an assumption that ordinary people do not belong in such places; they do not belong there because the place belongs to somebody else. To own land is clearly a privilege; the easiest way to deny other people a privilege is to assert that they do not want it anyway; and if they obviously do want it, that they would wreck it if they did have it. In a society in which privilege is based to a very large extent on the ownership of property, acceptance of the notion that only ownership confers rights becomes an important support of the status quo. As the demand for the right of access to privately-owned land entails a qualification of the exclusive right of ownership of one sort of property, not only landowners are likely to feel threatened by it. A similar sense of threat will be felt by all those whose aim is to defend the existing social system, and who reject any change which tends towards the equalisation of privilege. Speaking in the debate on the 1939 Access to Mountains Bill, Captain Frank Heilgers, Conservative MP for Bury St Edmunds who, according to his *Who's Who* entry, farmed over 1,000 acres in West Suffolk, claimed that the Bill attacked the whole principle of owning land and that it was a device for obtaining land nationalisation without compensation. In the guise of 'helping the hiker' the Bill really 'aims at the nationalisation of property'. He went on to at least partially contradict himself by saying that he thought that the argument that the Bill was the thin end of the nationalisation wedge, an 'argument which had always been used against it', was somewhat exaggerated. However, his comments do illustrate the thought processes of the opposition to access and why the debate it provoked went far beyond questions of personal taste in recreation.

His seconder, Col. R. S. Clarke, member for East Grinstead, also saw the Bill as a direct attack on the rights of property and made the interesting observation that rights were no less rights if they were not always exercised. 'If the privileges granted by a landowner are abused, he has the right of saying, "If they cannot behave themselves, I will close the area" '. If he does that people learn a lesson.'[25] In such a situation the landowner retained social superiority – the right to teach the lower orders lessons. It was often argued by opponents of access that a law was unnecessary as there was already access to most open country without a legal right. They tended to exaggerate the extent to which this was true, but it was undoubtedly the case that many landowners were prepared to tolerate people who were technically trespassers. This did not, however, diminish the importance to landowners of their rights to exclude people if they chose. It is not therefore surprising that what seemed particularly to upset the Duke of Atholl, in the story Tom Stephenson relates in his chapter on the way access was denied in the Highlands of Scotland, was that the students claimed a *right* to walk through Glen Tilt.[26]

The idea that rights of ownership in land should remain undiminished was not only questioned by ramblers and mountaineers. *The Times* commented on Bryce's 1884 Bill:

is it not a matter of compromise? Surely the lords of the soil cannot claim so absolute a monopoly of the earth's surface and of the most beautiful parts of it, as wholly to shut out the poor holiday folk, the artist, and the naturalist. Surely the many have rights as well as the few, and they that wish to see are entitled to legislative protection as much as they that wish to kill also.[27]

In 1924 the *Manchester Guardian*, a far more consistent supporter of access, dismissed as fanatical those who maintained that there was no difference 'between asking for the freedom to cross a man's barren mountain and asking for freedom to trample on another man's suburban garden of geraniums'.[28] In the access controversy, two social groupings met to whom land was a special kind of property. On the one hand there were people to whom it was a means of legitimising social and political power. On the other hand there were those who held that access to open country was the heritage of those who had minds which could appreciate it.

These are, roughly speaking, the conflicting ideas which met head on in the process which resulted in the 1939 Access to Mountains Act. As will be seen from Tom Stephenson's chapter on the subject, the rights of property won hands down. That the argument was not simply one of landowners versus ramblers was demonstrated clearly in the process, for the 'compromise' which emerged was managed from within the amenity movement by Sir Lawrence Chubb of the Commons Society. To see the issue as one of progressive versus conservative is much nearer the mark. Landowners and wealthy grouse shooters had (and have) considerable economic and political power but they could also count on a wide alliance of people to whom the defence of the status quo was the ruling political perspective.

Chubb is shown throughout to be a man of conservative views and his part in the story shows clearly that one did not have to be the owner of a grouse moor to take the view that, in Tom Stephenson's phrase, 'the rights of the rambler were a featherweight against the rights of property'.[29]

A process of compromise between a powerful lobby asserting that the rights of the landowner come first and a less powerful one pressing for more freedom, in recreation at least, for the unlanded population, set against a background assumption that the least possible change is the most desirable option, explains the disappointing nature of the access provisions of the National Parks and Access to the Countryside Act of 1949. The Hobhouse Committee, on which Tom sat, recommended that planning authorities should be required to define on a map all areas of uncultivated land, including beach and foreshore, and that when those areas had been determined the public should have a right of access to them. Reading the internal documents of the government departments involved, now available at the Public Record Office, is like trying to fit together a jigsaw puzzle with many missing pieces, but a good deal does emerge about the pressures and assumptions which produced an act with provisions for access to uncultivated land which allowed sleeping dogs to rest soundly.[30]

The issue of an 'Amenities Bill' was being discussed within the Ministry of Town and Country Planning as early as November 1947. Sir Philip Magnus, a 'temporary principal' official at the ministry at the time, prepared a paper in that month in which he commented that both the National Parks and Footpaths and Access Reports had been received with approval and little concrete criticism. However, he noted that 'the chorus of appreciation which greeted the appearance of the Reports was punctuated here and there by cautionary notes, particularly in respect of agriculture and forestry interests', whom he considered to be formidable enemies. Furthermore, although he recognised that there was no reason why a government bill should not succeed, 'the agricultural interest is, by common consent, a first priority today'. It was therefore essential to reach a compromise between these opposed interests.[31] Hence, even at this early stage, under a government in which landowners were as little represented as ever before or since, the ground rules were laid down stressing the importance of the agricultural lobby and the necessity for compromise.

The Minister, Lewis Silkin, had shown himself to be sympathetic to the ramblers' demands for access to mountains and moorland. Tom records that he spoke at a rally called to condemn the 1939 Bill at Leith Hill. Early in 1948 a paper prepared for him to present to a committee considering the government's legislative programme stated: 'On the subjects of footpaths and access to uncultivated land I am in general agreement with the recommendations of the Hobhouse Committee and I should propose to give most of their suggestions statutory effect in any legislation I may be authorised to prepare.' It was expected that the subject of access would be controversial, but at this stage the minister clearly saw himself following the Hobhouse line:

The procedure suggested by the Hobhouse Committee, i.e. designation of suitable uncultivated land as 'access land' by order of the local planning authority, appears to be the right sort of procedure. Certainly the involved and piecemeal methods of designation on the initiative of individuals provided by the Access to Mountains Act has proved utterly unworkable.

There was, however, a need for more consultation with the Ministries of Agriculture and Health.[32]

Whatever the result of these consultations, by the end of May 1948 there are signs that the 'general agreement' with access recommendations of the Hobhouse Committee was under review. A memorandum to the Deputy Secretary at the Ministry, Evelyn Sharp, begins:

You asked me to find out how far the Minister has committed himself to legislation on *access* as such. The answer is that, in the eyes of the Ramblers' Association, he 'promised' new access legislation within the lifetime of this Parliament (quotation from the Association's report of what the Minister said to a deputation in December 1945). This is pretty definite; on the other hand, the language used in our official Press Notice about the same meeting between the Ramblers and the Minister is a little less specific:- 'He (the Minister) hoped that it would be possible in due course to introduce legislation dealing with access to mountains and moorlands, rights of way, national parks and the control of outside advertisements'. (I suppose that, from a somewhat Jesuitical view, one can argue that 'new access legislation' – especially when read in isolation as in the Ramblers' account – sounds more committing than 'legislation dealing with access' as in the official version.)[33]

It is hard to see this as anything other than a retreat in preparation.

The new line is laid out in a memorandum presented by Silkin to the legislation committee dated June 1948. Under the provisions for access, he stated:

I do not propose to make it obligatory on planning authorities to define all uncultivated land for this purpose. I think that it would be a vast and unnecessary undertaking and the Ministry of Agriculture and the Forestry Commission have both represented that it would be exceedingly difficult to define with any certainty land where unrestricted public access would not be harmful to agriculture and forestry interests.

Instead, particularly as he himself was not convinced of the need for any general right of access to land in private ownership, he proposed to enable planning authorities to declare a public right of access to specified areas of uncultivated land in National Parks.

He goes on to acknowledge that these provisions do not go much beyond those of the 1939 Act, 'which is criticised largely because of its piecemeal approach'. It would, however, mean that planning authorities would have the responsibility of defining access areas, rather than interested parties; it would provide for compensation of landowners and:

I would further not propose to re-enact the clause in the Act which provides that the trespass on an area to which the public has access should be a criminal offence during any times or periods in which the right of access is withdrawn. This clause was the one which gave the greatest offence in the Act of 1939.[34]

The processes of policy formation within Whitehall and government thus resulted in the Hobhouse proposals being watered down, even in the most favourable political climate for a root and branch change which had thus far come about. Policy was formed against a background which was more prepared to accommodate the wishes of 'the agricultural interests' than the needs of the public for countryside recreation. Furthermore, the infant Bill was subject to a general assumption that the least possible change would be for the best. A reply to a protest from the Ministry of Town and Country Planning about the way the Bill had been drafted by the Office of the Parliamentary Counsel shows how far from any new thinking that part of the Whitehall machine, at least, was. It was all a matter, the rather pained reply said, of how far they were going to stick to the 1939 Act; 'it seemed to me that from a parliamentary point of view you would on the whole be in a stronger position if you were to follow that Act as closely as would allow you to get what you wanted'.[35]

When speaking at the Leith Hill rally to protest against that 1939 Act, Tom Stephenson had said that what was needed was a minor social revolution.[36] The balance of political forces and, perhaps equally importantly, the habits of thought current in Whitehall were not going to deliver a revolutionary approach, albeit a minor one, to access to uncultivated land, even under a government which had a claim to be regarded as 'the people's government' some access campaigners saw as their best hope.[37] The story of the journey of the 1949 Act from ideal to statute book is one of social groups divided by their economic interests, social attitudes and political reflexes, and this may go some way to explaining why the campaign for access to mountain and moorland has proved so long, costly of time and effort, and has provoked such passion on both sides. It also explains why, in spite of the considerable achievements in providing and maintaining access to mountain and moorland under the 1949 Act, in many areas of Britain the freedom James Bryce and other campaigners yearned for is still an aim rather than an accomplished fact.

References

1   Access to Mountains (Scotland), Bill 122, 28 February 1884. See p. 131.

2   *Hansard*, 4th Ser. Vol. 2, Cols. 92–101, 4 March 1892.

3   Letter from Portuguese National Tourist Office to Alan Mattingly, 13 August 1980, Tom Stephenson collection, Access Europe file, Ramblers' Association Archives, hereafter RAA.

4   Letter from P. Schweizer of the Swiss Embassy to Alan Mattingly, 6 August 1980, Tom Stephenson collection, Access Europe file, RAA.

5   Letter from the Spanish Ambassador to Alan Mattingly, 30 July 1980. Tom Stephenson collection, Access Europe file, RAA.

6   Letter from Miss M. B. van Wijngaarden, Royal Netherlands Embassy, to Alan Mattingly, 4 August 1980, Tom Stephenson collection, Access Europe file, RAA.

7   Bo Rosén, 'The right of common access in Sweden', Commons, Open Spaces and Footpaths Preservation Society *Journal*, Vol. 20, No. 7, Spring 1980, and Bo Lindevall, 'The right to roam in Sweden', *The Rambler*, No. 13, June/July 1988.

8   [G. Beaumont], *The Beggar's Complaint against Rack-rent Landlords, Corn Factors, Great Farmers, Monopolisers, Paper Money Makers, and War, and Many other Oppressors and Oppressions* by One Who Pities the Oppressed, 2nd ed. (Sheffield, 1812), p. 22. See p. 59.

9   A member of the Hayfield and Kinder Scout Ancient Footpaths Association, *The Guide to Hayfield and Kinder Scout* (Manchester and London, 1877), pp. 17–18. See pp. 64–5.

10   *Report of the Commissioners of Inquiry into the condition of the Crofters*

and Cottars in the Highlands and Islands of Scotland 1884, XXXII–XXXVI. Macrae's evidence is in Vol. XXXV, pp. 1988–92, questions 31183–260. See p. 124.

11   See Ch. 1.

12   *The Pioneer or Grand Consolidated Trades Union Magazine*, No. 7, 19 October 1833. See p. 60.

13   Donald W. Lee, *The Flixton Footpath Battle* (Manchester, 1976), pamphlet.

14   Paul Salveson, *Will yo' come o' Sunday Morning? The 1896 Battle for Winter Hill* (Bolton, 1982), pamphlet.

15   Paul Rodgers, *A Lecture on the Origin, Progress, and Results of the Sheffield Mechanics' Institution* (Sheffield, 1840), p. 21.

16   G. S. Phillips, *Walks around Huddersfield* (Huddersfield, 1848), p. 16. (This book was recently republished by Beardsell Books, Holmfirth.) See p. 66.

17   *Ibid.*, p. 23.

18   'An unorthodox ramble', in Sheffield Clarion Ramblers' *Handbook*, 1916–17, pp. 48–50.

19   Howard Hill, *Freedom to Roam* (Ashbourne, 1980).

20   Stephen Morton to editor, 11 May 1988. See also D. Rubinstein, 'The struggle for ramblers' rights', *New Society*, 15 April 1982.

21   *Hansard*, 4th Ser., Vol. 2, Col. 91, 4 March 1892. See p. 133.

22   Harry Hopkins, *The Long Affray, The Poaching Wars 1760–1914* (London, 1985).

23   'Access to Mountains Bill Memorandum, submitted to Sir George Chrystal, KCB, Secretary to the Minister of Health, on behalf of Water Supply Undertakings by the British Waterworks Association', British Waterworks Association *Proceedings*, Vol. 21, 21st Ser., Official Circular No. 163, April 1939, p. 298. See p. 104.

24   *Hansard*, 3rd Ser., Vol. 324, Col. 1286, 13 April 1888.

25   *Hansard* (House of Commons), 5th Ser., Vol. 342, Cols. 764–77, 2 December 1938.

26   See p. 123.

27   *Times*, 25 March 1884.

28   *Manchester Guardian*, 15 May 1924.

29   See p. 23.

30   See p. 143.

31   Memorandum from Sir Philip Magnus to Mr E. S. Hill, Ministry of Town and Country Planning, 3 November 1947, PRO, file HLG 29 334.

32   Draft of paper to be taken by Lord President's Committee on forthcoming legislation, 23 April 1948, PRO, file HLG 29 334.

33   G. Price-Jones to Deputy Secretary (Evelyn Sharp), 31 May 1948, PRO, file HLG 29 334.

34   Memorandum by Minister of Town and Country Planning, presented to Lord President's Committee, June 1948, PRO, file CAB 124 444.

35 Memorandum from P. H. Sirs, Office of the Parliamentary Counsel to E. V. Thompson, Solicitors' Department, Minister of Town and Country Planning, 1 December 1948, PRO, file CAB 124 445.

36 See p. 177.

37 See pp. 186–7.

Chapter 1

Early ramblers

Long before the start of the campaign for access to mountains and moorlands, or of any need for a campaign, people had begun to climb the hills. A long article in *The Gentleman's Magazine* of August 1747 describes an ascent of Cross Fell (2,930 feet), the highest point in the Pennines, 'a mountain', according to the author, 'that is generally ten months bury'd in snow and eleven in cloud'. In a postscript he adds, 'Being the 13th August, and a long drought; and a hot season, we were not able to find the least relics of snow, in places most likely for it; which is very extraordinary.'[1]

Another ascent of the mountain was made in about 1830, led by a mining engineer from Alston. This seems to have been something of a safari, with extra suits of clothes and a tent, plus ample food and excellent grog, and presumably logs for a blazing fire – all carried on horseback. A little after sunrise they struck their tent and used it as a screen, 'to the windward side of a large stone flag which we raised for a table and placed stone seats around'.[2] Pennine Way walkers can still see this stonework just beneath the northern lip of the mountain, near Crossfell Well, known in those days as 'Gentleman's Well'.

Wordsworth is usually credited with popularising the practice of walking for pleasure, but his guide to the Lake District, first published in 1810,[3] was preceded in 1778 by Thomas West's guide, which ran through ten editions in the next thirty years.[4] But before the publication of these and similar works, in the early days of the Industrial Revolution, there were ramblers afield, some of whom would have been unable to read such books had they been within their reach. These ramblers were humble and mainly illiterate factory workers who, despite their long working hours and appalling poverty, found time and opportunities to explore the countryside around their homes.

Wordsworth would have looked askance at them; at least he would not have welcomed them in the Lake District. When opposing the building of the Kendal–Windermere railway in 1844, he wrote:

Instead of tempting artisans, labourers and the humbler classes of shopkeepers to ramble at a distance, let us rather look with lively sympathy upon persons in that condition, when upon a holiday, or on a Sunday, after attending divine worship, they make little excursions with their wives and children among neighbouring fields, whither the whole of each family might stroll, or be conveyed at much less cost than would be required to take a single individual to the shores of Windermere by the cheapest conveyance.[5]

In a second letter, he said Ambleside, Grasmere, and the neighbourhood had been favoured by the residence of gentry whose love of retirement had been a blessing in those vales, for they ministered to the temporal and spiritual necessities of the poor. Many of these friends of the poor would quit the country if the railway came.[6]

The 'kindly, cheery' Mrs Wordsworth, according to Harriet Martineau, thought 'a green field with buttercups would answer the purpose of the Lancashire cotton operatives'.[7]

Many of these early ramblers were really countrymen at heart, only one remove from rural life. As J. L. and Barbara Hammond wrote, 'For the first half of the nineteenth century the industrial town was absorbing the English peasant used to an open air life, learning from the landscape, in touch with nature, moving and thinking with its gentle rhythm'.[8]

Among the thousands of immigrants were, for instance, paupers from the wide Vale of Aylesbury and the gentle slopes of the Chilterns. In the years 1835–37 the Poor Law Commissioners transported on canal barges, over a four-or-five-day journey, 389 men, women and children from Buckinghamshire as fodder for Lancashire factories.[9] Perhaps the putrid, crowded cellars in which they lived, the heated, humid mills where they worked, the stinking streets and the smoke-laden sky drove them to seek green fields and clean air. George Linnaeus Banks, a journalist and versifier, celebrated his leaving Manchester in 1848 by writing of its:

> Courts and alleys miasmatic
> Haunts too vile for even beasts
> Where from foetid base to attic
> Rottenness unsated feasts.[10]

Fortunately open country was within easy reach and Archibald Prentice, a Manchester journalist writing of that city in 1826, said: 'there are so many pleasant footpaths, that a pedestrian might walk completely round the town in a circle which would seldom exceed a radius of two miles from the Exchange'.[11] Many manufacturing towns such as Bolton, Burnley and Oldham, Todmorden and Hebden Bridge, Huddersfield and Halifax, were similarly located with the countryside near at hand. In 1826, according to Prentice, 'thousands and tens of thousands whose avocations render fresh air and exercise an absolute necessity of life, avail themselves of the rights of footway through the meadows and cornfields and parks of the immediate neighbourhood'.[12]

This may have been an exaggeration, but there is other evidence of increasing use of footpaths which led landowners to close (often illegally) rights of way which they had previously tolerated. An act of 1815 enabled two magistrates to close any path they considered unnecessary. It was probably closures under this Act which in June 1824 led to the formation of an Association for the Protection of Ancient Footpaths in the vicinity of York,[13] and in 1826 the Manchester Association for the Preservation of Ancient Footpaths. Prentice, one of the founder members of the Manchester society, described it as a pleasant association of 'tories, whigs and radicals, and one which . . . spread among the country gentlemen a wholesome terror of transgressing against the right of the poor to enjoy their own without anyone to make them afraid'.[14]

On more than one occasion that 1815 Act was criticised in Parliament, and in 1831 one MP, supporting a petition from Manchester against the state of the law for stopping up footpaths, claimed, 'It was a common thing to hear one magistrate saying to another, "Come and dine with me, and I shall expect you an hour earlier as I want to stop up a footway." '[15]

This closing of footpaths, the enclosure of commons and manorial wastes, and the harsh administration of the game laws provoked some bitter complaints. In the early days of the nineteenth century a pamphlet published in Sheffield said: 'in former times the poor could gather a few nuts in season, without fear or dread of molestation: but nowadays we frequently see warning papers put up in the streets threatening nutters with prosecution should they dare to gather nuts on certain proscribed grounds – Poor Beggars'.[16]

'To a contemplative and humane mind it must be a galling sight',

said the writer, 'to behold a bench of magistrates and a table full of
lawyers with their curled wigs and black gowns, besides attorneys,
constables and witnesses, all spending their time over a poor hungry
wretch who has done nothing worse than that of shooting or hanging a
hare.'[17]

Another protest was recorded in October 1833:

Do you not think, gentlemen, that there is a soul in an artizan, and that he had
some little guess of the rogues' tricks that are being played upon him? Have
we not seen the commons of our fathers enclosed by insolent cupidity, – our
sports converted into crimes, – our holidays into fast days? The green grass
and the healthful hay-field are shut out from our path. The whistling of birds
is not for us – our melody is the deafening noise of the engine. The merry
fiddle and the humble dance will send us to the treadmill. We eat the worst
food, drink the worst drink, – our raiment, our houses, our every thing, bear
signs of poverty, and we are gravely told this must be our lot.[18]

Not all those early ramblers were illiterate, for among them were
many keen naturalists. As the early Alpinists gave the cloak of science
to their ascents, so these ramblers went forth as students of natural
history.

'Nothing', claimed a writer in 1873, 'could be more remarkable
than the way in which love for plants developed among the operatives
of Lancashire towards the close of the last century and the first half of
the present century.' The village of Eccles, six miles from Manchester, was, he said, probably the first botanical centre in Lancashire. In
about 1777 there was a flourishing botanical society there with about
forty members, and a little later similar societies were formed in
Ashton-under-Lyne, Oldham and other towns for those who, after a
day's work, could not travel on foot to attend meetings in Eccles.[19]

There were many tributes paid to these amateur naturalists. At the
meeting of the British Association for the Advancement of Science at
Manchester in 1842, Adam Sedgwick, Professor of Geology at Cambridge, described a walk he had taken through the city streets 'amidst
the smoke of the chimneys and the roar of the engines'. He told of the
artisans he had met and went on, 'In talking to men whose brows were
smeared with dirt and whose hands were black with soot, I found
upon them the marks of intellectual minds; and the proofs of high
character; and I conversed with men, who in their own way, and in
many ways bearing upon the purpose of life, were far my superiors.'[20]

Engels had 'often heard working men, whose fustian jackets

scarcely held together, speak upon geological, astronomical and other subjects'.[21] Mrs Gaskell, in her novel *Mary Barton*, declared:

There is a class of man in Manchester, unknown even to many inhabitants, and whose existence will be doubted by many, who may yet claim kindred with all the noble names that science recognises. I said 'in Manchester', but they are scattered over the manufacturing districts of Lancashire. In the neighbourhood of Oldham there are weavers, common handloom weavers, who throw the shuttle with unceasing sound, though Newton's *Principia* lie open on the loom, to be snatched at in work hours, but revelled over at mealtimes or at night . . . It is perhaps less astonishing that the more popularly-interesting branches of natural history have their warm and devoted followers among this class. There are botanists among them equally familiar with the Linnean or the Natural system, who know the name of every plant within a day's walk from their dwellings; who steal a holiday of a day or two when any particular plant would be in flower, and tying up their simple food in their pocket handkerchiefs, set off with a single purpose to fetch home the humble-looking weed.[22]

An expert appraisal of these men was published in the *Survey of Manchester and its Region*, prepared for the meeting in that city of the British Association for the Advancement of Science in 1962. 'The Manchester district', it said,

was the scene of one of the most remarkable manifestations of popular science which has ever been recorded. Beginning from the establishment of the Linnean system the weavers and other artisans of Lancashire began to concern themselves with natural history, and especially with local flora. In every town and indeed small villages botanical societies were established . . . such societies met in taverns on Sunday afternoons, usually once a month. Most of them acquired small libraries, and their herbaria were sometimes very substantial. District associations were formed, and at the great annual meetings as many as two hundred members would attend. With only the rarest exceptions these men were self-educated manual workers, mostly textile operatives, but with a sprinkling of craftsmen from other trades and a few gentlemen's gardeners.

It is comical to see with what astonishment the Victorians of the 'respectable' classes observed these proceedings. The ability of poor botanists to pronounce and correctly apply the Latin names of plants was wonderful enough, but their ability to meet at the Golden Lion without scandalously misconducting themselves was, to their insufferable contemporaries, by far the greater marvel.

These men lived for the most part in grinding proverty, but they explored the area more thoroughly than any comparable area has ever been explored, they supplied information to authors of several important reference books, and one of them, a clog-maker named Buxton, himself published a botanical guide which will always be a primary source of information about plant distribution in the early industrial period.[23]

The 'clog-maker' was Richard Buxton, who described himself as a 'bat-maker', a maker of children's shoes. Under pressure from his friends, he included in his botanical guide a brief and very modest account of his life and work.[24]

He was born in 1786 and at the age of twelve began learning the trade of batmaker. Unable to read at sixteen, he bought a spelling book and later learned the first principles of the Linnean system from Meyrick's *Herbal*.[25] He never earned more than 15*s* [75p] a week from his trade and delivering newspapers on Saturdays. Nevertheless, he made excursions to Derbyshire, the Craven district of Yorkshire and North Wales, though some of these journeys were at the expense of 'a gentleman who had just begun to study botany and who appeared very anxious in its pursuit'.[26]

For some years Buxton rambled alone until he began to meet other botanists, most of them as impecunious as himself. One day in 1826, on Kersal Moor, he approached a man and asked him if he were botanising. 'The man', said Buxton, 'was John Horsfield, handloom weaver, the President of Prestwich Botanical Society.'[27] Buxton mentions many others of his fellow naturalists. There was 'the present father of botany among the working men of Lancashire, my ever-cheerful and kind-hearted friend, John Mellor of Royton, near Oldham, who as a working-man, has travelled more over England and Scotland than any other botanist with whom I am acquainted'. Then there were John Martin of Tyldesley, weaver, who paid particular attention to the genus *Carex*; James Percival, junior, of Prestwich, mechanic, who promised to become an excellent botanist; Thomas Towneley of Hulme, shoemaker, a good naturalist. He also mentions John Nowell, a twister-in of Todmorden, a noted specialist in mosses, and Samuel Gibson, whitesmith of Hebden Bridge, a keen geologist who discovered a new fossil which was named after him as *Goniatites gibsonii*.[28]

Of himself Buxton wrote, 'Originally of anything but a strong constitution, I have now reached the age of sixty-two years; and, although by no means robust, I can yet make a ramble of thirty miles a day and enjoy the beauties of nature with as much zest as ever I did in my life.'[29]

He invited his fellow-workmen living in the back streets and narrow alleys of the large towns to go into the green fields and fresh air and, whenever they could, to take their wives and children with them. The fields and woods, although the rich man's heritage, might still be the poor man's flower garden. He hoped the lords of the soil would allow pent-up dwellers in the crowded cities to view the beauties of creation, and he asked them at least to preserve the old footpaths if they declined to allow new ones to be made.[30]

Another friend of Buxton, with whom he rambled hundreds of miles, was James Crowther, a leading member of Manchester Botanical Society. Crowther was born in a cellar in Manchester and, like Buxton, had a life of poverty, never earning more than £1 a week. To finance his botanical pursuits, after a long day in the mill, he would go down to the canal basin at Knott Mill to earn a few coppers acting as porter to passengers arriving on the Duke of Bridgewater's packet from Liverpool.

He was a strong walker and sometimes, after a day's work, would walk fifteen or twenty miles in search of some species, but would be back at work next morning. Often he was chased by gamekeepers, but usually outran them. He knew that if he were caught there was the possibility of being tried for trespassing in pursuit of game.[31]

The founding of the Manchester Society for the Preservation of Ancient Footpaths in 1826 has already been mentioned. That society, or some of its members, may have been responsible for the House of Commons, in 1833, approving a motion 'that a Select Committee be appointed to consider the best means of securing open spaces in the vicinity of populous towns, as public walks and places of exercise, calculated to promote the health and comfort of the inhabitants'.[32] Richard Potter, a founder member of the society, paid tribute to it during the debate. Without its exertions, Potter believed, there would have been very few footpaths left within ten miles of Manchester.[33]

With unusual rapidity, the Committee reported in May of the same year. They noted that in the last half-century the population of the large towns had greatly increased. There had been many enclosures of open spaces, and little or no provision had been made for public walks or open spaces. The Committee found 'That as respects those employed in three great manufactures of the kingdom, cotton, woollen and hardware, creating annually an immense property, no provision has been made to afford them the means of healthy exercise or cheerful amusement with their families, on their holidays or days of rest.'[34]

The Committee recommended the establishment of places for athletic exercise in the vicinity of large towns. 'It cannot be necessary', they said,

to point out how requisite some public walks or open spaces must be to those who consider the occupations of the working classes who dwell there, confined as they are during the weekdays as mechanics and manufacturers, and often shut up in heated factories; it must be evident that it is of the first importance to their health on their day of rest to enjoy the fresh air, and to be able (exempt from the dust and dirt of public thoroughfares) to walk out in decent comfort with their families; if deprived of any such resources, it is possible that their only escape from the narrow courts and alleys (in which so many of the humbler classes reside) will be the drinking shops, where in short-lived excitement they may forget their toil, but where they waste the means of their families, and too often destroy their health. Neither would your Committee forget to notice the advantage which the public walks (properly regulated and open to the middle and humbler classes) give to the improvement in the cleanliness, neatness and personal appearance of those who frequent them. A man walking out with his family among his neighbours of different ranks will naturally be desirous to be properly clothed, and that his wife and children should be also, but this desire, duly directed and controlled, is found by experience to be of the most powerful effect in promoting civilisation and exciting industry.[35]

As often happens, some years passed before the recommendations of the Select Committee had any effect. The Government in 1841 provided £10,000 to encourage the provision of public walks and parks, but until 1847 local authorities could not use rates for that purpose without securing a special Act of Parliament. Manchester raised a public subscription and, with £3,000 from the government fund, established in 1846 three parks in Manchester and Salford at a cost of £25,000.[36]

This municipal benevolence should perhaps be put into context by bearing in mind that three years before the Select Committee reported, Kinder Scout and adjacent moors had been enclosed. According to a little booklet written by an anonymous member of the Hayfield and Kinder Scout Ancient Footpath Association, published in 1877, a great part of the enclosed area had been known as 'King's land' on which access was not restricted. The public, said the writer, 'imagining that what was once their own is now their own, have not infrequently come into unpleasant collision with gamekeepers.'[37]

The lands, he said, were surveyed and allotted to the owners of contiguous lands.

No allotment, however, so far as we know, was made to the poor, or for their benefit; and it seems that since this time more than forty acres of what was known as 'Poor Man's Piece', and 'Poor Man's Wood', have disappeared from many modern maps.

The award of acres may be thus tabulated:

To the rich according to their riches	2,000 acres
To the poor according to their poverty	0 acres
Moreover, minus upwards of	40 acres.[38]

By the time that enclosure was made a new force had arisen, one that was in many places to encourage the interest of townsmen in the countryside. The first Mechanics' Institute was founded in 1823 and thirty years later there were about 800, more than a third of them in Cheshire, Lancashire and Yorkshire.[39] The original purpose of the Institutes was to produce more efficient workmen. The object of the Manchester Institute was 'to instruct the working classes in the principles of the arts they practise and in other branches of useful knowledge, excluding party politics and controversial theology'.[40]

From their early days the Institutes were suspect; church and chapel feared them as propagandists of free-thought, the Tories believed they would give working men ideas above their station, while Engels thought the teaching of the natural sciences might draw the working men away from their opposition to the bourgeoisie. Acquaintance with those sciences, he said, was useless for the worker who never got the slightest glimpse of nature because of his long working hours.[41]

Mabel Tylecote, in her book *The Mechanics' Institutes of Lancashire and Yorkshire before 1851*, quoting from the Annual Report of the Yorkshire Union of Mechanics' Institutes for 1846, points out that something was done to break down the barriers surrounding those who lived in the larger towns and to acquaint them 'with the countryside and the ways of life of persons of another class and of people living in a different type of community'.[42] Some of the Institutes, according to Tylecote, arranged visits to country places of interest. More than 2,000 members of the Institutes of Beverley, Bridlington and Driffield, in July 1847, joined an excursion to Flamborough Head by land and sea. Huddersfield Institute in the same year arranged excursions to Blackpool, the Lake District, and the Isle of Man. Keighley Institute, in 1850, organised a visit to Studley Royal, Fountains

Abbey, Ripon, and Harrogate which was joined by several hundred members and friends.[43]

At the Sheffield People's College Henry Clifton Sorby, a geologist, lectured on the formation of local rocks and on the geology of the Malvern Hills.[44] At the Mechanics' Institution in the same city, in May 1840, a speaker referred to 'the beautiful scenery in the midst of which our town is situated. I have said before that there is no teacher like nature. What voice so likely to touch the chords of our hearts as the voice of the hills and valleys; our murmuring rivers, or our warbling woods and our silent moors.'[45]

Similar sentiments were expressed by G. S. Phillips, secretary of the Huddersfield Institute, which, he claimed, was the largest institution for popular education in England. In a booklet with the title *Walks round Huddersfield*, he wrote, 'There can be few towns in the manufacturing districts more delightfully situated than our good town of Huddersfield.' He went on:

I esteem it an unspeakable privilege to live in a land of so much beauty and grandeur; and when I think of the occupations of the people of this neighbourhood, which confine them day after day in closed workshops, I am likewise grateful to the good and bounteous Master on their account and thank Him for the most part in silent reverence. For whoever may own the land, no man can own the beauty of the landscape; at all events no man can exclusively own it. Beauty is a kind of property which cannot be bought, sold or conveyed in any parchment deed, but it is an inalienable common right; and he who carries the true-seeing eyes in his head, no matter how poor he may otherwise be, is the legitimate lord of the landscape.[46]

Many of the Institutes were taken over towards the end of the century by the local education authorities to serve as evening institutes and technical colleges. That happened with the Burnley Institute started in 1834 by three foundry workers, 'to facilitate and promote the diffusion of useful knowledge among the operative mechanics and other inhabitants of Burnley and its neighbourhood'. For nearly a century, including its absorption in the Municipal Technical College, this Institute continued to attract working men and women, especially to its natural history section. 'It grew', said the Annual Report for 1912, 'until it became famed throughout the country as a training ground for men of high talent, and the hope and inspiration of many a working lad.'[47]

Branch schools were started in the 1880s in neighbouring towns and villages and students walked to them from miles around. One student in 1886 was Philip Snowden, later to become the first Labour Chancellor of the Exchequer. Another about that time was Ernest Evans, who became Natural Science Master of the Institute, and 'one of the most influential teachers of natural science subjects in the north of England'.[48]

At the age of thirteen, in 1868, Evans was working twelve hours a day in a Barnoldswick mill.[49] From there he walked over the swarthy heights of Pinhaw Beacon and its neighbours and over the contrasting green limestone fields of Craven. For the next twenty years he worked as a cotton weaver, except when blacklisted for his trade union activities. He was appointed in 1889 to teach botany at the Institute, and he remained on the staff of the Burnley Education Authority until he retired in 1920. By 1893 he was responsible for all the natural science classes and in 1898 the Annual Report of the Institute said: 'Mr Evans has now 131 students doing excellent work in physiology, biology, geology and physiography'.[50]

Evans was a great rambler and many of his students rambled with him. He was above all a practical naturalist, making frequent field excursions and introducing his students to geological features; folding and faulting of the rocks, anticline and cyncline, the occurrence of fossils and lingering relics of the Ice Age, including glacier-carried fragments of rock from Galloway and the Lake District found embedded in the boulder clay of the Ribble Valley. So too he would draw attention to the variations in the flora coinciding with the underlying strata, and he was familiar with little-known habitats of the globe flower and grass of Parnassus, bird's-eye primrose, bog-myrtle, butterwort, sundew, and many other species. 'On those excursions', said one writer, 'Evans was at his best, for his knowledge was unparalleled, and his enthusiasm unbounded. He knew every crag and moor, every hill and valley and clough for miles round Burnley.'[51]

In 1891 a weaver, who had studied under Evans, gained the first national scholarship in geology ever to be awarded in this country. He was followed by a long succession of Lancashire cotton operatives proceeding via Evans's classes to the Royal College of Science in London.[52] Weavers and other workers, working from 6 a.m. to 5.30 p.m., would hurry home for a meal and a quick wash and change, and then to evening school from 7 p.m. until 9.35 p.m. For four nights in the week, thirty weeks in the year, they would doggedly plough through a four-year course before sitting for the coveted scholarship.

Each year the chosen few, not necessarily the most learned, would pass on to the Royal College of Science, and after further training there, would go out, some to the far corners of the earth, as skilled scientists. Of those left behind, many maintained a lifelong interest in natural history, and a habit of rambling in the adjacent countryside and father afield in their brief holidays. Evans was undoubtedly to some extent responsible for the popularity of rambling in north-east Lancashire, though many of the present-day ramblers may never have heard of him.

As one who studied under him and walked many miles with him, I learned much from his wide knowledge and his enthusiasm in the field. I particularly remember the Annual Boxing Day rambles he led. This meant an early tram from Padiham to Burnley and then a walk across the Sabden Valley hollowed in soft shales between resistant beds of millstone grit. Over the Nick of Pendle we went down to the limestone quarries of Chatburn to note the grooving and scratching of the hard rock by the passage of the ice sheet. Our sandwiches we ate with pint pots of tea in a small pub in Grindleton. Then a visit to a disused limestone quarry (now, I believe, filled with dumped refuse) to see a textbook example of folded strata. Next we crossed the Ribble Valley and mounted to another quarry at the top of Sawley Brow with more folded strata. Thence by field paths to Downham and Twiston where once one Pudsey mined silver to mint his own coins. Then over a spur of Pendle Hill to the village of Barley, where, in the fading light, we had to see a glacier-transported boulder of white limestone conspicuous in a gritstone wall.

At Barley we were joined by others who had walked out from Burnley and Nelson for a 'High Tea' or, in local speech, a 'knife and fork tea'. After that there was a sing-song, and then a walk of six miles to Burnley, along country lanes, with no danger of being mown down by motor cars. So ended a round of about twenty-five miles. For me it still meant a tram ride to Padiham and a cycle ride of four miles.

One incident unlikely to have occurred anywhere else might be recalled to illustrate Evans's influence. The Burnley Natural History Society, which consisted mainly of Evans's students, past and present, used to arrange a syllabus of lectures and rambles. On one of those Saturday afternoon rambles in June 1912, a young Burnley weaver was the botany leader. On the outskirts of the town we met a coalminer squatting on his haunches examining what, at first sight, appeared to be a dandelion. Soon the young weaver and the collier, in his pit dirt, were discussing in learned detail the characteristics of the flower until they were agreed upon its genus and species. 'You are a botanist?' asked the weaver. 'Well, a bit of one, like,' was the reply. He had studied botany and geology under Evans a dozen years previously. Twenty years later such men were among the founders of North-east Lancashire Federation of Rambling Clubs.

Contemporary with Evans, and only six miles away in the little town of Colne, was a young Congregational Minister, who for the next half-century was to play a prominent part in the open-air movement. Of Thomas Arthur Leonard, founder of the people's holiday movement, it was said that 'he led the children of Colne out of Blackpool into the mountains'. In June 1891, he took members of the rambling club connected with his chapel for a four days' holiday in the Lake District at a cost of 21s (£1.05) a head, including railway fare.[53]

In those days the Lancashire cotton mills closed down in Wakes week for holidays without pay. Then most of the workers, who since the first payday after the Wakes had been saving their sixpences and shillings, often in the works club, would go in droves to Blackpool, Morecambe, and the Isle of Man. 'Clearly', thought Leonard,

the great majority of young folk did not know how to get the best out of their holidays. This was the more remarkable as Bonnie Colne, as we called our town, stood amongst the beautiful uplands of the Pennines, with Charlotte Brontë's moors on the one hand and the wilds of Pendle Hill and Ribblesdale on the other, and was almost within sight of the mountains of the Lake District.[54]

The success of similar holidays in later years led to the founding in 1897 of the Co-operative Holidays Association, 'to provide recreative and educational holidays, by purchasing or renting and furnishing houses and rooms in selected centres, by catering in such houses for members and guests and by securing helpers who will promote the intellectual and social interests of the party with which they are associated'.[55] What would today be regarded as a 'do-gooder' flavour in the objects proved no deterrent in those late Victorian days, and successful holiday centres were opened in a number of places. Leonard then resigned from his ministry to become secretary of the CHA, as it was to become widely known and affectionately regarded by thousands whom it had introduced to walking holidays in this country and abroad. At the beginning of the present century the Association could provide a week's holiday at its popular Newlands Centre for

22s 6d (£1.12).[56]

Not all CHA members shared Leonard's spartan outlook, and in 1913 he resigned from the secretaryship to form a new organisation, the Holiday Fellowship. He felt that there was a need for another body to develop the movement yet farther. 'We felt also', he wrote, 'that despite our working-class origins we were becoming middle-class in spirit and conservative in our ideas. Our centres tended to be of the conventional order, and the adventurous centre of simple, economical ways was not popular.'[57]

When Leonard retired from the secretaryship of the HF in 1926 he had, through the two bodies, opened seventy holiday centres and started many thousands walking for pleasure.[58] He was then sixty-two, but for another twenty years he continued to serve the open-air movement, championing various causes, throwing out new ideas and serving on several committees. He was in at the beginning of the Youth Hostels Association, and one of its early vice-presidents; first chairman and then first president of the Ramblers' Association; and more than anyone else he pressed for realisation of the Pennine Way* long-distance footpath; he presided at the conference of open-air organisations in 1938 at which the Pennine Way Association was born. Even in his eightieth year he started a new organisation to provide family holidays.†

His life's work in providing people's holidays also had an indirect effect on the growth of rambling organisations. Both the CHA and HF formed local groups or rambling clubs and these were often the mainstay of the ramblers' federations. When the RA emerged in 1935 there were some 150 CHA and HF groups and they produced some of the leading personalities in the access to mountains campaign, including Stephen Morton of Sheffield, who convened the first meeting which led to the formation of the National Council of Ramblers'

---

*The Pennine Way can be said to be Tom Stephenson's best-known memorial. It originated in an article he wrote for the *Daily Herald* published on 22 June 1935 under the headline 'Wanted, a Long Green Trail'. The idea for the article came from a letter he had received from two American women who had walked the Appalachian Trail in the eastern United States and wondered whether there was anything similar in England. This was the stimulus for Tom Stephenson to sketch a walk of some 150 miles from Edale in the Peak District to the Cheviots. It struck an immediate chord among ramblers, the Pennine Way Association being one result. It took thirty years to overcome resistance to the idea, some of it chronicled in this book. It was officially opened in April 1965.

†This was Family Holidays Ltd, described in Charles Johnson, *The History of the Holiday Fellowship*, Vol. 1 (London 1981), pp. 105–6.

Federations, George Mitchell of London, the first honorary secretary of the Council and of the RA, Alfred Embleton of Liverpool, its first honorary treasurer, and Edwin Royce of Manchester, the grand old man of the campaign for access to mountain and moorland.

References

1 'A Journey up Cross-fell Mountain,' *Gentleman's Magazine*, Vol. 17, 1747, pp. 384–5.

2 Thomas Sopwith, *An Account of the Mining Districts of Alston Moor, Weardale and Teesdale* (Alnwick, 1833), p. 47.

3 Wordsworth's guide first appeared as an unsigned introduction to Joseph Wilkinson's *Select views in Cumberland, Westmoreland and Lancashire* (London, 1810). It was first published under Wordsworth's name as *A description of the scenery of the Lakes in the North of England* (London, 1822).

4 Thomas West, *A Guide to the Lakes* (first published London, 1778).

5 *Morning Post*, 11 December 1844.

6 *Morning Post*, 20 December 1844.

7 Harriet Martineau, *Biographical Sketches*, 2nd ed. (London, 1869), p. 404.

8 J. L. and Barbara Hammond, *The Bleak Age*, rev. ed. (West Drayton, 1947), p. 36.

9 Arthur Redford, *Labour Migration in England, 1800–1850* (Manchester, 1926), pp. 91–3.

10 Quoted in E. L. Burney, 'George Linnaeus Banks, 1821–1881', *Manchester Review*, Vol. 12, No. 1 (1971), pp. 1–13.

11 Archibald Prentice, *Historical Sketches and personal recollections of Manchester* (London and Manchester, 1851), p. 289.

12 *Ibid.*

13 *Yorkshire Gazette*, 17 July 1824.

14 Prentice, *op. cit.*, pp. 291–2.

15 *Hansard*, 3rd Ser., Vol. 5, col. 651, 3 August 1831.

16 [G. Beaumont], *The Beggar's Complaint against Rack-rent Landlords, Corn Factors, Great Farmers, Monopolisers, Paper Money Makers, and War, and many other Oppressors and Oppressions*, By One Who Pities the Oppressed, 2nd ed. (Sheffield, 1812), p. 22.

17 *Ibid.*, p. 97.

18 *The Pioneer or Grand National Consolidated Trades Union Magazine*, No. 7, 19 October 1833.

19 James Cash, *Where There's a Will There's a Way! or Science in the Cottage. An account of the labours of naturalists in humble life* (London, 1873), pp. 10, 11.

20 J. W. Clark and T. McKenny Hughes, *The Life and Letters of the*

Reverend Adam Sedgwick (Cambridge, 1890), Vol. 2, p. 46.

21   Friedrich Engels, *The Condition of the Working Class in England in 1844*, trans. and ed. W. O. Henderson and W. H. Chaloner, 2nd ed. (Oxford, 1971), p. 272. (First published London, 1892.)

22   Elizabeth Gaskell, *Mary Barton: a tale of Manchester life* (Harmondsworth, 1970), p. 75. (First published London, 1848.)

23   K. J. Dorman and J. H. Tallis, 'Interesting features of the local vegetation and flora', in C. F. Carter (ed.), *Manchester and its Region. A Survey Prepared for the Meeting of the British Association for the Advancement of Science in Manchester, 1962* (Manchester, 1962), p. 86.

24   Richard Buxton, *A Botanical Guide to the Flowering Plants, Ferns, Mosses and Algae, found indigenous within sixteen miles of Manchester* (London and Manchester, 1849).

25   William Meyrick, *The New Family Herbal; or Domestic Physician* (Birmingham, 1789).

26   Buxton, *op. cit.*, p. x.

27   *Ibid.*, p. vi.

28   *Ibid.*, p. ix.

29   *Ibid.*, p. xii.

30   *Ibid.*, *pp. xii–xiii.*

31   Cash *op. cit.*, pp. 9, 83.

32   *Hansard*, 3rd Ser., Vol. 15, col. 1053, 21 February 1833.

33   *Ibid.*, col. 1057.

34   *Report from the Select Committee on Public Walks*, 1833, Command Paper 448, p. 4.

35   *Ibid.*, pp. 8–9.

36   Hammond, *op. cit.*, p. 233.

37   A member of the Hayfield and Kinder Scout Ancient Footpaths Association, *The Guide to Hayfield and Kinder Scout* (Manchester and London, 1877), pp. 17–18.

38   *Ibid.*, pp. 16–17.

39   Frank Smith, *The Life and Work of Sir James Kay-Shuttleworth* (London, 1923), p. 254.

40   Wilfrid H. Thomson, *History of Manchester to 1852* (Altrincham, 1967), p. 315.

41   Engels, *op. cit.*, p. 271.

42   Mabel Tylecote, *The Mechanics' Institutes of Lancashire and Yorkshire before 1851* (Manchester, 1957), p. 274.

43   *Ibid.*, p. 275.

44   G. C. Moore Smith, *The Story of the People's College, Sheffield* (Sheffield, 1912), p. 59.

45   Paul Rodgers, *A Lecture on the Origin, Progress, and Results of the Sheffield Mechanics Institution* (Sheffield, 1840), p. 21.

46   G. S. Phillips, *Walks round Huddersfield* (Huddersfield, 1848), pp.

15–16. (A fascimile edition has recently been published by Beardsell Books, Holmfirth.)

47 Tylecote, *op. cit.*, p. 263.

48 A. E. Wales, 'A great scholar whose name will endure', *Burnley Express and News*, 14 April 1956.

49 *Ibid.*

50 A. E. Wales, 'Through hard times to a true vocation', *Burnley Express and News*, 21 April 1956.

51 A. E. Wales, 'How a fine teacher's influence grew', *Burnley Express and News*, 28 April 1956.

52 *Ibid.*

53 T. Arthur Leonard, *Adventures in Holiday Making; Being the story of the rise and development of a people's holiday movement* (London, [1934]), p. 20.

54 *Ibid.*, p. 19.

55 *Ibid.*, pp. 27–8.

56 *Ibid.*, pp. 40–2.

57 *Ibid.*, pp. 53–4.

58 *Ibid.*, p. 74–6.

1 Edwin Royce

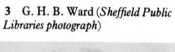

3 G. H. B. Ward (*Sheffield Public Libraries photograph*)

2 T. A. Leonard

4 Frank Head

5   The burial place of Murdoch Macrae

6   Maggie Gruer, who provided accommodation for ramblers in the Cairngorms despite prohibitions

7   Hugh Dalton and Madge Stephenson on a walk in the Lake District, 1950

8   Benny Rothman, Tom Stephenson and Stephen Morton, Cavedale, 1986
(*Peak Park photograph*)

9 Barbara Castle speaking at a rally to mark fifty years of the Pennine Way in 1985. In the tent are Sylvia Franks, secretary of North East Lancashire area of the RA, Mike Harding and Tom Stephenson

Chapter 2

The origins of the Ramblers' Association*

Numerous rambling clubs sprang into being in the last quarter of the nineteenth century. One of the earliest was the Sunday Tramps, founded in 1879 by Leslie Stephen, well known as a critic, biographer and mountaineer, who led its members on fortnightly rambles in Kent and Surrey. They were a small band of writers, lawyers and philosophers and the like and talking was as much part of their excursions as walking. The novelist George Meredith wrote, 'when that noble body of scholarly and cheerful pedestrians, the Sunday Tramps, were on the march, with Leslie Stephen to lead them, there was conversation which would have made the presence of a shorthand writer a benefactor to the country'.[1]

George Meredith entertained the Sunday Tramps to dinner after some of their rambles at his home at Box Hill and they were given hospitality at other intellectual households in the area. 'But on principle Stephen objected to our being "pampered" as he would say, and generally bread and cheese at the village ale-house, or sandwiches, which we had been bidden to bring with us, were our fare.'[2] The 252nd and last walk of the original Tramps was in March 1895, although the club was reformed at the beginning of this century.

Other ramblers were united in field clubs, naturalist societies and camera clubs. Among the oldest rambling clubs still functioning are the Manchester YMCA Rambling Club (1880) and, in London, the Forest Ramblers (1884) and Polytechnic Clubs (1888). There were probably more rambling clubs in Manchester than in London, but it

*This chapter was left unfinished by Tom Stephenson and I have compiled it from fragments written by Tom and material he gathered for it. I have made every effort to be faithful to his intentions as far as these could be discerned, but the result cannot be taken entirely as Tom's own view of the events described.

was in London that the first Federation of Rambling Clubs was formed, in March 1905.[3]

Representatives of about twenty clubs attended a meeting called by Lawrence Chubb, secretary of the Commons Society, and J. A. Southern of the Highbury United Rambling Club.[4] In the chair was Sir Robert Hunter, an eminent legal authority on commons and rights of way and for many years honorary solicitor for the Commons Society. He was elected president of the Federation, a post he held until his death in 1913 when he was succeeded by Sir Frederick Pollock, another famous lawyer and member of Stephen's Sunday Tramps.[5] Chubb and Southern were appointed joint secretaries.[6]

The earliest available records of the Federation are to be found in its *Handbook* published in 1913. The list of officers reads like a page from *Burke's Peerage*. The list of vice-presidents included Lord Avebury, Lord Eversley, Lord Farrar, the Earl of Meath, and Sir Jeremiah Colman. That fondness for noble patronage persisted for many years. As late as 1962, when the Federation had become the Ramblers' Association's Southern Area, one of its vice-presidents was the Duke of Sutherland, whose ancestors had perpetrated one of the cruellest of the Highland Clearances.[7] By a curious coincidence a member of its executive committee, Mr. J. A King, was a descendant of Donald McLeod, who recorded his 'gloomy memories' of the clearances.[8]

The objects of the Federation according to the 1913 *Handbook* were to maintain and preserve ramblers' rights and privileges, secure more favourable travelling facilities, which meant negotiating such things as cheaper fares for ramblers with the railway companies, and generally to protect the interests of ramblers. As time went on, the Federation developed quite distant outposts, although it was based on London. In a letter written to T. A. Leonard in September 1931, George Mitchell, then its secretary, said, 'this Federation is the only one south of Birmingham, but it has affiliated clubs in Bristol, Cardiff, Darlington and Newcastle on Tyne among other places'.[9] In the 1940s the Federation's boundaries extended from the Wash to Dorset and covered seventeen counties.

George Mitchell's letter goes on to demonstrate the way in which rambling clubs in many other parts of the country had begun to see a need to federate in order to represent the general interests of ramblers within a particular area. He goes on, 'in Lancashire almost each town has a Federation, Manchester, Liverpool, Bolton, North Lancashire and now I hear Oldham wants an organisation of its own'.

The Manchester Federation had its beginnings at a meeting in November 1919, at the Clarion Café. In those days there were numerous Clarion Cafés, clubs and clubhouses linked with the *Clarion*, a socialist weekly paper. Six clubs were represented at the meeting, which decided to form a Ramblers' Council. Soon after this a 'conference of ramblers on railway fares' led to the formation of a Manchester and District Federation of Ramblers. At a joint meeting in December 1921 it was resolved to amalgamate the two bodies as from 1 January 1922.[10] At an 'inaugural conversazione' on 21 January 1922 the Ramblers' Federation (Manchester and District) was formed with a membership of thirty-eight clubs and thirty-seven individuals.

The importance of the access to mountains issue to Manchester ramblers was shown immediately, as this new grouping took it up and circularised, with some persistence, forty-nine MPs. With remarkable optimism the secretary's report on the first year's work concluded 'given enthusiasm, and a willingness to devote time and intelligence to the demand, there is no reason to doubt that the Access to Mountains Bill will become law during the next year or two.'[11]

Liverpool Federation was the next in line. At a preliminary meeting in November 1922 it was agreed to recommend the formation of a Federation of Liverpool and District Rambling Clubs. According to the minute book thirty people were present and a retiring collection raised 3s 11d (about 20p). As with the Manchester Federation, one of the objects was 'to urge the public right of access to mountains and moors'. The idea of national organisation for the rambling movement was also current at the time, some ten years before one came into being, at least in Liverpool. The Federation was 'to take such steps as are deemed advisable for the closer organisation of the national movement'.[12]

In Sheffield in March 1926, G. H. B. Ward, who had founded the Sheffield Clarion Ramblers in 1900, convened a meeting of local clubs to ascertain whether they favoured the formation of a Sheffield federation of rambling clubs.[13] At a second meeting in May eighteen clubs decided to form such a body. Ward was appointed chairman, a position he held until he died in 1957, and Stephen Morton became its first secretary.[14] With grouse moors inside the city boundary, with Kinder Scout, Bleaklow, and other keeper-patrolled moors within easy reach, one of its main objects was to campaign for free access to mountains and moorlands. Another, as in Liverpool, was to work for a national organisation for ramblers.[15]

Others followed. In 1930 federations were in existence in Birmingham, the West Riding of Yorkshire, Nottinghamshire and Derbyshire, Lincolnshire, and north-east Lancashire. A Cumberland Federation was formed in 1932 and changed its name to the Lake District Federation in 1933. A West of England Federation was also founded in 1932, South Wales in 1933 and the East Riding of Yorkshire in 1938.

Moves to link these federations into a national organisation began with Manchester, Liverpool, and Sheffield, where they soon began to hold joint meetings. In 1927 the Manchester and Sheffield Federations called a countryside and footpath conference at Hope, Derbyshire. This was attended not only by the three northern federations and the Peak District and Northern Counties Footpath Preservation Society but also by the London Federation, the Commons Society, and the Society for Checking the Abuse of Public Advertisements, an organisation which campaigned against the insensitive siting of advertisements in the countryside.

The Manchester Federation's *Handbook* commented, 'for the first time, a general expression of opinion and policy was obtained on the preservation of footpaths, rights of way, etc., litter nuisance, "uglyfication" of the countryside, access to mountains and moorlands'.[16]

So successful was the conference that it was decided 'that steps should be taken to organise for the next and following years a conference upon a wider basis, one which would include all societies concerned with the preservation of the countryside and the freedom of access thereto'. For this purpose a committee was formed, with Arthur Hewitt of the Manchester Ramblers' Federation as secretary, on which the ramblers' federations were represented. The committee included two representatives of the Leicestershire Footpath Association who offered to find accommodation for the meeting in Leicester. The offer was accepted and a local committee was set up. The ramblers' federations appear to have had little further say in the proceedings.

The conference was held on 12 and 13 October 1928 under the auspices of the National Trust, SCAPA, the Commons Society, the Council for the Preservation of Rural England (CPRE), the Federations of Rambling Clubs, the Peak and Northern Counties Footpaths Preservation Society, and the Leicestershire Footpath Association.[17]

R. A. Glen of the Commons Society, an eminent authority on highway law was billed to speak on 'The Rights of Way and Access to

Mountains Bill'.* According to the printed report he made no reference to access to open country in his speech. A Manchester delegate is reported as having referred to conditions in the Peak District where ramblers were threatened with guns and revolvers. He then moved that the conference urge the government to give facilities for the passage of the Access to Mountains Bill in the forthcoming session.

Mr Glen is reported as replying that 'it would be very unwise for the conference to deal with the Access to Mountains Bill. There would be a difference of opinion on it, and they wanted their resolutions to be unanimous. He suggested that they should refer the question to the CPRE for consideration. It was a very contentious Bill as it stood.' Another delegate suggested that the conference should refer the Access to Mountains Bill to the CPRE for examination and that the result should be reported to a future conference. This was agreed.[18]

So, at an early point in their history, the northern ramblers learnt that they were not likely to receive much support from existing amenity organisations for an access to mountains campaign.

In 1929 the conference was organised by the CPRE and held in Manchester on 10 and 11 October. This conference, after some discussion, did carry a resolution urging the government to give facilities for the Access to Mountains Bill in the next session. The author of *Federation Notes* in the Manchester and District Federation's annual *Handbook* commented:

the unfriendly attitude towards this measure, manifested at Leicester last year, was again evident, but the weight of northern opinion told on this occasion thanks to the persistence of our President Mr Stanley Jast. It was stated on behalf of the CPRE that the Bill was a contentious measure. We can hardly believe that the CPRE expects to make omelettes without breaking some eggs. We submit respectfully that the CPRE should decide whether such a Bill is needed or not, and if the former they should, if the present Bill does not provide sufficient safeguards for the landowner, advise them where it is lacking. There is a growing suspicion among Northern ramblers that the Countryside Conference is not a wholly disinterested body, but is being captured by a class concerned only in the preservation of rich men's amenities.[19]

One delegate who left the conference with that impression was Stephen Morton, who had been deputed to speak on access to

---

*The story of the series of access to mountains bills is told in Chapter 6.

mountains and moorlands. He found little support at the conference and concluded that a solution to the problem could only be advanced by an organisation made up solely of ramblers' federations. It had become clear that societies devoted to footpath preservation and scenery protection were not, and were not likely to become, supportive of ramblers' views on access.

The Sheffield and District Ramblers' Federation therefore decided to contact other ramblers' federations with a view to forming a national federation of ramblers. There was by no means unanimity among ramblers' federations that such a national body should be formed, at least at that time. In January 1930 a joint conference of the Manchester, Sheffield, and Liverpool Ramblers' Federations decided that 'the time was not yet ripe for the formation of a National Federation'.[20] However, the Liverpool Federation appear to have changed their minds later in the year, for their secretary wrote to Mitchell in October asking what news he had about a standing council of ramblers' federations. 'I know that the idea is not approved by all the Federations, but we are hoping to see the Council functioning before long.'[21]

Further meetings were held at Birchfields, Hope, in Derbyshire and the foundation of a national body was agreed on in 1930. For the first year G. H. B. Ward acted as chairman, and Stephen Morton as secretary, to allow time for the objects and constitution to be worked out and officers and committee selected. This interim framework was dissolved and the National Council of Ramblers' Federations was established at a conference at Longshaw, near Sheffield, in 1931.

Agreement was still not achieved smoothly, however. The Manchester Federation clearly had doubts about a national body and put a motion to the conference that two unions should be formed, one northern, one southern, with a joint consultative and co-ordinating council. An exchange of letters between T. A. Leonard and George Mitchell suggests that Manchester was wary of too much power in a national organisation going to the London Federation. T. A. Leonard wrote of the Manchester ramblers, 'what probably weighs most in their minds is the centring of the union in London. If the centre could be in the north I think a good deal of the resistance would disappear. And why should this not be so? Do you see any objection?'[22]

Mitchell did see objection, and in his reply to Leonard suggests that, with so many federations in the north, London might not even get a seat on any executive which was eventually elected.

The argument, although plausible, is quite fallacious inasmuch as any National Organisation which might be formed would not be controlled by Manchester, or London members, or any other place for that matter . . . So far as London wanting to be the headquarters of a National Organisation, there is no particular desire on our part for this, but owing to circumstances over which present day ramblers have no control the City happens to be the seat of Government for the present.[23]

At the Longshaw conference, held on 26 and 27 September 1931, the Manchester resolution for northern and southern bodies was discussed along with two resolutions for a national organisation. A small sub-committee was formed to work out an agreed resolution. The Manchester delegation appear to have been satisfied for, when the conference resumed, Arthur Hewitt of Manchester moved that a National Council of Ramblers' Federations be formed and this was carried unanimously.[24] The meeting also agreed to a resolution 'That the District Federations be asked to organise indoor public meetings in favour of access to mountains.' Alf Embleton, a representative of Liverpool Federation, showed a firm preference for a populist approach to the campaign by suggesting that meetings should be held at seaside resorts like Blackpool or Southport during the summer rather than holding indoor meetings which might be poorly attended.[25]

The access to mountains campaign started out as and continued to be a prime concern of the fledgling organisation. In the following year, 1932, the National Council discussed the current position of the campaign. A letter from Sir Charles Trevelyan MP was read by the chairman, T. A. Leonard, stating that he thought there was little prospect of success for the Access to Mountains Bill in the present Parliament, or of the Prime Minister or any other member of the government meeting a deputation. The meeting decided to concentrate on encouraging federations to hold local demonstrations, and to offer advice as to how this could be done most effectively. At this meeting a sub-committee was set up to concentrate on matters concerning access to mountains, a sub-committee which was to play an important part in the story of the campaign for access legislation.[26]

The Annual Report of 1934 recorded an attempt at a negotiated solution. It stated that the Committee was working with the Commons Society and that a meeting had taken place attended by them, representatives of the Central Landowners' Association and

Land Agents' Society, and Peak District and Northern Counties Footpath Preservation Society, the Derbyshire Footpaths Preservation Society, the Derbyshire Community Council, and various local authorities with water-gathering grounds. The position of the amenity societies seems to have been very moderate, compared to the ideal of a right to access to all uncultivated land. They had 'urged that the time had come for granting the public permissive ways, under proper safeguards'. The landowners' representatives 'received these views and promised to consider in sympathy any definite proposals of an experimental nature which might be put before them'.[27] In the end these negotiations came to nothing, but the National Council of Ramblers' Federations continued to involve itself in negotiations, lobbying, and demonstrations, such as the famous series held in Winnats Pass, near Castleton in Derbyshire, to further the campaign for access to mountains.

However, there were clearly still strains in the relationship between the Manchester Federation and the National Council. When the Council decided to become the Ramblers' Association in 1935, Manchester decided not to join. One of the reasons for this seems to have been their continued distrust of the commitment of some of the federations to the campaign for access to mountains – they feared that the organisation would be dominated by people who were more concerned with footpaths and national parks.[28] Stephen Morton appears to have tried to pre-empt any such development by moving a resolution at the annual National Council meeting in 1936 that it should be placed on record that the Access to Mountains Bill was the main concern of the Association and this was agreed. It is also clear from these minutes that not all members of Manchester Federation's leadership felt the same. The Council agreed 'with acclamation' that Edwin Royce of Manchester should be vice-chairman of the RA for the ensuing year – not, presumably, against his will.[29]

The Manchester Federation finally joined the RA in December 1939 after an informal meeting between its officers and members of the RA's executive committee.[30] By this time all the rambling organisations had gone through the trauma of the 1939 Access to Mountains Act* and the country was at war. The RA greeted hostilities with a manifesto which stated the ramblers' approach to the new situation firmly:

*The passing of this Act and the controversy surrounding it are described in chapters 8 and 9.

It will be in the national interest that those citizens who can do so should get into the countryside at regular intervals. There is nothing so beneficial to health, nerves and general well-being as a good walk in the country, especially to people who live in towns and those whose work imposes a great strain on them. The Ramblers' Association therefore hopes that every effort will be made by government and local authorities and by owners and occupiers of land to maintain rights of way and to provide reasonable freedom to roam over uncultivated land.[31]

References

1 F. W. Maitland, *Life and Letters of Leslie Stephen* (London, 1906), p. 357.

2 *Ibid.*, p. 360.

3 *The Rambler*, September 1905. Copy in Tom Stephenson collection, RA History file, RAA.

4 *The Rambler*, June 1904. Copy in Tom Stephenson collection, RA History file, RAA.

5 *Ramblers' Handbook* (London, 1914).

6 *Ramblers' Handbook* (London, 1924, 1925).

7 Ramblers' Handbook (London, 1962).

8 Donald McLeod, *Gloomy Memories of the Highlands* (Inverness, 1883).

9 George Mitchell to T. A. Leonard, undated (in reply to Leonard, 15 September 1931), Tom Stephenson collection, RA History File, RAA.

10 A. W. Hewitt, *The Ramblers' Federation, 19 years of progress in Manchester and District* (Manchester, 1938), pamphlet.

11 Harold E. Wild, 'Genesis', in *Twenty-Five Milestones* (Manchester, 1948), pamphlet.

12 Liverpool and District Ramblers' Federation, First Annual Report and Balance Sheet, for year ending 31 December 1923, Tom Stephenson collection, RA History file, RAA.

13 Sheffield Clarion Ramblers' Club, *Annual 1927–28* (Sheffield, 1927, pp. 150–1.

14 Sheffield Clarion Ramblers' Club, *Annual, 1928–29*, pp. 125–6.

15 Sheffield Clarion Ramblers' Club, *Annual 1927–28*, p. 150.

16 *Ramblers' Federation Handbook*, Official Yearbook of the Ramblers' Federation (Manchester and District) (Manchester, 1929), p. 12.

17 Report of the Countryside and Footpaths Preservation National Conference and Exhibition, supplement to *Out of Doors*, Vol. 111, No. 4, December 1928.

18 *Ibid.*, p. xiv.

19 'Federation notes', *Ramblers' Federation Handbook, op. cit.*, p. 9.

20 Minutes with letter to George Mitchell from Alf Embleton, 22 January

1930, Tom Stephenson collection, RA History file, RAA.

21 Letter to George Mitchell from N. S. Waterworth, 29 October 1930, Tom Stephenson collection, RA History file, RAA.

22 Letter to George Mitchell from T. A. Leonard, 15 September 1931, Tom Stephenson collection, RA History file, RAA.

23 Letter to T. A. Leonard from George Mitchell, undated, Tom Stephenson collection, RA History file, RAA.

24 Minutes of the National Conference, held at Longshaw Lodge, Derbyshire, on 26 and 27 September 1931, RAA.

25 *Ibid.*

26 National Council of Ramblers' Federations, Report and Minutes of the meeting held at Derwent Hall, Ashopton, Derbyshire, on 1 and 2 October, 1932, RAA.

27 Draft Annual Report, 1933–34, Tom Stephenson collection, RA History file, RAA.

28 Andrew Dalby, 'Foundation and first steps', in Ann Holt (ed.), *Making Tracks, A celebration of fifty years of the Ramblers' Association* (London, 1985), p. 12.

29 Minutes of the Annual Meeting of the Council held at Comford Court, Matlock on 14 and 15 March 1936, RAA.

30 Dalby, *op. cit.*

31 Enjoyment of the Countryside in Wartime, A Manifesto from the Ramblers' Association, Tom Stephenson Collection, RA History file, RAA.

Chapter 3

Trespassers will be prosecuted

Enough timber to have launched a small armada must have gone into making those thousands of 'Trespassers will be prosecuted' notices, which, for more than a century and a half, have been such a ubiquitous feature of our countryside. We called them 'wooden liars' because trespass is a civil matter, not a criminal offence, so a trespasser cannot be prosecuted, only sued. More honest, if equally galling, notices prohibiting entry bar the way of the rambler in many of the most beautiful parts of their native land. In 1967 Lancashire County Council published a memorandum on the Forest of Bowland in which they included a map showing the location of prohibitive signs, most of them on the Sefton Estate.[1] On a beautiful, unfenced moorland road across that estate, every few hundred yards, there was a stark notice: 'Private'.

Leslie Stephen, founder of the Sunday Tramps rambling club, was a great trespasser and wrote:

I looked out for notices that trespassers would be prosecuted. That gave a strong presumption that the trespass must have some attraction. Cyclists could only reflect that trespassing for them is not only forbidden but impossible. To me it was a reminder of the many delicious bits of walking which, even in the neighbourhood of London, await the man who has no superstitious reverence for legal rights.[2]

Among the lawyers who were members of the Tramps was Sir Frederick Pollock, president of the Federation of Rambling Clubs from 1913 to 1919. He is credited with devising the formula with which the Tramps responded to charges of trespassing. 'We hereby give you notice,' said the formula, 'that we do not, nor doth any of us, claim any right of way or other easement into or over these lands, and we tender you this shilling by way of amends.' It was said to be most effective when repeated after the leader in solemn chant by a large party of Tramps, and when sung in unison the effect on the gamekeeper was said to have been devastating.[3]

The formula may have worked in the Home Counties, but whether it would have soothed the savage breast of a Derbyshire keeper is questionable.

Probably more effective than trespass boards were notices similar to this:

BEWARE

MANTRAPS AND

SPRING GUNS

A few such notices, almost certainly bluffs, like those warning of 'Snakes in this Wood', existed well into this century, though those diabolical machines had been declared illegal in 1827. The mantrap was like a giant rat-trap with spiked jaws. If a poacher trod on the plate, which might be buried under leaves, the jaws were released and crashed into his leg, probably smashing the bone, and there he might die before being discovered. In the County Museum at Dorchester there is a display of these instruments. One of them is described as 'humane'. It has no jaws, and so did not lacerate the flesh; merely smashed the bone.

The spring gun consisted of an upright steel rod to which a trip wire was attached. If the wire were disturbed it released a weight which fired the gun and sent a charge of shot along the line of the wire. One type could be fixed to fire at the poacher's legs or his head. They could be fearsomely effective. In 1810 the statesman Lord Palmerston, no friend of poachers, was out on a day's shooting when he stepped on a trip wire. The gun did not fire, but for the rest of the day, it is said, he was nervous whenever a bramble caught his leg.[4]

The use of such instruments was accepted, but not without dissent.* One unsporting MP said in the House of Commons, 'better the whole race of game was extinct than that it should owe its preservation to such cruel expedients'.[5] Sydney Smith, in his usual forthright style, wrote that:

---

*Harry Hopkins in *The Long Affray; The Poaching Wars 1760–1914* (London, 1985) describes the social effects of the obsession of the British aristocracy with blood sports and points to the way the rambler has taken over something of the niche of the poacher in the demonology of gamekeepers and landowners (see p. 301).

there is a sort of horror in thinking of a whole land filled with lurking engines of death . . . the lords of manors eyeing their peasantry as so many butts and marks, and panting to hear the click of the trap and to see the flash of the gun. How many human being educated in liberal knowledge and Christian feeling, can doom to certain destruction a poor wretch, tempted by the sight of animals that naturally appear to him to belong to one person as well as another, we are at a loss to conceive.[6]

Robert Peel, as Home Secretary, when supporting the Bill for the abolition of spring guns, was of a similar opinion:

if a spring gun was to be defended as a punishment for trespass, a man might also defend the springing of a mine, by which a whole gang of poachers might be destroyed at once. He for one could not approve the power of punishing with death a trespass which, even if a man were convicted, would only bring upon him a punishment of three months imprisonment. If persons were anxious to preserve game let them keep a physical force sufficient for that purpose.[7]

In 1907 there was a spring gun in Mytton Wood, Whalley, Lancashire. Several times I, with other lads of the village, confident we could outrun the gamekeeper, tried in vain to fire the gun by prodding the wire with sticks which (we hoped) were long enough to keep us out of the line of fire. It never did fire and it may be that the gun was not charged at that time.

It was a different story when, in 1953, members of the Sussex Pathfinders Ramblers' Club encountered a gun which was charged. Robert Crewdson and Frank Gregory were in the lead when there was a loud report from the undergrowth. Gregory felt a strong blast against his right side and found blood running down his face. Crewdson was also bleeding from numerous face wounds. Another member of the party found a spring gun hidden in the bracken. A gamekeeper was accused of setting a spring gun and causing grievous bodily harm and was committed for trial. In his defence it was said that he had by mistake loaded the gun with a twelve-bore cartridge, instead of a blank. He had been using these alarm guns, as he called them, for twenty years without incident. They were not meant to injure anyone, but to warn him that poachers were trespassing. The solicitor for the prosecution said that if the intention were only to warn of the presence of poachers, that could have been effected equally well by having the cartridge pointing to the ground or away from the ride where people might walk. However, a police witness said that the apparatus was correctly described as an alarm gun, and that these guns were openly on sale, and were in common use for the purposes of giving alarm. The gamekeeper was acquitted.[8]

There are many well-authenticated records of ramblers being assaulted by gamekeepers, and no doubt there were many others never reported. In 1932 a leaflet put out by ramblers' organisations stated:

members of our federations have been menaced by a revolver-flourishing gamekeeper on Bleaklow; . . . others of our members have had unpleasant experiences on the moors of Derbyshire, the West Riding of Yorkshire, North Wales, and in the Trough of Bowland (e.g., Fairsnape Fell, Bleasdale; and Abbeystead Fell, near Lancaster). For the best defence of their rights some shooting landlords employ undesirable types of keeper who do not hesitate to assault walkers and use foul language.[9]

The story of what happened to one rambler when he set out for a walk on a spring morning is instructive of the climate of the time. The BBC broadcast the following message in April 1930:

The Derbyshire police are anxious to get in touch with the motorist who at about 3.45 p.m. on Good Friday was hailed by a rambler at Woodhead, Derbyshire, and gave him a lift towards Sheffield . . . The man had previously violently assaulted a gamekeeper and fractured one of his legs, and information as to his identity or whereabouts should be communicated to the Chief Constable of Derbyshire or any police station.

The wanted man was 21-year-old Donald Burt, who reported to his local police station immediately after hearing the broadcast. On Good Friday morning he had left the Yorkshire Bridge Inn near Bamford to trace the River Derwent to its source. This led him over Bleaklow, then (as it was until the coming of the Pennine Way thirty-five years later) a strictly preserved grouse moor; thirty-seven square miles of heather and a peat groughs without a single right of way; the largest area in England without a public path and only sixteen miles from the centres of Sheffield and Manchester.

When the case came to court the prosecution said that the gamekeeper and his assistant were standing on the road near Woodhead station when they saw Burt descending the moor. The assistant went to meet him and questioned him about trespassing, and then walked down with Burt to his superior. Burt was said to have struck him, whereupon he fell twelve feet and broke his left leg, Burt, it was claimed, had then hit the assistant and run away. Burt denied the charges against him. He had feared a 'rough-house' and run off. Upon reaching the road he was detained by a local resident and it was then he heard the keeper say his leg was broken, and he said to his captor, 'let me go and let's go back to help him.' As they were doing so the assistant came towards them and struck at Burt, who warded off the blow, hit back, and then bolted.

The prosecution claimed that Burt had struck a left-handed blow, but the defence then revealed that Burt had suffered a compound fracture of his left arm the previous November. The bones in his forearm were united by a metal plate and his left thumb was still dislocated – it would have been impossible for him to strike a blow with his left arm. The police prosecution failed. If Burt had not been able to engage a solicitor and a barrister the story might have had a very different ending.[10]

It was sometimes possible to defeat gamekeepers using less expensive means. Fifteen years previously G. H. B. Ward and a party of his Sheffield Clarion Ramblers had an encounter at Woodhead with a gamekeeper. They had arrived at Woodhead Station at 7.30 a.m. on a January Sunday in 1915. In those days ramblers, many of whom would have started work at 6.00 a.m. on six days of the week, found it no hardship to catch a train at about the same time on the seventh day.

As Ward tells the story, there was a tempting smell of frying bacon as they passed the gamekeeper's cottage. The man evidently did not finish his breakfast, for soon he came charging after the party, pushed through them and grabbed Ward by the collar of his sweater. He said they were not going that way. In his free hand he held a thick 'knock-nobbler', and Ward asked his friends to grab that arm, lest the keeper should use the stick. They did so, and released Ward. There was more abuse from the keeper, who made a second dash at Ward. This time he was removed and laid on his back. Ward told him that they were going on their trespass way and that, if he interfered with them any further, they would bundle him into the middle of the swollen stream.[11]

Eric Byne, in his book on the High Peak, has recorded another incident in which keepers came off second best. Byne and seven other youngsters set out one Sunday morning to walk from Bradfield to Edale via Edwen Beck and Abbey Brook. They found themselves, says Byne,

confronted by four burly keepers armed with guns and cudgels, who lost no time in attacking. They rushed at the boys with howls of abuse, intent on beating them up. What followed must have come as a surprise. None of the boys was large, but all eight were members of Footit's ju-jitsu Gymnasium at Hillsborough, and after the shock of the first scuffle they succeeded in disarming the men and tossing them into the brook. This happened three times until the keepers were completely cooled down, after which they retreated along the opposite bank.[12]

The ramblers' federations received many complaints about keepers' behaviour and sometimes brought cases to court. In August 1927 the Manchester and District Ramblers' Federation received a report of an incident which had occurred two days previously. Members of the Hans Renold Rambling Club had been walking in the Woodlands Valley in Derbyshire when two of their members were shot by a farm hand. One rambler received three wounds in the arm, one in the thigh, and another three wounds in his leg. The Federation took up the case and supplied signed statements to the Superinten-dent of Police at Chapel-en-le-Frith. The case came to court, the man was fined with costs, and he published an apology in the High Peak Reporter.[13]

However, courts were sometimes lenient in their view of assaults on ramblers. On the other side of the Pennines, in August 1930, William Jones, a 19-year-old hammer-driver, met, near Roche Abbey, one of Lord Scarborough's gamekeepers. The result for Jones – a smashed nose. The keeper was charged with causing grievous bodily harm and at the trial a medical witness said that there was a definite hole in the bridge of Jones's nose which could not have been caused by a bare fist. Jones said that the keeper had struck him with the butt end of his gun and knocked him to the ground. The bench found the keeper guilty and he was fined £4. This sentence should perhaps be compared with the keeper's next appearance in the same court, this time as complai-nant. A 47-year-old miner was charged with assaulting him and stealing seven rabbits. The miner was given seven days' imprison-ment for the assault and two months for the theft.[14]

Coming nearer to our own time, in 1965, a young woman was injured by a farmer while climbing with a friend. The farmer had ordered them to leave, and as they had been preparing to do so had thrown a stone which hit her head. As a result she spent two days in hospital. The magistrate called it a stupid and reckless action, but set the fine at £5 as the farmer would have to bear the costs of two hearings.[15]

Cases could not always, however, be brought to court. The *Handbook* of the Sheffield Clarion Ramblers for 1941–42 gives an insight into the attitude of at least some police officers at the time. Frank Spriggs wrote to Castleton (Derbyshire) Police as follows:

On Monday 12th August (1940) I was walking from Peak Forest through Goosehill Hall, Castleton, and when I reached a wall along the Rowter Farm to the Dirtlow Rake track, I could not find a stile, and so I climbed over a wall to find a continuation of the path which is clearly shown on the one-inch OS map. I was stopped by two men who took up a threatening attitude, used strong language and told me to get back. I immediately did as they told me, but had hardly turned when the taller man hit me a heavy blow with his fist on the left side of my head above the ear.

As I am a cripple with a paralysed arm I was unable to do anything but hurry away, and I ran to the police station at Castleton . . . the police officer at Castleton did not appear to take my statement seriously and suggested that if I had been trespassing the farmer was entitled to take what steps he thought necessary to remove me.

The Sheffield Federation were advised by lawyers that an action for assault was unlikely to succeed unless supported by witnesses, and the case was taken no further.[16]

Justice, it has been said, is open to all – like the Ritz Hotel. It must have been something of a surprise to the Duke of Rutland to find himself taken to court, in 1892, by Daniel Harrison, a saw-handle-maker from Sheffield. Harrison brought the action against the Duke, Lord Edward Manners, and three gamekeepers, claiming damages for assault, false imprisonment, and the obstruction of a public highway.

For Harrison it was said that on 6 October 1891, while he was walking along a public footpath, the three gamekeepers assaulted him and prevented him continuing on his way. Later on the same day, a gamekeeper, having a stick, a gun, and two sporting dogs, assaulted him and beat him and with gestures and violence compelled him to return on his way. On 8 October, as he was walking on the highway between Ringing Low and Hathersage, three keepers assaulted him, threw him on the ground, and held him there for about three-quarters of an hour. The keepers were acting under the orders of the Duke of Rutland and Lord Edward Manners. Harrison claimed £300 damages, and asked for an injunction restraining the defendants or their agents from preventing him exercising his lawful rights. Harrison's Counsel said the case was brought to vindicate the rights of the public to use highways over moors owned by the Duke of Rutland. The defendants seemed to believe that whatever the public rights, they, at any rate, had the paramount right to shoot across the public highway.

The defendants held that Harrison was not walking on the highway for a lawful purpose but was trespassing. He was on the highway for the purpose of interfering and had threatened to continue to interfere with the defendants, who were lawfully exercising sporting rights over the moors belongong to the Duke of Rutland. Any assaults were lawfully committed for the purpose of preventing trespass and unlawful interference. The defendants denied all liability, but paid 5s into court and said this was sufficient to satisfy the plaintiff's calls for action. By way of counter-claim the Duke of Rutland asked for an injunction restraining the plaintiff from continuing interference and trespass.

In the witness box Harrison told of an encounter with Lord Edward Manners on 6 October. Harrison had said that if the gunmen continued firing over the roadway he would summons them. Lord Edward Manners had said, 'You can go to the devil if you have a mind.' Harrison said, 'Thank you, my Lord, but I will walk along the road when I think proper.' His Lordship then said he would have him stopped and if he was shot it would be upon his own head. On 8 October Harrison was again on the moors when he saw three keepers and three constables standing on the highway between him and the butts. One said, 'You are not going any further.' Harrison said, 'Well, I shall try to go.' The three keepers then pulled him on to the ground and sat upon him. They weighed about forty stones between them and held him so tightly that he was almost choked. He asked the constables to interfere but they only laughed. He told them he would report them and asked for their numbers. One constable said, 'I will give thee a number on top of thi' head.'

Under cross-examination Harrison admitted that in 1884 he was convicted of trespassing over the moors. Counsel for the defendants said that it was only after being convicted for poaching that Harrison sought to revenge himself by interfering with the sporting rights of the Duke and his friends. Harrison had lingered in front of the butts to destroy a fair and legitimate sport. Counsel for Harrison said that this was the first time in the history of English law that anyone had suggested that a person who owned the adjoining land was entitled to the soil of the highway, and that the public in passing over the highway in any way they chose were trespassers upon that highway, and were to be stopped, to be put upon the ground on the orders of some landowners, because they interfered with the sacred rights of sport.

In summing up, the Lord Chief Justice said that it was beyond question that Mr Harrison was on a public highway. All the Queen's subjects had the absolute right to go along it. Suppose there was a beautiful view to be obtained from a particular spot. Not all the dukes in the country should prevent a man walking up and down the road for the purpose of admiring the view. Naturally it was important to the owners of the moors that they should be able to drive their birds, but they must exercise rights subject to the rights of the public. If they could not drive without interfering with the absolute right of the public they must drive some other way. They must exercise their rights subject to the rights of the public. The question was therefore one of deciding damages.

The jury found that the 5s paid into court was sufficient damages.[17] Harrison was not satisfied and took his case to the Appeal Court, where he fared no better. In fact the Appeal Court Judges were less sympathetic to him in their opinions on the law of passage on a public highway. Although he lost his battles, Harrison won a measure of immortality, for in the law books dealing with highways – passing and repassing – there is listed as a leading case *Harrison* v. *Rutland*.[18]

Harrison, as a working man, obviously could not have met all the legal expenses he incurred. G. H. B. Ward took an interest in the case and thought that Harrison had some anonymous wealthy backer. However that may be, Harrison still battled on. In 1907, then described as a farm labourer, he was in court again, charged with breach of an injunction restraining him from interfering with the shooting on Hallam Moor. He had apparently been up to his old tricks of walking in front of the guns.[19]

In the mid-1950s Manchester Corporation Waterworks Committee had a gamekeeper on their Longdendale Moors who was notorious for his vigorous and abusive approach to trespassers. One Sunday evening in Edale I met two lads who had been ordered off Westend Moss by him. He told them that if he ever met that fellow Stephenson he would wring his bloody neck. On the following Sunday, Phil Daley, chairman of the Peak Park Board Access Committee, his wife Eileen, who was a magistrate, and I set out from Crowden to follow the Pennine Way, which at this time had been diverted from the original line by Laddow Rocks to a route over Tooley Shaw Moor to the summit of Black Hill. We were sitting on the top of Westend Moss at about 1,700 feet, when we saw the keeper and his two big black labradors racing towards us.

Before he had fully recovered his breath he asked where the bloody hell we were going and had we no more sense than to come up there in the middle of the nesting season. When we said we were following the Pennine Way he replied that we were nowhere near the Pennine Way. Then he began denouncing that fellow Stephenson who was no rambler, but simply made money out of writing about rambling. He went on for some time on this theme and then I said, 'Well, I am Stephenson.' He looked at me and quick as a flash said, 'Well, I knew you were. I was only pulling your leg.' I told him that I had heard that he was going to wring my neck. To this he said, 'I was in a bad temper that day, and fed up with ramblers on the Pennine Way.' We succeeded in convicing him that we were on the Pennine Way as diverted and he accompanied us to the summit of Black Hill. There he shook hands all round and departed.

I wrote to the National Parks Commission, predecessor of the Countryside Commission, informing them of this incident and of reports of the similar experiences of other ramblers. I added, 'One would have thought it possible to have completed a footpath agreement in the seven months that have elapsed since the Minister's decision was announced. In any event, Manchester Corporation might have been expected to have informed their gamekeeper that this was an intended right of way and that walkers should not be prevented from following the route.'[20]

The Commission replied, 'You will be glad to know that, as a result of your representations, the Ministry themselves have asked Manchester Corporation to inform their gamekeeper that this is an intended right of way, and that walkers should not be prevented from following the route as originally proposed by the Corporation.'[21]

After the Peak District of Derbyshire, the most restricted area of moorland in the country was probably the Forest of Bowland on the borders of Lancashire and what was then the West Riding of Yorkshire, though other parts of the West Riding ran it close, particularly the Chatsworth and Saville Estates, and the gathering grounds of the Bradford and Leeds Corporations. In August 1966 representatives of the Lancashire County Council Planning Committee met a deputation from the RA. The deputation referred to a Parliamentary

Question put by Peter Jackson, MP for High Peak, asking what action was being taken to secure greater public access to open country[22] and presented a number of signed statements from ramblers who had been prevented by gamekeepers from walking on Abbeystead Moors. One statement told of sixteen members of the Morecambe and Heysham Holiday Fellowship Rambling Club who, having left a road at Abbeystead, walked about half a mile up a path towards the moors when they heard shouting through a loudhailer. At first they couldn't distinguish the words and then they heard, 'Are you coming down or do we have to fetch you? We'll set the dogs on you and they'll tear you to pieces.' The ramblers returned to the road and met a man who said he was the head keeper to the Earl of Sefton. He was carrying a hailer under his arm and when one of the ramblers protested about his manner, and the threat he had made, he said he didn't think he had done anything wrong.[23]

The deputation were given a long and sympathetic hearing, but nearly seven years were to pass before the County Council succeeded in negotiating access agreements for a few thousand acres.

Cases of violence towards ramblers on the part of gamekeepers and others, such as those mentioned above are, after all, the actions of a small minority. This account is not meant as an indictment of keepers in general or to suggest that they are by nature sadistic brutes. It is included to make clear the very real risks run by ramblers who, by accident or design, trespassed, or, sometimes, exercised their right to walk on a public right of way, the existence of which was not convenient to a landowner. I have found many gamekeepers very friendly, and sometimes very helpful folk. I have never encountered any violence beyond, when I was a lad, a clip on the ear or a tap from a stick on my behind. Such slight punishment was probably not so much for trespass as for insolence from a young Mr Knowall, who refused to believe that a mountain or a wide sweep or moorland could be owned by anyone. As a lad I was friendly with a gamekeeper in the village of Slaidburn, in the Forest of Bowland. Often I would join him for an eight-o'clock Sunday breakfast, after a thirteen-mile trek from my home. We would spend the day together on the fells, and then I would walk back home. Sometimes he would accompany me with his bicycle as far as the Moorcock Inn, then a small whitewashed house on Waddington Fell, and then cycle home. On one occasion we met three men who knew me, and who hastily assumed that I was under arrest. Until the situation was explained to them they were prepared to do battle if necessary to secure my release.

Often enough I have been ordered off a moor, not always politely. Sometimes, though, there would be a persuasive suggestion of retreat, or even of an acceptable detour.

In Scotland I have found helpful gamekeepers. There was one in the Applecross district who directed me to a short cut running near a shooting lodge. He told me that if anyone questioned me I was to say I knew I was on a public right of way. Then there was the gamekeeper who advised me of the day when I was unlikely to be intercepted on the ascent of Ben More Assynt, and there was a head keeper who gave me a lift to Achnasheen, saving me ten miles of road walking. He told me on the journey that the previous day he had watched me through his telescope, scrambling on a forbidden mountain.

A well-remembered incident occurred sixty years ago on the summit of Great Whernside, in Upper Wharfedale. On a June afternoon I was basking at the summit when a keeper approached with a gun and a dog. He said: 'Dost tha' know tha' art trespassing?' I said, 'Aye, what are you going to do about it, prosecute or shoot?' He replied, 'Nay, its aw reet as long as tha' knows.'

References

1 RAA, Bowland File.
2 Sir Leslie Stephen, 'In praise of walking', in *Studies of a Biographer*, Vol. 3 (London, 1902), pp. 276—7.
3 *Times*, 18 January 1930.
4 Jasper Ridley, *Lord Palmerston* (London, 1970), p. 70.
5 *Hansard*, 1st Ser. Vol. 36, Col. 925, 9 June 1817.
6 *The Edinburgh Review*, Vol. 35, No. 69, 1821, p. 134.
7 *Hansard*, 2nd Ser., Vol. 15, Cols. 719–20, 27 April 1826.
8 *Ramblers News*, No. 17, Spring 1954, p. 13; *Evening News*, 24 February 1954; *Evening Standard*, 24 February 1954.
9 Manchester and District Ramblers' Federation, in conjunction with Glasgow, Liverpool and Sheffield Ramblers' Federations, *Access to Mountains and Moorlands* (Manchester, 1932), pamphlet.
10 Sheffield Clarion Ramblers' *Handbook*, 1931–32, p. 107.
11 Sheffield Clarion Ramblers' *Handbook*, 1948–49, p. 44.
12 Eric Byne and Geoffrey Sutton, *High Peak* (London, 1966), p. 151.
13 Manchester Ramblers' Federation Minutes, 16 August, 13 September, 27 September 1927; 22 February 1928.
14 Sheffield Clarion Ramblers' *Handbook*, 1931–32, p. 138.
15 *Rucksack*, Vol. 3, No. 1, winter 1965–6, p. 13.

16   Sheffield Clarion Ramblers' *Handbook*, 1941–42, p. 134.

17   *Sheffield Daily Telegraph*, 5 August 1892; *Sheffield and Rotherham Independent*, 5 August 1892.

18   *Justice of the Peace*, Vol. 57, No. 18, 1893, pp. 278–81; *Law Times*, Vol. 94, No. 2593, 1892, p. 128.

19   Sheffield Clarion Ramblers' *Handbook*, 1955–56, p. 53.

20   RAA, Longdendale File, letter dated 3 August 1955.

21   RAA, Longdendale File, letter dated 16 September 1955.

22   *Hansard* (House of Commons), 5th Ser., Vol. 730, Written Answers Col. 9, 20 June 1966.

23   RAA, Boulsworth File, note of incident.

Chapter 4

The water authorities

Almost as rigorous as the sporting interests in their prohibition of walkers on the moors were some of the water authorities. To allow ramblers on their gathering grounds, they said, might lead to pollution of their reservoirs and perhaps cause a typhoid epidemic. Some authorities, like Bolton, Bradford, Huddersfield, and Manchester, while banning ramblers, leased their moors for grouse shooting. The shooters, the keepers and the beaters were, presumably, pure and uncontaminated, or, as one rambler put it more crudely, they were a superior race devoid of bowels and bladders.

On the other hand, some authorities, without any ill consequences, allowed access not only to the gathering grounds but also to the edges of their reservoirs as, for instance, in the Lake District to the shores of Buttermere, Crummock Water and Ennerdale Water, natural lakes from which domestic supplies are abstracted.

Some authorities took water from adjacent rivers, most notable of them being the Metropolitan Water Board, which drew much of its water from the Thames although, farther upstream, it had received the sewage effluent of large towns such as Oxford and Reading. Even so, the London water supply was claimed to be bacteriologically one of the purest in the world. That was not the opinion of Sir William Kay, for more than fifty years chairman of Manchester City Water undertaking. A member of an RA deputation to his committee reminded him of the Metropolitan Water Board's claim. With a facial expression of extreme disgust, he replied, 'Don't talk to me of London water. I wouldn't drink the stuff. It's probably been through half-a-dozen pairs of kidneys before it reaches you.'

Until it installed a filtration plant in 1965 Manchester had a dual policy. By its Parliamentary Act of 1879 authorising the conversion of the natural lake of Thirlmere into a reservoir, it was required to allow public access to the adjacent mountains, including Helvellyn. By contrast, its moors in the Longdendale gathering grounds were left for shooting, ringed with 'Trespassers Will Be Prosecuted' notices, and patrolled by keepers to ward off intruders, which they did effectively, if not always politely.

For the liberty to ascend Helevellyn we are indebted to the Open Spaces Society, then known as the Commons, Open Spaces and Footpath Preservation Society, for obvious reasons usually abbreviated to 'Commons Society'. When work started in 1847 on the Longdendale reservoirs there were no amenity societies striving for the public good, but when the Thirlmere Bill was before Parliament in 1879 the Society was fourteen years old. With influential friends at Westminster, it effectively threatened to oppose the Bill unless a clause were added to the effect 'that the access heretofore enjoyed on the part of the public and tourists to the mountains and fells surrounding Lake Thirlmere shall not be in any manner restricted or interfered with by the Corporation.'[1] In 1892 Birmingham Corporation introduced a bill to enable them to purchase some fifty square miles of common land at the head of the rivers Elan and Clairwen in Mid-Wales. The Commons Society was again to the fore, and secured the addition of a clause saving the commoners' rights and giving the public the right to roam over the area.

The water authorities' point of view was that they had a statutory duty to provide a pure and wholesome water supply, and they had to take all possible steps to prevent pollution. The greatest danger came from carriers of enteric diseases. If such a person urinated or defecated on a water gathering ground, said the authorities, the bacteria so released might proliferate and reach the piped water supply and so start a serious epidemic.

In April and June 1935, the CPRE made two abortive approaches to the British Waterworks Association with the hope of gaining some measure of access to gathering grounds. At a meeting in June, in addition to the CPRE, the Camping Club, the Commons Society, the RA, and the YHA were represented. On the other side were representatives of Cambridge, Cardiff, Edinburgh, Leeds, Liverpool, and Manchester water undertakings. The CPRE representative, Captain E. P. Richards, speaking 'as a walker and water engineer', submitted what he called a fair and impartial report. This was erroneously taken by the water undertakings as an agreed policy statement by the deputation, though it had not been endorsed by the RA.

The RA had been represented by its chairman, T. A. Leonard, and J. A. Southern, a member of the executive committee. Kenneth Spence, who was to become a vice-president of the RA the following year, had been there acting on behalf of the CPRE and YHA. Both Leonard and Spence seem to have felt the meeting was hopeless. Leonard wrote later to Spence:

As I looked at those people opposite us I felt convinced that everyone had a car, used it extensively, had never known what it was like to walk over a mountain on a hot day and come down by a sparkling spring and had the joy of dipping his face and arms in it. They hadn't it in them to realise the strong human appeal that exists on our side.

When the water authorities came into the open with legislation, he went on, 'We must have a good case based upon the latest bacteriological lines.'[2]

Spence wrote to George Mitchell, the RA secretary, that he thought the meeting had been an appalling business. He feared that Richards's verbose document had only complicated the issue. It seemed to him that the water authorities would not grant one inch more liberty, and they threatened to seek powers to limit existing access. What the RA needed, he realised, was some expert medical support, and he felt it would not have been difficult to get. It was, he wrote, 'imperative that all outdoor movements should fight tooth and nail for complete access in the case of any new areas being turned into catchment areas'.[3]

Lawrence Chubb, who had attended the meeting as secretary of the Commons Society, wrote to H. G. Griffin, secretary of the CPRE, that the conference had been disappointing. Although the water authorities had overstated their case he thought it would be hopeless to try to convince them that public access was without danger. He did not agree with Spence's view (he had been sent a copy of Spence's letter) regarding future gathering grounds. The outdoor movement, he felt, would never be able to secure any general right to wander over areas which were private property and not subject to any customary or legal right of access. He added, 'What some of our most enthusiastic friends will not bring themselves to realise is the danger of weakening the present position by putting forward untenable claims. We must be reasonable above all things.'[4]

The water authorities regarded the presence of *Bacterium coli* above a certain level in the water as evidence of pollution which was possibly faecal. The foundation of the RA case was laid in an article written by Edwin Royce and H. H. Symonds, a retired Liverpool headmaster and pioneer of the RA, YHA, and the Friends of the Lake District, and published in *Rambling* in January 1936. The authors quoted experts to the effect that *B. coli* is widely distributed, can be isolated from air, dust, water and soil, and is found in all warm-blooded animals. 'If *B. coli* is found in, say, Thirlmere', they wrote,

it does not follow that this bacillus necessarily indicates the presence of typhoid, dysentery or cholera bacilli, or that the *B. coli* is due to the pollution of the water by human faeces: the offenders may equally well be animals or birds, such as sheep, dogs, grouse or seagulls. Therefore to forbid all access to a lake or catchment areas, because *B. coli* has been found there, is an illogical proceeding.[5]

One reader impressed by the Royce–Symonds article was Frank Head, a young Sussex man who had taken a post in Manchester to be nearer the Lake District. He was an organic chemist by training and realised that the only way to combat the water authorities was to meet them on their own ground, backed with the relevant technical know-ledge. He set out to qualify himself in that direction by a study of the works of accepted authorities on water supplies and water pollution. By so doing he became an expert witness for the RA on numerous occasions. His study of recognised bacteriological, medical, and water engineering publications seemed to support the view that the possi-bilities of pollution of a reservoir by ramblers on a gathering ground were exceedingly slight. Bacteria, accustomed to living at human body temperature, had to survive exposure on open moorland, endure further exposure in cold, running water, storage in a reservoir and, perhaps, filtration and chemical treatment before reaching the water mains. The possible occurrence of such a chain of favourable (for the bacteria) circumstances seemed remote.

Even the British Waterworks Association, when opposing the Access to Mountains Bill in 1939, were not content to rest their case on pollution alone. Among their general objections they included 'the tendency of such areas (i.e. mountains and moorlands) to become a resort for undesirable characters among whom immorality and licen-tiousness is rife'.[5]

In 1943 I, together with H. H. Symonds and Edwin Royce, favoured the idea of pressing for investigation of the pollution ques-tion by a government committee of scientific and technical experts.

Phil Barnes, a Sheffield rambler famous for his trespassing activities, and John Dower, author of the famous report on National Parks, feared that bacteriologists, who were the real experts, would be outnumbered by water engineers on such a committee. It might therefore report in favour of continued, or even greater restriction on access. Such a committee, the Gathering Grounds Sub-committee of the Central Advisory Water Committee of the Ministry of Health, was, in fact, set up in 1946 by Aneurin Bevan, Minister of Health, 'to investigate the question whether the public should be allowed access to gathering grounds owned or controlled by water undertakers and the extent to which it is desirable that afforestation and agriculture should be permitted on gathering grounds'.[7] As Barnes and Dower had feared, water engineers were in a majority.

Frank Head and Phil Barnes submitted written and oral evidence to the Committee, the written statement being mainly the work of Frank Head. The RA's evidence stated that adequate means existed for purifying highly polluted river water, and that some degree of public access had to be tolerated even by those authorities which relied upon the protection of raw water rather than upon filtration and chemical treatment. The RA was concerned with securing access for the public to gathering grounds in uncultivated mountain and moorland country. It recognised the necessity to protect public water supplies from gross pollution, but claimed that reasonable public access and some measure of agricultural use in catchment areas were not inconsistent with that need.

Slight pollution, they said, was of little significance unless the bacteria of enteric diseases were present, and extremely few of the persons concerned would be carriers of such diseases. The presence of *B. coli* was no proof of human pollution, but might be due to the excreta of birds and animals. Seagulls, in particular, had come under suspicion as possible carriers of typhoid germs from sewage outfalls to reservoirs.

Most pathogenic bacteria, they said, would perish during a long sojourn in a reservoir. Long storage, indeed, was a reliable method of purifying water. Chlorination or other chemical treatment should provide further protection against pollution. Chlorine was cheap, and it could no longer be argued that water undertakings could not afford to construct the necessary buildings, since all authorities were compelled to install chlorine plant during the war. London and other towns derived pure and wholesome supplies from polluted rivers, and it should be a relatively easy matter to safeguard the much purer raw water supplies on the moorland authorities. All the larger under-takings possessed the necessary plant for that purpose. Thus there was no sufficient reason for sterilising large areas of gathering grounds by excluding the rambler and discouraging farming. Great Britain was too small a country for large areas to be rendered entirely unproduc-tive of food, or some of our most inspiring country to be kept inaccess-ible to the public.

In the proposed national parks in mountain or moorland districts large areas of the best scenery formed gathering grounds. It was inconceivable that wild uncultivated land within national parks should continue to be forbidden territory. It was just as inconceivable that land of that type owned or controlled by public bodies should be any less accessible than areas privately owned.[8]

Similar evidence was presented for the CPRE and CPRW, the Standing Committee of National Parks, the Commons Society, the Friends of the Lake District, and the Caravan Club.

The sub-committee reported in 1948 and, to a surprising degree, endorsed many of the arguments of the RA.[9] They said that no system designed to prevent human access to gathering grounds was likely to be completely endorsed in practice. The sub-committee thought it significant that no case of transmission of disease by pollution of a large reservoir had been reported, even in cases where there was no effective filtration or sterilisation. Where water was stored for more than a month many germs would normally die. Very few germs survived efficient filtration, and those that did could be dealt with by chemical sterilisation, though chlorination of unfiltered water was not satisfactory.

The sub-committee found wide differences in opinions and practice among water engineers and authorities. Burnley prohibited access except where there were public footpaths and considered restriction on public access essential. Manchester considered total exclusion to be ideal but a limited degree of access had to be tolerated. Sheffield did not regard the presence on the gathering grounds of small.parties of pedestrians as serious in view of the purifying effect of storage, filtration, and sterilisation. Bristol's representative regarded it as unlikely that raw water would suffer to any appreciable degree from access under proper control, nor would it necessitate any extension of existing measures for purification. The Irwell Valley Water Board's manager thought all farming activities should be prohibited; the

Derwent Valley Board considered that cattle should not be allowed to graze along the water's edge, though no restrictions on sheep were necessary.

Strong hostility to the idea of public access to gathering grounds was expressed by Manchester Water Committee's representatives. The report quotes them as having said that the corporation had gone many miles for pure water which, owing to its excellent quality, did not need to be filtered; and that it would be unreasonable to add substantially to the costs by installing the filtration and treatment which, it was said, would be necessary if the public were to have unrestricted access to the gathering grounds; they asked why their customers should pay more for their water merely to provide recreation for others. To some of us in the RA that seemed a fine piece of Manchester cynicism or arrogance, and a regard of the Lake District as an outer suburb of the city: a place where they could take a natural lake like Thirlmere and, with a huge embankment, convert it into a reservoir often rimmed with bleached shorelines of mud: where they could abolish farming use of the land, drape the lower hillsides with monotonous conifers, close an ancient hostelry, and complain because they were required by Parliament to allow the public access to the adjacent hills. So, too, in later years they dammed Haweswater and drowned the village of Mardale with its famous inn, the Dun Bull. In more recent times they acquired the right to tap Ullswater and Windermere, but by that time they had installed a filtration plant.

In their conclusions, the sub-committee suggested that water entering a reservoir should be kept free from gross pollution, and the reservoir itself, and in some cases the feeder streams, should be so protected as to prevent fresh sources of pollution entering it directly and short-circuiting the purifying effect of storage, and between reservoir and consumer there should be efficient filtration and sterilisation. 'Subject to such reasonable safeguards', the sub-committee considered 'that gathering grounds should be so managed as to make the maximum contribution to the general welfare by providing facilities for healthy recreation and the production of food and timber.'

They would prohibit bathing and only allow boating, fishing, or access to the banks under a system of control. Subject to necessary limitations for the discouragement of large crowds, they could see no justification on grounds of water purity for prohibiting access by walkers, cyclists, or motorists to the remainder of the gathering grounds.

So it seemed the battle was won, but for some years the water engineers still clung to their old-fashioned prejudices. In May 1949 Lewis Silkin, Minister of Town and Country Planning, moved an amendment to the National Parks and Access to the Countryside Bill, following representations from the RA, to ensure that gathering grounds would not automatically be excluded from access orders. 'There has been', he said, 'a report on access to gathering grounds from which it appears that fears which had been expressed by local authorities and all sorts of people in the past about the dangers to be feared from access to gathering grounds were almost entirely unfounded, and that it would be quite safe to give access.'[10]

Another member, Hugh Molson, then said he had received two telegrams from water authorities. They were disturbed about the amendment and asked that they should be consulted. Silkin said he had also received a telegram. It was open, he continued, for any authority to make a case against any access order which was applied for. If it was established that there were good reasons for the land being excepted, then those reasons would be taken into account.[11] That ministerial commitment was duly noted by the water authorities for use in later years at public inquiries.

The first in the field against public access to its gathering grounds was Huddersfield Corporation, which, at a public inquiry in May 1954, objected to the designation of an alternative 'bad weather' route for the Pennine Way from Black Hill to Wessenden Head. The Corporation objected on the grounds of possible pollution of their Digley Reservoir. Since this was of recent construction, with long storage, filtration, and chlorination, the RA thought that if the objection were upheld it would make nonsense of the recommendations of the Gathering Grounds Sub-committee Report. That view was shared by the Peak Park Planning Board, the Standing Committee on National Parks*, the British Mountaineering Council, the Commons Society, the Peak District and Northern Counties Footpaths Preservation Society, and the Youth Hostels Association, all whom gave evidence at the inquiry. The RA nationally was

---

*The Standing Committee on National Parks was founded in December 1935 to press for the establishment of national parks. The 1931 Addison Report on National Parks, discussed in Chapter 10, had provoked no response from the government and the Standing Committee sought to keep its ideas alive and argued for a central authority and state funds. Among the founder members were H. H. Symonds, Edwin Royce, T. A. Leonard, and Kenneth Spence.

represented by its honorary solicitor and me with the Manchester Area represented by Frank Head, Sheffield by Phil Barnes and the West Riding by Arthur Adamson who had, extremely valuably, had twenty-two years' experience as a member of Leeds Corporation Waterworks Committee.

The RA argued much the same case as it had to the Gathering Grounds Sub-committee. At the end of the inquiry the Inspector decided to walk part of the disputed route. He was accompanied by the Town Clerk of Huddersfield and several of the witnesses. We had only gone a few yards from the road near the Isle of Skye Inn (now demolished) when we were stopped abruptly by a gamekeeper and his son. He was instructed by his employer, he said, to turn back anyone who was without permission. He said the ground had been patrolled seven days a week for the past twelve years, and there had been many violent encounters with ramblers. Some of us told him we had walked that way frequently without seeing him. In the fortnight before the inquiry the route had been walked by H. H. Symonds, Gerald Haythornthwaite of Sheffield CPRE, Phil Barnes, and Frank Head. I had walked it three times, to take photographs which were submitted to the Inquiry.

Fortunately the Inspector persisted in trespassing, and the gamekeeper was hopelessly outnumbered. For us it was a welcome encounter, enabling the Inspector to see for himself the kind of reception to which ramblers were accustomed.[12]

With some elation we welcomed the Minister's decision that the risk of harm to the water supply were so remote that the Corporation's objection could not be supported. The official decision letter said:

evidence was given by expert witnesses on behalf of the Peak Park Planning Board and the Ramblers' Association that a simultaneous breakdown of Huddersfield's three lines of defence for the purity of their water supply was most improbable and that the acidity of peat water was unfavourable to the survival of pathogenic organisms. Any accidental pollution of the feeder streams, if it did occur, would be extremely slight and would be within the margin of safety allowed by the methods of storing and treating the water.[13]

Any joy over the Huddersfield decision was short-lived. Soon we were faced with another inquiry. Manchester Corporation was objecting to the proposed route of the Pennine Way northwards from Longdendale to Black Hill. A few of us in the RA were aware this was looming. In 1953, while I was still a member of the National Parks

Commission, a member of the Ministry of Housing and Local Government staff wrote a letter which was so unfortunately worded that if it had been published it might have led to a first-class row in Parliament and the press.

Manchester Corporation wrote to the Ministry objecting to the proposed line of the Pennine Way from Crowden to Black Hill. The Ministry replied that they saw no reason to vary the route and asked Tintwistle Rural District Council to proceed with a compulsory footpath order against Manchester Corporation. The Corporation wrote back protesting and adducing the stock arguments about pollution. The Ministry's reply of 17 November contained the following revealing passage: 'through an unfortunate misunderstanding our water experts had the wrong path in mind. Now that they are clear as to the line of the approved route *they are on your side* and we are, therefore, again consulting the National Parks Commission about it' (my emphasis).

The following day the Commission received a letter from the Ministry stating:

as you will gather, there was some misunderstanding about the line of the approved route, but it is now clear that our experts are firmly on the side of the Corporation and advise that the path would be a danger to Manchester's water supply. In the face of their advice it would be quite impossible for our Minister to confirm a public path order for this section. It seems, therefore, that the only way to expedite the completion of this section of the route will be for you to work out an alternative line which the water undertakers will accept and to submit a varying report.

The 1949 Act had provided for the Minister to ask the commission to consider varying the line of a long-distance path, and if they refused to do so he had the power himself, after consultation with the Commission, to make a varying order. The correspondence made clear, however, that for all practical purposes the issue had been settled without there having been any consultation with the Commission. At my request a meeting was arranged at which the Ministry's technical experts met a sub-committee of the Commission, which I chaired. They were unable to refute our contentions that, if there were any danger of pollution from the disputed route of the Pennine Way, there was also a danger from the existing public footpath from Crowden over the Chew Valley and immeasurably greater danger from two roads and a railway line which ran alongside the reservoir. The outcome of all this was that the full Commission, at their next meeting, unanimously agreed that the reasons adduced by the Minister's representatives did not afford any valid pretext for varying the route. The Commission also 'took strong objection to the sequence of events by which the Minister had prejudged the issue with Manchester Corporation without consulting the Commission; and desired that in communicating their views to the Minister this should be placed on record'.[14]

The first public indication of Manchester Corporation's objections appeared in January in the *Manchester Guardian*. The paper's local government correspondent wrote that Manchester Corporation feared the suggested route would lead to pollution of the Longdendale Reservoirs. This view

appears to have won the support of the Ministry's Water Division. In consequence the Minister had referred the matter back to the National Parks Commission which is understood to have re-affirmed its opinion that the original route is the one to be preferred, and that the grounds of Manchester's opposition are not strong enough to warrant any alteration. It is open to the minister, if he thinks fit, to vary an approved route, but as yet no definite decision has been announced.[15]

In February I joined a deputation led from Manchester RA by Frank Head to the Manchester Corporation Waterworks Committee, to plead for public access to the Longdendale gathering grounds. According to the official report, 'a frank and friendly exchange of views took place'.[16] The deputation came away feeling that although they had been given a good hearing there was no foreseeable hope of access to the Longdendale moors. We had, however, done better than we knew, for the official report to the City Council from the Waterworks Committee recommended that filtration plant should be installed and access restrictions then be reconsidered.[17] However, a motion calling upon the Waterworks Committee to withdraw its objection to the Crowden Brook section of the Pennine Way was lost when it came before the full City Council in May 1954.[18]

The public inquiry was held in Glossop Town Hall in July. Speaking for Manchester Corporation, the Deputy Town Clerk said that the National Parks Commission had adopted the route of the Pennine Way without consulting the water undertakings concerned. Use of the proposed route would increase substantially the risk of pollution of Manchester's water supply, and in declining to accept this risk, the corporation was acting in accordance with the recommendations of the Gathering Grounds Sub-Committee of the Central Water Advisory Committee.[19] The Corporation's Water Engineer thought that there was sufficient and reasonable access already to the gathering grounds. Over the past century the Waterworks Committee had pursued a vigorous policy directed toward the ideal of the greatest possible degree of protection of the water supply at its source. They thought it better to 'prevent pollution rather than to tolerate contamination and then rely on fallible mechanical methods to remedy the harmful results of pollution'.

Under cross-examination, he agreed that there was some risk from Torside Clough, where the route crossed several feeder streams close to the reservoirs. He also agreed that the Water Committee had tolerated for fifty years the risk of pollution from the road alongside the spring watercourse, which took much of the Crowden water direct into supply, without storage or filtration, and that no attempt had been made to fence the existing Greenfield Path or to bridge its crossing over feeder streams near the reservoirs.[20]

The RA, in its evidence, said they did not question the need for maintaining a pure water supply, and recognised that Manchester Corporation had a statutory duty in that respect. Nevertheless, they maintained that the possibilities of users of the Pennine Way polluting the reservoirs were theoretical and unsubstantiated by the history of Longdendale or other large reservoirs. Even if the possibilities were admitted they were immeasurably less than those which could arise from the roads and the railways alongside the reservoirs, or from the existing public footpath up the Crowden Valley. On the north side of the reservoirs there was an important and much used road, the A628. This crossed the feeder streams entering from the north and crossed on a viaduct some 300 yards long an arm of the Woodhead reservoir. On the south side a secondary road carried considerable traffic. Also on the south side was a Sheffield to Manchester railway line (in those days a passenger line carrying something like 20,000 passengers weekly). On emerging from the Woodhead tunnel it crossed the river Etherow and three other streams flowing into the Woodhead reservoir. West of Crowden station drainage from the line, including lavatory washings, seeped through the ballast, thence into streams entering Torside reservoir. These risks of pollution were far greater than any risk from the use of the Pennine Way and they had been accepted by Manchester Corporation, despite the lack of filtration, and, until recent times, of chlorination. For all practical purposes, the use of the Pennine Way could add no further, measurable risk.[21]

Perhaps the weightiest evidence in the Inquiry came from a medical witness called by the RA. Dr Wilfred Fine, Deputy Physician Superintendent of Newsham General Hospital, Liverpool, dealt with the incidence of typhoid and paratyphoid. He said that there had been a decline in typhoid cases in recent years, and consequently a decrease in the number of carriers. Dr Fine said that on the most adverse view, there were 2.9 carriers per million of the population in this country. In the age group not exceeding forty-four years (the group most likely to use the Pennine Way) there were probably three carriers in four million. The population of great Britain in that age group was about thirty million. Taking an annual usage by 10,000 members of this group it would take 300 years for three million people to pass. As there were only three carriers in four million people of this age group, in 300 years, in round figures, two carriers could be expected to pass along that part of the Pennine Way.[22]

While Dr Fine was giving evidence, one of the Manchester officials was heard to say, 'we haven't got a case, but we shall win'. He proved no false prophet. The Minister's decision was given in a letter in which he noted with pleasure that Manchester Corporation were not opposed to any path over their gathering grounds, but were suggesting a route for the Pennine Way that would be reasonable for walkers, while safer for their water supplies than the approved route. The opinion of his own technical advisers supported the Corporation's contention that in the absence of filtration the presence of walkers so close to the Crowden Great Brook would appreciably increase the risk of pollution. He did not think it reasonable that the public should be exposed to this additional risk, small though it might be, and he had decided that the route of the Pennine Way should be varied at this section. When the Corporation's proposals for filtration had been carried through, it would be reasonable for the National Parks Commission to put proposals to him for varying the route.[23]

The decision was what we in the RA had expected, and we fully endorsed a leader in the *Manchester Guardian* which said, 'the minister's decision to uphold Manchester's objection to the Crowden Valley section of the Pennine Way is a nonsensical one – though not unexpected after the odd manner in which the case had been conducted'. The leader concluded with the pertinent question, 'Does the minister now intend, until Manchester filters its water supply, to close all those paths, roads and railways over its gathering grounds and if not why not? Surely he and the Corporation must be consistent in their misplaced zeal.'[24]

More than ten years were to pass before Manchester completed its filtration plant in Longdendale, and in 1965 the Pennine Way was restored to the originally approved route from Laddow Rocks to Black Hill. In the same year the Corporation entered into an access agreement with the Peak Park Planning Board granting public access to some thirty square miles of the Longdendale moors. So the old 'Trespassers Will be Prosecuted' signs were replaced with signs declaring 'Open Country' – land to which the public have access for air and exercise.

The next trial came when Lancashire County Council in 1955 made two access orders applying to 1,494 hectares on Boulsworth Hill, rough moorland 1,700 feet high within easy reach of north-east Lancashire ramblers. It provided a ridge walk of about three miles commanding wide views including Pendle Hill, the Ribble Valley, Bowland Fells, and the Pennine Heights of Ingleborough, Pen-y-ghent, Fountains Fell and the Malham and Wharfedale Moors. The land was used for sheep grazing and grouse shooting, and in some parts as gathering grounds of Colne and Keighley Borough Councils and Trawden Urban District Council.

The water undertakings and sporting interests objected to the orders and a public inquiry was held in March 1956. Phil Barnes supported the County Council on behalf of Lancashire Branch of the CPRE and I did so for the RA.[25] The water authorities said they did not have all the recognised lines of defence against pollution – protection at source, long storage, filtration, and sterilisation.[26] A witness for the shooting interests claimed that indiscriminate access would spoil the grouse breeding and made shooting impossible. Emmott Moor, he said, was 'particularly vulnerable: a walker on Coombe Hill might clear the moor of grouse for a day by the drop of a handkerchief.'[27] Emmott Moor is edged by a road along which in those days several cars would pass in each hour. We were not told how the grouse managed to survive such frequent alarms.

The Ministry took fifteen months to reach a conclusion. The letter giving the decision stated that in the interests of public health and protection of public water supplies it would be wrong to allow public access. However, there was one notable comment: 'the Minister would not regard as conclusive against general access the arguments which were put forward on behalf of the sporting and grazing interests.'

Although the Minister decided not to confirm the orders, he suggested that the County Council 'should consider providing a new footpath linking the land to the north and the land to the south of the area covered by the orders, with a branch path leading from the ridge down to the public road from Trawden village'.[28] That was in 1957 and, although Lancashire County Council made repeated efforts to negotiate a path, twenty-one years were to lapse before any positive action was taken. In the meantime much of the land had been acquired by the North West Water Authority which, on access issues, seemed to be as antediluvian as the old Manchester Water Committee. All the authority would concede on Boulsworth was a permissive path three miles long and forty metres wide – and that even this path should be closed during the whole of May while the grouse were nesting.

Alan Mattingly, speaking as RA Secretary at a North-East Lancashire RA meeting in Blackburn in February 1977 said:

to deny access during the whole of May is a completely new departure which we find quite unacceptable. Apart from anything else, it is quite unnecessary. Research studies have demonstrated that public access is not harmful to the grouse during the nesting season and that 'public access', to quote a study carried out by the University of Newcastle, 'has virtually no effect on grouse populations and consequently on grouse bags'.[29]

Like other water suppliers the North-West authority give little, if any heed, to the section of the Water Act 1973 which reads:

Every water authority and all other statutory water undertakers may take steps to secure the use of water and land associated with water for the purpose of recreation and it shall be the duty of all such undertakers to take such steps as are reasonably practicable for putting their rights to the use of water and of any land associated with water to the best use for those purposes.[30]

This chapter has been limited to the issue of access to gathering grounds, but it should be mentioned that the RA has been actively concerned with the wider problems of water supplies and their effect on the environment. It has appeared at many inquiries and before Select Committees of Parliament concerned with the construction of new reservoirs. From its Countryside Fund, it has contributed generously towards the legal costs incurred by the amenity organisations in such representations.

References

1   W. H. Williams, *Commons, Open Spaces and Footpaths Preservation Society, a short history of the society and its work* (London, 1965), p. 15.
2   RAA, Access – Water File, letter from T. A. Leonard to K. Spence, 25 June 1935.
3   RAA, Access – Water File, letter from K. Spence to G. Mitchell, 22 June 1935.
4   RAA, Access – Water File, letter from L. Chubb to H. G. Griffin, 27 June 1935.
5   E. Royce and H. H. Symonds, 'Pollution of reservoirs', *Rambling*, Vol. 1, No. 5, January 1936, pp. 4–7.
6   'Access to Mountains Bill Memorandum, submitted to Sir George Chrystal, KCB, Secretary to the Ministry of Health, on behalf of Water Supply Undertakings by the British Waterworks Association', British Waterworks Association *Proceedings*, Vol. 21, 21st Ser., Official Circular No. 163, April 1939, p. 298.
7   Gathering-Grounds Sub-committee of the Central Advisory Water Committee, Ministry of Health, Report, *Public Access to Gathering Grounds, Afforestation and Agriculture on Gathering Grounds*, 1948.
8   RAA, Access – Water File, typescript written evidence to Gathering-Grounds Sub-committee of the Central Advisory Water Committee.
9   Gathering-Grounds Sub-committee, Report *op. cit.*
10   *Hansard* (Standing Committees), Session 1948–49, Vol. 2, National Parks and Access to the Countryside Bill, Col. 872, 24 May 1949.
11   *Ibid.*, cols. 872–3.
12   *Manchester Guardian*, 20 May 1954.
13   RAA, Pennine Way – Holmfirth File, decision letter from Ministry of Housing and Local Government, 14 July 1954.
14   RAA, Access – Water File, letter from the author to T. S. Monkhouse of the *Manchester Guardian* (for guidance, not for publication), 18 December 1953.
15   *Manchester Guardian*, 21 January 1954.
16   Manchester Waterworks Committee Report to the City Council, *Public Access to the Gathering Grounds of the Waterworks Undertaking*, Council Circular Item No. VI, 11 March 1954, para. 16.
17   *Ibid.*, paras. 15, 17.
18   *Manchester Guardian*, 6 May 1954.
19   *Manchester Guardian*, 30 July 1954.
20   *Ibid.*
21   RAA, Longdendale File, typescript Proof of Evidence, Tom Stephenson.
22   *Manchester Guardian*, 31 July 1954: RAA, Longdendale File, notes
23   RAA, Longdendale File, decision letter from Ministry of Housing and

Local Government, 29 December 1954.

24 *Manchester Guardian*, 31 December 1954.

25 RAA, Boulsworth File, correspondence.

26 *Manchester Guardian*, 22 March 1956.

27 *Manchester Guardian*, 21 March 1956.

28 RAA, Boulsworth File, decision letter from Ministry of Housing and Local Government, 28 June 1957.

29 RAA, Press Release E4700, 24 February 1977.

30 Water Act 1973, Section 20 para. 1.

Chapter 5

The Highland story

As in the rest of Britain, much of the land in Scotland was once held in common, and as late as 1847 there were some 37,000 acres of common pasture land in the Highlands.[1] 'The inland, the upland, the moor, the mountain, were not really occupied at all for agricultural purposes, or served only to keep the poor and their cattle from starving.' As cultivation increased, though, 'our lawyers lent themselves to appropriate the poor man's grazing ground to the neighbouring baron'. And, although 'the lord never possessed any of the common, when it came to be divided, the lord got the whole that was allocated to the estate and the poor cottar got none. The poor had no lawyers.'[2]

In the latter half of the eighteenth and the early part of the nineteenth century, sheep-rearing was developed on a large scale in the Highlands. The landlords found that farmers, given an adequate acreage, could pay far higher rents than could be wrung from peasants scraping a bare existence from the soil. So began the Highland Clearances, that barbarous and ghastly period in Scottish history when the natives were swept off the land and whole parishes and glens were depopulated. Thousands of impoverished farmers and their families were evicted, their houses burnt down in front of them. Old men and women, women nearing childbirth, children and invalids, were left roofless to make a bed in the heather or on the inhospitable sea shore.*

---

*Tom Stephenson's view of the Highland Clearances follows one tradition in the history of the Scottish Highlands, one which saw them simply as the expulsion of a helpless peasantry by a corrupt and anglicised aristocracy. This a view has a modern exponent in John Prebble's *The Highland Clearances* (London, 1963). However, more recent and detailed scholarship has found the clearances a more complicated phenomenon.

These clearances were for sheep farms, not for deer forests which had not then appeared on a great scale. This explains why the Earl of Malmesbury could say in his Memoirs that in 1833, 'a stranger could shoot and fish over almost any part of the Highlands without interruption, the letting of the *ferae naturae** being unknown to their possessors'.[3] The Laird of Glenmoriston in 1773, according to Boswell, did not hinder anyone shooting deer on his mountains.[4]

But by the 1840s deer forests were replacing the sheepwalks. The land had been over-grazed and would support only dwindling flocks. Australian wool was flooding the market and, with falling prices, farmers could no longer meet the rents which had been so grossly swollen during the sheep booms. Thomas Johnston, who in later years became Secretary of State for Scotland, wrote, 'land run to waste, land misused, land devoted to anti-social practices, yields more rent to private owners than land tilled by peasants. And so, say the lairds, the peasants must go.'[5]

Johnston commented:

if there was no money in sheep there was money in sport. Plutocrats from America . . . brewers from England . . . successful gamblers from a scoop in the Kaffir market, cotton capitalists, satiated aristocrats; mighty Nimrods from the Piccadilly clubs; nay even the Gaekwar of Baroda hired the Highlands for a solitude, swept away the shepherds, and at certain stipulated periods of the year came with French cooks and in tartan kilts to slaughter deer and grouse and rabbits. There had always been a considerable number of wild deer in the Highlands; but the depreciation in rent value of the sheep runs and the increasing number of idle rich people in the towns who were satiated with the tamer pleasures and yearned for 'noble blood sports', were the causes of that extraordinary increase in the acreages devoted to sport, of

---

Patterns of landholding were, in any case, more complicated than Tom Stephenson implies, as is shown by Robert A. Dodgshon in *Land and Society in Early Modern Scotland* (Oxford, 1981). As to the Clearances themselves, Eric Richards's two-volume *History of the Highland Clearances* (London and Canberra, 1982 and 1985) sees landlords and tenants caught in an irresistible web of economic pressures. J. M. Bumsted's *The People's Clearance, Highland Emigration to British North America 1770–1815* (Edinburgh, 1982) makes the point that the early phases of emigration were undertaken against the wishes to the landlords and that it is patronising and over-simplified to view the Highlanders as passive victims. However, brutality and exploitation were certainly part of the story; James Hunter's *The Making of the Crofting Community* (Edinburgh, 1976) chronicles the lot of those who stayed and their efforts to ease it.
*Ferae naturae means literally 'wild animals', but is used to indicate game suitable for blood sports.

those further clearances of the rural working class and of that persistent drainage through immigration of our best blood and brawn.'⁶

When in 1845 an Edinburgh Society was formed 'for protecting the public against being robbed of its walks by private cunning and perseverance', Lord Cockburn, the Lord Advocate of Scotland, thought it was fifty years too late. 'When I was a boy,' he wrote,

nearly the whole vicinity of Edinburgh was open. Beyond the Causeway it was always almost Highland. Corstophine Hill, Braid Hill, Craiglockart Hill, the Pentland Hills, the sea side from Leith to Queensferry, the river-side from Penicuick by Roslin and Hawthornden to Lasswade, the Valley of Habbie's How and innumerable other places now closed, and fast closing, were all free.

The law to prevent enclosure and theft, he said, was dear, and 'each Justice protected his brother, knowing that he would shortly require a job for himself. Thus everything was favourable to the way-thief, and the poor were laughed at. The public were gradually man-trapped off everything beyond the high road.'⁷

That Edinburgh society was soon embroiled well beyond the city purlieus in a protracted legal battle with the sixth Duke of Atholl. That gentleman, who owned nearly 200,000 acres of land in Perthshire, half of it deer forest, tried in 1847 to prevent Professor Bayley Balfour and a party of botanical students from passing through Glen Tilt on what was held to be an old drove road and a public right of way.

The encounter was commemorated in a humorous ballad published in 1873. A verse gives the flavour of the whole.

> The battle it was ended then,
> Afore t'was focht ava' man;
> But noo some ither chaps are gaen
> To tak the Duke to law, man.
> Ochon! your Grace, my bonny man
> An' ye had sense as ye ha'e lan'
> Ye'd been this hour
> Ayont the po'er,
> O' lawyers dour
> An' let Balfour,
> Gang through the Hielan' hills, man . . .⁸

After a futile approach to the Duke's agent, the Edinburgh Society decided to take the case to court in the names of three of its members. The action came before the Court of Session in December 1849. The pursuers (the Scots legal term for the people raising the action) claimed that the road had been used from time immemorial by the public on foot and on horseback, and by drovers with their cattle and sheep. It was well known as 'the road from Blair Atholl through Glen Tilt to Braemar' and was the only direct road between those places. There was evidence that in the past the road had been maintained at the public expense, though the Duke and his predecessors had made, with or without authority, lengths of new road connecting sections of the old road, and the new sections had been freely used by the public. The Duke, they said, had for some years back attempted to obstruct and deprive the public of use of the road, and he had employed gamekeepers forcibly to interrupt and threaten travellers lawfully passing along the road. Since the proceedings began he had interrupted and turned back the pursuers themselves.

They therefore asked for a declaration that the road in dispute, so far as it passed through the property of the Duke, was a public road and they and all others were entitled to a free and lawful use and enjoyment thereof. The Duke challenged the right of the pursuers to maintain the action on the grounds that they did not really reside in the vicinity of the road and had no local interest or patrimony, nor had they acquired any interest by frequent or constant use of the road.

The judge ruled against the Duke and sustained the title of the pursuers to insist on the action.[9] This left undecided the question of the right of way as was emphasised when the Duke petitioned for leave to appeal. In granting the petition the Lord President made clear where his sympathies lay. He said:

this case most deeply involves the interests of the Duke of Atholl, for it is well known that the use of a public road through such a forest as this will entirely destroy the comfort and materially decrease the value of the forest. I for one and everyone who knows anything of such Highland estates, can feel no astonishment that the proprietor should resist this action to the utmost of his power. If a proof is to be allowed of inveterate usage it must lead to a most extensive and expensive investigation on both sides. He went on to say though, that 'if these pursuers have heard that they were entitled and have been in immemorial usage to go through Glen Tilt, I do not object to reserve the right to them pending the appeal; that is a very different thing from allowing it to the whole public of Scotland to do so, which would be out of the question.'[10]

The Duke's appeal to the House of Lords was heard in June 1852. On behalf of the Duke the Solicitor-General suggested that there was no authority or principle which could justify a proceeding by private parties in vindication of a right merely public. A perfect stranger having no connection at all with Glen Tilt might maintain that right and the owners of land in Scotland would be exposed to perpetual vexation. However, the Law Lords rejected this argument and agreed that the pursuers had a right to bring their case.[11] That, however, never proved necessary. After the House of Lords decision the Duke appears to have lost interest in the case, and the right of way through Glen Tilt has remained unchallenged down to the present day.

While the case was wending its slow way through the courts, in 1850, the Duke took the law into his own hands when he and his servants forcibly intercepted two Cambridge undergraduates who were descending Glen Tilt; an exploit which caused him to be savagely lampooned in *Punch*.[12]

One of the students told the story in a letter to *The Times*.

It is generally thought that in this land of liberty and civilisation wild men of the woods and savages have long been extinct: the following account of an adventure which lately befell myself and a fellow student on a tour in the Highland will show the fallacy of the supposition.

On Friday, August 30th, we shouldered our knapsacks and left Castletown of Braemar with the intention of walking to Blair Atholl through Glen Tilt, a distance of thirty miles. We might have gone by another road through Blairgowrie and Dunkeld, but as this road was upwards of sixty miles in length, and we were informed by all persons of whom we inquired at Braemar that though the Duke of Atholl, in spite of the decision of the Court of Session, was still endeavouring to stop all who made use of the bridle-road or foothpath through Glen Tilt, yet he would not dare to use violence if one insisted on a right of passage, we determined to take the shorter road.[13]

The students had just began to feel that they would succeed without difficulty when they were stopped by a gillie. They tried to proceed but were prevented by the gillie, who said he was acting on the Duke of Atholl's orders. They therefore insisted on seeing the Duke in person. They found the duke 'puffing and blowing in a great state of excitement'. The letter continues.

Finding him determined to oppose our progress vociferating 'You must go back! Why didn't you stop sir?' I again took out my pocket book, and preparing to write, said 'What is your name?' 'I am the Duke of Atholl' he replied, upon which we immediately tendered him our card (which he read and pocketed) and stated that we wished to proceed to Blair Atholl. However, he insisted that we must 'go back' to which we urged that the Court of Session had decided that there was a right of way through Glen Tilt, and, therefore, we could not be stopped. He replied angrily 'It is not a public way, it is my private drive! You shan't come down; the deer are coming, the deer are coming!' Upon this we expressed our willingness to retire behind the lodge till his sport was ended, but he said we had been impertinent, we claimed it as a right, and we should not go down an inch.

The students seem to have been misinformed about the outcome of the Court of Sessions case; as we have seen, the outcome was only that there was a right to bring the case, not that there was a right of way. However, the Duke, using 'oaths and other violent expressions, such as you would scarcely expect to hear from the lips of a gentleman', despite the presence of ladies, ordered his servants to detain the students by main force. A gillie advised them to wait until nightfall, then proceed. This they did and, after a somewhat unnerving walk in the dark, reached their hotel.

The Times was evidently more radical in those days than it has been in recent years. It devoted a long leader to the incident in which it said, 'The public have as perfect a right of "way" through the Vale of Glen Tilt as the Duke of Atholl has to the possession of any acre of the property which constitutes his estate. The right in the one case, as the title in the other is the mere creature of law.' The leader concluded, 'the two Cambridge students would have an easy remedy against the Duke of Atholl if they cared to bestir themselves in the business. Certainly it would be rendering the public a service to bring this hotheaded, foolish man to his senses.'[14] It is a pity the students did not so bestir themselves, for nearly a century later the Duke's descendants were still opposed to any idea of access to mountains legislation.

For the beginnings of such legislation we must turn across the country, to the shores of Wester Ross where an arm of the Atlantic, Loch Duich, extends up Glen Shiel, almost lapping the feet of the Five Sisters of Kintail. Johnson and Boswell descended Glen Shiel in September 1773 on their way to the Isle of Skye. It was there that Johnson declared Boswell's 'immense mountain' to be 'no more than a considerable protuberance'. At Invershiel they were refreshed with two wooden dishes of milk, one of them whipped like a syllabub. While they rested they were circled by men, women and children, all Macraes, none of whom could speak English. Some were as black and wild as American savages, though Boswell noticed 'one woman was as comely almost as the figure of Sappho'.[15]

More than a century later a descendant of those Macraes was to make legal history. He was Murdoch Macrae, a poor Highland shoe-maker living in a small cottage at Carn Gorm, Morvich, at the head of Loch Duich. Poor in wealth, but not in courage, he defied an American millionaire, William Louis Winans, who prosecuted him for allowing a pet lamb to stray on Winans's deer forest.

I. R. Mackay of Inverness, who has made a study of 'The Pet Lamb Case', states that Macrae may have seemed to Winans and lawyers 'an insignificant person although a potential deer poacher and a small time Land League agitator'. Macrae gave evidence to the Napier Commission in August 1883 and it is known that in 1888 he was a member of the Lochalsh, Kintail and Glen Shiel Branch of the High-land Land Law Reform Association.* He could not read or write and spoke no English, giving his evidence in court in Gaelic.[16]

Winans had leased from Whitsuntide 1882, for twenty-one years, the whole of the Kintail estate of about 25,000 acres including the Five Sisters of Kintail. The lease stipulated that the landlord, James Thompson Mackenzie, should be allowed until 15 August to remove the occupants of farm buildings. In September of that year, the buildings being still occupied, Winans applied for an order to give him immediate possession of the houses and other heritages forming part of the estate 'free from the occupation of the defender's [Macken-zie's] shepherds, servants and occupants of all other buildings on the estate'. The 'other occupants' were cottars, including Murdoch Macrae.[17]

MacKenzie said that the cottars occupied their houses and a small piece of land under a tenure customary in the Highlands. He had no right and no wish to remove them. His agent had written to Winans before the lease began stating that 'there are at Lochside about half a dozen families living in small huts with a quarter to half an acre of potato ground for which they pay no rent' and he did not want these people, who were natives of the place, to be removed.[18]

The Court of Session hearing in June 1883 decided that the shep-herds should go, but with regard to the eviction of the cottars the

---

*The Napier Commission was a commission of inquiry set up under the chairmanship of Baron Napier 'to inquire into the condition of the Cro^ ᵒrs and Cottars in the Highlands and Islands of Scotland' (Parliamentary Papers, Vols. XXXII–XXXXVI, 1884) in February 1883 following unrest among crofters, particularly in Glendale on the Isle of Skye. Murdoch Macrae (whose name is given as Murdo Macrae) gave evidence on 3 August 1883 (questions 31183–31260). At the same time the Highland Land Law Reform Association was founded and soon became the organisational framework for the crofters' protests. See James Hunter, *op. cit.*

judges were unanimous in dismissing the action. The Lord Justice-Clerk said that it did not in the least follow from the lease that the landlord was bound to depopulate the whole district.[19] The Lord Ordinary said that the decree which Winans sought was to compel Mackenzie to institute proceedings against the cottars who were not parties to the action; legal proceedings which, as regards them, would be harsh and unreasonable, and which Mackenzie said would be contrary to the good faith between him and them.[20]

However, this rebuff clearly left Winans in no mood to give in gracefully. In July 1884, Winans's agent wrote to Macrae accusing him of letting a lamb graze on his employer's land. Unless he promised to desist Winans would apply for an interdict. Ignoring an interdict would amount to contempt of court and render the offender liable to imprisonment. 'According to Winans' definition and ruling', observes I. R. Mackay, 'the deer forest extended to the high water mark of Loch Duich, which meant that it extended to the very doorsteps of the cottars' houses so that, on stepping outside, they were immediately trespassing on the forest.'[21]

Macrae ignored the letter and on 30 July the Sheriff's Court at Dingwall granted an interim interdict against him forbidding him to graze any lambs, sheep, cattle, or other beasts on Winans's land.[22] Macrae may also have ignored the interdict, for in December 1884 Winans stated that instead of pressing for a perpetual interdict he would accept an undertaking from Macrae that he would not trespass in future. Macrae refused to give such an undertaking and in January 1885 Winans applied at the Sheriff's Court for an interdict. The case was heard by the Sheriff-Substitute, who not only refused the interdict but also recalled the interim interdict granted in July 1884 and awarded costs to Macrae. Winans, of course, promptly lodged an appeal which was heard by the Sheriff-Principal. The tables were turned. The Sheriff overruled the decision of his Assistant, and found that, although Macrae had removed his sheep when asked to do so by Winans's head gamekeeper, he had later turned them out again. Macrae had also turned out to graze in the forest a lamb which had previously been home-fed and had refused to remove it. Macrae told how he found this animal, the famous 'pet lamb', when he was cutting peats:

I found a lamb. I identified it as my own lamb. It was about thee weeks old at the time. The lamb was in a very poor state . . . I took the lamb home. I didn't drive it before me, but took it in my arms . . . My wife used to feed it with milk when we had milk, and when we had none she used to beat up eggs and sugar . . . It gradually grew stronger by the nursing of my wife. It would follow any one of the children.

He denied he had ever driven the lamb on to the forest land. The Sheriff found Winans entitled to an interdict and to costs against Macrae.[23]

It has often been said that this ruling led to an outcry and the raising of a public fund to enable Macrae to appeal, but there is no mention of such a fund in the Scottish papers of the time. I. R. Mackay says there is some evidence that Mackenzie, the landowner, helped pay the costs.[24] Mr A. E. Macrae, of Letterfearn, grandson of Murdoch, was of the same opinion.[25]

Macrae's appeal came before the Court of Session in June 1885. There Winans found that his millions had no weight in the scales of justice, or if they had, they weighed against him. Mackenzie, the landowner, said that when he heard that Winans, with his 200,000 acres of shooting, was going to bring this action for the trespass of a pet lamb, it seemed so ridiculous that he did not believe it.[26]

The court found that Winans had failed to prove that Macrae had trespassed by putting a lamb to grass on the forest land, or that he had threatened to put more sheep or cattle thereon. The court, therefore, sustained the appeal, recalled the judgement of the Sheriff Principal, affirmed the judgement of the Sheriff-Substitute, and found Macrae entitled to expenses in the Inferior and in the Court of Session. So Winans had his knuckles rapped. But perhaps he had the last laugh, for during the proceedings Macrae said he had put the lamb away on the day that the petition was served on him, as he understood that if he did not do so he would be imprisoned.[27] The case became a *cause célèbre*, and one frequently referred to by campaigners for the right of access to mountains as an illustration of the way local people, not just visitors, suffered from the closing-off of the hills.

Highland opinion of Winans was revealed in a brief paragraph in *The Times* which said:

the actions of Mr Winans in closing up a road at Guisachan had caused great indignation in the north. It is reported by a Beauly correspondent that on Saturday evening, while Mr Winans was proceeding through the village of Tomich near Guisachan, stones were thrown at him. It is added that he immediately offered a reward of £500 for the capture or discovery of the guilty persons.[28]

As this incident shows, even denied his interdicts Winans found other means to keep his vast acreage inviolate. He and his fellow sportsmen set out to keep the Highlands as remote and inaccessible as possible. Trollope's description of the shooting estate of Crummie-Toddie in *The Duke's Children* is as much history as fiction.

Everything has been made to give way to deer and grouse. The thing had been managed so well that the tourist nuisance had been considerably abated. There was hardly a potato patch left in the district, not a head of cattle to be seen. There were no inhabitants remaining, or so few that they could be absorbed in game-preserving or cognate duties. Reginald Dobbes, who was very great at grouse, and supposed to be capable of outwitting a deer by venatical wiles more perfectly than any other sportsman in Great Britain, regarded Crummie-Toddie as the nearest thing that there was to a Paradise on earth. Could he have been allowed to pass one or two special laws for his own protection, there might still have been improvement. He would like the right to have all intruders thrashed by the gillies within an inch of their lives; and he would have had a clause in his lease against the making of any new roads, opening of footpaths, or building of bridges.[29]

Rights of way were obstructed or abolished. Inns were closed and such tenants as remained in the deer forests, mainly gamekeepers and other servants of the owners, were forbidden to provide accommodation for visitors, though some of them would do so on the quiet if they liked the look of you. Thus, as Alfred Russel Wallace, that self-effacing contemporary of Charles Darwin, wrote, 'the whole people . . . are shut out from many of the grandest and most interesting scenes of their native land, gamekeepers and watchers forbidding the tourists or naturalists to trespass on some of the wildest Scottish mountains'.[30]

Ernest Baker, a writer and mountaineer, referred in 1924 to the accommodation problem. He said farmhouses, once convenient halting-places in the neighbourhood of the Cuillin on the Isle of Skye, were forbidden to take in lodgers. He referred to the long tramp across Scotland by the ancient route between the territory of the Mackenzies of Kintall and Beauly. 'This walk, he said:

from Beauly to the west coast by way of Glen Affric and the superb pass of Glen Lichd, may well claim to be the finest in the British Isles. Ten years ago, the last hostelry that made a walk of such length barely feasible, the long established Shiel Inn, was summarily closed – all the others had been shut up or robbed of their licences many years before. It is now some fifty miles between the nearest fully licensed houses on this ancient right of way. The right of way has thus become useless, for foresters who occupy the only habitations in the upper parts are strictly forbidden to give anyone a bed, and camping out would hardly be permitted. Tourists going to Kintail to explore the mountains have found absolutely nowhere to lay their heads and have had to remove without delay to the less inhospitable climbing districts.[31]

Some of the tenants quietly ignored the restrictions imposed upon them. Some of my generation, who walked the twenty-one miles from Aviemore through the Larig Ghru to Inverey, long remembered the kindly, whimsical Maggie Gruer, her hospitality and gargantuan meals. Though forbidden to provide accommodation, Maggie proudly boasted that she had never turned a rambler away from her door.

In Glen Shiel itself, the battleground of Winans v. Macrae, I found a warm welcome on several occasions in the 1930s at the School House, where the husband ran the house and a small market-garden, while his wife taught in the school next door. There was another address in Glen Shiel where I would certainly have stayed had I known of it. In 1930 or 1931 Edwin Royce stayed with a Mrs Macrae at Carngorm Cottage, Morvich, beside the former home of Murdoch Macrae.[32] Her husband was the son of Murdoch. Surprisingly, the name Macrae meant nothing to Royce (as I discovered fifteen years later), otherwise he might have learned some details never recorded.

In those days, while public money was being spent on a 'Come to Scotland' campaign, one could buy in Fort William picture postcards of a noticeboard then prevalent in the Highlands. It read:

> Visitors are stongly advised
> to keep the path after
> the 12th August so as not
> to disturb the deer

> The modern rifle carries
> far and makes little noise.
> The soft-nosed bullet
> inflicts a very nasty wound

In October 1935, when camping on the shores of Loch Assynt, I saw a similar notice in the cottage window of the Post Office at Inchna-damph in Sutherlandshire.

Scottish ramblers, climbers, and youth hostellers seemed meekly to accept such conditions. The Scottish Rights of Way Society thought there was no need for access to mountains legislation. The Scottish

Youth Hostels Association said blandly, 'all the Torridon mountains should be avoided during the stalking season. The keepers are very strict, and the Forestry Commission desire that our members should not wander in the neighbouring deer forests.'[33]

For all that, more and more ramblers were finding their way into the innermost recesses of the Highlands. As Eric Linklater wrote:

a circumstance of some interest in connection with the history of the Clearances is that within recent years the Highlands have been re-invaded by human beings. It is, it is true, only a seasonal invasion, but it is vigorous, youthful, multi-hued, cheerful, vulgar, and every year more numerous. The invaders are called hikers and complaints have been heard that they disturb the grouse and annoy the deer for whose sake the hills were made so large and the glens so lovely. But many of the hikers must be descendants of evicted Highlanders who sought refuge in the Lowland cities and in contrast to those who complain of their behaviour, I find it very pleasant to think of them worrying the deer that replaced the sheep that dispossessed their fathers. I should like to see hikers more numerous and brightly shirted than ever on every mountain in Scotland; for if they scatter the grouse and pursue the deer far enough, the Highlands may be available again for their rightful heritors of the earth, who are men.[34]

That is still awaited and the mountains remain in the jealous possession of the lairds and sportsmen. The Countryside (Scotland) Act 1967 gave planning authorities powers to secure public access to areas of countryside as defined in the Act, but at present there are no apparent prospects of a legal right of access across all open country in Scotland.*

References

1 Thomas Johnston, *The History of the Working Classes in Scotland*, 4th ed. (Glasgow, 1946), pp. 155–6.

2 Cosmo Innes, *Lectures on Scotch Legal Antiquities* (Edinburgh, 1872), p. 155.

3 James Howard Harris, 3rd Earl of Malmesbury, *Memoirs of an ex-Minister. An autobiography* (London, 1885), p. 41.

4 James Boswell, *The Journal of a Tour to the Hebrides with Samuel*

*The situation with regard to access in Scotland has not changed since Tom Stephenson wrote this section. If anything, the situation has got worse as more forestry has spread into open country and as estate owners have tried to restrict access to moors, particularly during the long deerstalking season (Alan Mattingly, Director of The Ramblers' Association, personal communication, 10 May 1988).

Johnson (London, 1785), entry for 1 September 1773.

  5   Johnston, *op. cit.*, p. 210.
  6   *Ibid.*, pp. 208–9.
  7   Lord Cockburn, *Journal of Henry Cockburn. Being a continuation of the Memorials of his Time, 1831–1854* (Edinburgh, 1874), Vol. 2, pp. 104–5.
  8   Douglas Maclagan, *Nugae Canorae Medicae: lays by the Poet Laureate of the New Town Dispensary* (Edinburgh, 1850).
  9   *Court of Session Cases*, Dunlop, 328, 12 December 1849.
  10   *Court of Session Cases*, Dunlop, 691, 9 February 1850.
  11   *Scots Revised Reports*, House of Lord Series, vol. 9, 1850–57. (Edinburgh, 1899), pp. 193–200.
  12   *Punch*, 1850.
  13   *Times*, 15 October 1850.
  14   *Times*, 17 October 1850.
  15   Boswell, *op. cit.*
  16   I. R. Mackay, 'The Pet Lamb Case', *Transactions of the Gaelic Society of Inverness*, Vol. 48, 1972–74, p. 187, reprinted as a pamphlet, Inverness, 1978.
  17   *Court of Session Cases*, Rettie, 4th Ser., Vol. 10, No. 151, p. 941, 8 June 1883.
  18   *Ibid.*, p. 944.
  19   *Ibid.*, p. 948.
  20   *Ibid.*, p. 946.
  21   Mackay, *op. cit.*, p. 191.
  22   *Court of Session Cases*, Rettie, Vol. 12, No. 172, 3 June 1885, p. 1051.
  23   *Ibid.*, pp. 1055–8.
  24   Mackay, *op. cit.*, pp. 195–6.
  25   A. E. Macrae, telephone conversation with the author, 17 November 1980.
  26   *Court of Session Cases*, Rettie, Vol. 12, No. 172, 3 June 1885, p. 1062.
  27   *Ibid.*, pp. 1061–5.
  28   *Times*, 21 October 1885.
  29   Anthony Trollope, *The Duke's Children* (London, 1881), p. 218.
  30   Alfred Russell Wallace, *Land Nationalization, its necessity and its aims*, 3rd ed. (London, 1892), p. 84.
  31   Ernest A. Baker, *The Forbidden Land, a plea for public access to mountains, moors and other waste lands in Great Britain* (London, 1924), pp. 10–11.
  32   Edwin Royce, 'Wildest Caledonia', *Ramblers' Federation Handbook, Official Handbook of the Ramblers' Federation* (Manchester and District), 1931, p. 36.
  33   Scottish Youth Hostels Association *Handbook 1935* (Edinburgh, 1935), p. 110.
  34   Eric Linklater, *The Lion and the Unicorn* (London, 1935), pp. 90–1.

Chapter 6

Parliament and access

It has often been claimed that the 'Pet Lamb Case', the millionaire Winans against crofter Murdoch Macrae, induced James Bryce, MP for Tower Hamlets, to introduce in 1884 his Access to Mountains (Scotland) Bill, but it could only have been one of many incidents so influencing him. He was aware of the feeling prevailing in the Highlands, of the lingering bitter memories of the Clearances, and of the resentment of the people at being turned off their native heaths for the still-expanding deer forests. The preamble to his Bill read:

Whereas large tracts of uncultivated mountain and moorland in Scotland, formerly depastured by sheep and cattle, have of late years been stocked with deer, and attempts have been made to deprive Her Majesty's subjects of the rights which they have heretofore enjoyed of walking upon these and other tracts of uncultivated mountain and moor land for purposes of recreation and scientific or artistic study.

And whereas doubts have arisen as to the respective rights of the owners of uncultivated mountain and moor lands in Scotland and of Her Majesty's subjects generally as regards the said use of such lands and the access thereto, and it is expedient to remove such doubts and to secure to Her Majesty's subjects the right of free access to such lands . . . subject to proper provisions for preventing any abuse of such right . . .

Clause 2 of the Bill said, 'no owner or occupier of uncultivated mountain or moor lands in Scotland shall be entitled to exclude any person from walking on such lands for the purposes of recreation or scientific or artistic study, or to molest him in so walking'.

According to clause 3, in any action founded on alleged trespass 'it shall be a sufficient defence that the lands referred to were uncultivated mountain or moor lands, that the respondent entered thereon only for the purposes of recreation or of scientific or artistic study, and that no special damage resulted from the alleged trespass'.

By clause 4 a person could be excluded from the land for being 'in pursuit of game, taking eggs or being accompanied by a dog; for damaging the land or vegetation, or buildings or fences; for disturbing sheep or cattle so as to cause damage to the owner; going on the land with any malicious intent or otherwise than for the purpose of recreation and scientific or artistic study'. Clause 5 excluded land in proximity to a dwelling house and to any plantation of young trees and clause 6 stated that it did not extend to England or Ireland.[1]

Parliament, as on many subsequent occasions, dismissed the Bill without debate, but *The Times* thought it worth a column on its leader page. The Bill, with its quaint title, it said, had a value quite apart from its chance of success. That in determining 'the comparative strength of the various forces now moving and ultimately forming the national character. What is the comparative weight of numbers and of rent? The sportsman is a survival of prehistoric times. The lover of the picturesque is a creature of modern civilisation, insomuch that some have doubted whether he existed in classical antiquity.'

Many tourists went northward every year in quest of beautiful scenery.

They find the Scotch Highlands not cheap, nor even everywhere accessible. They are confronted with a fortification of strong fences, locked gates, resolute gamekeepers, men of action, and the terrors of the law. They entreat, they parley, they offer to bribe, they bluster, they threaten and finally they retire with the loss of half a day and trudge the next hour on a hard road between fences and plantations. Their tempers are not improved by the disappointment.

Against the multitude of tourists were the handful that shot grouse or stalked deer. They were millionaires in comparison with the others. There were two opposing armies, the tourists on one side, and the letters and renters of shootings on the other.

'Their respective claims', said the leader, 'are not disposed of by saying that a refined national taste ought to prevail over the interests of capital, and over a taste shared by the trapper and Red Indian.' It is sometimes difficult to decide whether the writer is indulging in satire or whether it is *The Times* of the Establishment speaking. 'These deer stalkers and grouse shooters are the men who have been sacrificing their days and nights, their domestic and social comforts, their health, strength, and whole vitality, to the welfare of the nation, in

Parliament, in public office, and many a private concern hardly less important to the public interest.'

In conclusion the writer asks:

is it not a matter of compromise? Surely the lords of the soil cannot claim so absolute a monopoly of earth's surface and of the most beautiful parts of it, as wholly to shut out the poor holiday folk, the artist, and the naturalist. Surely the many have rights as well as the few, and they that wish to see are entitled to legislative protection as much as they that wish to kill also. On the other hand, numbers cannot claim utterly to destroy the rights of property; that is, the right to some exclusive use of it. The problem cannot be insoluble.[2]

In February 1888 Bryce tried again. It has been said that on this occasion he included England and Wales, but this is not so. This Bill follows the first word for word.[3] It received a second reading[4] by something of an accident – in a later debate Lord Elcho described how

we came down to the House at about ten minutes past 9.00 o'clock, and though I am willing to admit that we were not all actuated by benevolent motives towards the proposal of the hon. Member, we were surprised to find that not only had the Second Reading of the Bill been carried without a word from the hon. Member, but a great many other measures had also been carried.[5]

But this availed nothing and after several attempts to bring it forward the Bill was dropped.

Meanwhile a champion from Wales had entered the lists. T. E. Ellis, MP for Merionethshire, presented in April 1888 a Mountains, Rivers and Pathways (Wales) Bill, which said:

Whereas notwithstanding that according to ancient Welsh traditions and customs, mountains, lakes and rivers were deemed free, doubts have arisen in relation to uncultivated mountain land, rivers, lakes, streams and ancient pathways, concerning the respective rights of owners or tenants and Her Majesty's subjects generally as regard the use of such lands and waterways and the access thereto; and whereas such doubts check the healthful and recreational advantages to be derived by visitors to Wales, and tend to the detriment of the residents, and it is expedient to remove such doubts, and to secure to Her Majesty's subjects the right of free access to such lands and waterways for the purpose of recreation and the pursuit of science or art, subject to due limitation necessary for protecting the rights of landowners and tenants.

From the passing of this Act

The public shall have the free right to enter upon, and have access to mountain land, moor land or waste land, and to have access to or walk along the bed or bank of any river, stream, or lake, to ride in any boat, coracle or canoe upon any river or lake, for the purpose of recreation, wimberry gathering, sketching, or antiquarian research.[6]

In a brief speech at his Bill's second reading, Mr Ellis said any pathway that had been used for five successive years in the last forty-nine years should be again used by the public. There was every safeguard in the Bill for landowners and tenants. He was opposed by the member for Caernarfon, who claimed that the Welsh traditions about mountains being free and open were simply fancy, and had no foundation in fact. He could understand the lodging-house keepers might wish to fill their houses with people who would overrun the country, and do as much mischief as they possibly could. The debate was never resumed.[7]

The only time Bryce secured a debate was in March 1892 when he submitted a motion in favour of an access to mountains bill. All he asked on that occasion was

to bring forward the grievance and suffering caused to the people of Scotland, and in a lesser degree to the people of other parts of the United Kingdom by their exclusion from their right to enjoy the scenery of their own country, and to seek healthy recreation and exercise on their own mountains and moors. The grievance, no doubt, is greatest in Scotland. It is not too much to say that all over the Highlands, the hills are completely closed.

Complaints were most numerous respecting the country round Braemar where the process of sealing up the country was carried furthest. 'It is hardly possible,' he said, 'to stir off the roads in the neighbourhood of Braemar without being confronted by a gillie and threatened with proceedings by interdict. Even those superb mountains between the source of the Dee and the valley of the Spey are so closed that one is obliged to stalk gillies as the gillies stalk the deer.' The grievance, he said, was by no means confined to the Highlands. There had been cases in the Lowlands, such as the Pentland Hills. There were scarcely any districts where such complaints had not been heard. He had heard of the initiation of a similar policy in the Lake District and certain parts of Wales.

Bryce, who was an experienced mountaineer, president of the Alpine Club from 1899 to 1901, said he had climbed mountains abroad in almost every country and had never heard of a single case where a man had been prevented from freely walking where he wished. Even in the Alps, where the chamois was hunted, there had never been an attempt to exclude the pedestrian. He told the story of King Victor Emanuel of Italy, who was fond of the sport of pursuing the wild Alpine goat.

Occasionally it happened that members of the Alpine Club or other visitors arranged to climb a mountain on the day when the King proposed shooting there. All that the King did when he knew of such a party being in the neighbourhood was to send a messenger with his compliments asking them if they could make it convenient to go up another peak because he had arranged to shoot in that particular district.

He said, 'The king did not think of claiming a right but simply asked as a favour that people would defer their visit to a peak from a particular day.'

Eighty years ago, Bryce said, people could wander freely over Scottish mountains, and until recently there had been no attempt to interdict any person from walking over open moors or mountains. Then, as now, there were people who claimed that there was no need in Scotland for access legislation, but Bryce said there had been many petitions in favour of his Bill; some had been 'the natural and spontaneous voice of the people'. In addition to those from the districts affected there had been petitions

from the inhabitants of Edinburgh, Dundee, Paisley, Dunfermline, Inverness, and other towns in favour of the Bill. The Convention of the Scottish Royal Burghs have repeatedly petitioned in its favour, and similar requests have been made by the Royal Scottish Academy of Arts, the Society of Painters in Water Colours, the Glasgow Philosophical Society and the Glasgow Geological Society.

Although this lack of access was a serious inconvenience for the visitor to Scotland, it was, he said:

A far more serious grievance to the poor people who live there, and most of all to the poor crofter, who finds himself debarred from what his fathers enjoyed and finds himself hemmed in very often by barbed wire fences from going on land, which, by right and equity, is the property of the clan, although the title is vested in the landlord. It is a grievance severely felt that they should be excluded from what has been recognised as the property of the clan, and cannot venture to lodge a visitor who desires to climb the mountain.

One of the objections to the Bill was that it would injure sport. Bryce stated he had consulted many friends who were deerstalkers and one or two who owned valuable deer forests. It was admitted that no harm would be done to grouse shooting, and he had the opinion of deerstalkers that no substantial harm would be done; indeed an additional zest might be added, making it a little more difficult to pursue the sport. But, Bryce stated, even if it could be shown that access would injure sport, he would still say the people were entitled to that right.

On the question of compensation he said:

Property in land is of a very different character from every other kind of property. Land is not property for our unlimited and unqualified use. Land is necessary so that we may live upon it and from it, and that people may enjoy it in a variety of ways; and I deny therefore, that there exists or is recognised by our law or in natural justice, such a thing as an unlimited power of exclusion. . . . There is no such thing in the old customs of this country as the right of exclusion for purposes of the mere pleasure of the individual and there is no ground in law or reason for excluding persons from a mountain . . . we must not be asked to pay compensation for what we have never given away.[8]

In *Rucksack* of June 1981[9] I wrote deploring the slow progress in securing access to open country under the National Parks and Access to the Countryside Act of 1949. 'The RA', I said, 'must never be satisfied with pedestrian tramlines, but must insist on a legal right to walk on all uncultivated land.' I advocated trespass, taking care not to do any damage or intrude on anyone's privacy. To my surprise this brought several objections. One lady said my exhortation to constant trespass lowered us to the level of vandals and half-wits. She considered it a privilege to walk over land, if only by footpath.[10] Bryce agreed with me. He said:

We are by no means content to be kept to a specified limited path in the centre of a mountain. If, for instance, I were going to the top of a mountain, and saw in the distance the cliffs overhanging a loch, I am not to be prevented from going to that loch because it happens to be in a deer forest and off the footpath. That destroys all the sense of joyous freedom which constitutes the great part of the enjoyment of fine scenery.[11]

Bryce's seconder, the member for Aberdeenshire West, suggested that anyone who believed there was no public feeling on this issue should go to the north of Scotland or Braemar and that 'if any southerner going to the north to look for a seat is not sound on what is called 'Bryce's Bill' he may as well pack up his carpet bag and make immediate use of his return ticket'.[12]

The Solicitor-General for Scotland gave the government view, after remarking, 'although I think the grievance has been exaggerated, I do not at the same time doubt that there is a certain and I will admit a genuine grievance that people are not allowed to go on the hills when they would do no harm'. He concluded by saying the government would accept Bryce's resolution, but would reserve to themselves entire freedom of judgement as to the sufficiency of the privileges and the recognition of important interests involved.[13]

There was support for the idea that England should share in this legislation. The member for Eccles, Lancashire, rose to complain that in a populous part of Lancashire he had been stopped from going over a hill in May because he might interfere with the grouse.[14] His colleague for Gorton South-East said that he believed

that before many years are past we shall have a much more enlightened industrial class who will be able more and more to enjoy and understand the beauties of nature; it seems to me that Parliament should now make some effort to enable them to enjoy those privileges without in the least encroaching upon the rights of the landowners.[15]

Bryce gained his motion in favour of such a bill without a division and, the Conservative government having accepted the principle of the Bill, Bryce pressed for it to be taken further. In May 1892 a bill 'To Regulate the Access of the Public to Mountains in Scotland' was presented by the Lord Advocate and the Solicitor-General for Scotland and given a first reading.[16] However, even as a government-sponsored bill it never reached the statute book. Parliament was dissolved in June 1892 and at the general election the Liberals took office. Bryce was an important member of the Party. He had been Under-Secretary for Foreign Affairs in a previous administration and in the new government Gladstone appointed him Chancellor of the Duchy of Lancaster with a seat in the Cabinet. In 1894 he was President of the Board of Trade, and in 1905 Chief Secretary for Ireland. Why, it might be asked, did a man of such eminence in his party fail to obtain more support for his Access to Mountains Bill? The answer is simple. Many leading Liberals, like their Conservative counterparts, belonged to the 'huntin' shootin' and fishin'' class. Sir Charles Trevelyan was a champion of access and had his own grouse moor, but this was an uncommon combination.

Bryce submitted his Bill for the last time in 1898,[17] with the usual rejection. In February 1900 his younger brother, Annan, presented the same Bill, as he did in July 1906 and again in February 1908.[18] On this last occasion there was another bill on the Order Paper in the name of Charles Trevelyan, the Liberal MP for Elland in the West Riding, [19] mentioned in the last paragraph. The only difference between the two bills was that Trevelyan's did not include the words 'this Act shall not apply to England or Ireland'.

Trevelyan mentioned the 'Pet Lamb Case' as an instance of private selfishness so gross that no one defended it. That social scandal, grotesque in its enormity, had gone, but the law, or absence of law which permitted it, still remained. The general evil had increased in the last fifteen years, and it was now more difficult to walk freely in the wild places of Scotland and England. Sixty years ago, when people were free to wander all over the wild places of England and Scotland, only 35 per cent of the population lived in towns; now the figure was 75 per cent. In order to live a thoroughly healthy life in town it was necessary that the population should have country air and exercise. No one among the well-to-do population ever dreamt of staying the whole year in town. Every rich man either bought or hired some place to go where he had his special share of wild country, and where he could enjoy in the fullest and freest way the most beautiful wild places. A rapidly increasing mass of the population in the great towns were forming walking and climbing clubs and studying natural history during their rambles.

People in Switzerland, France, Germany, and Italy are free to go where they like in the wild places of their country. 'Who has ever been forbidden to wander over an Alp? Who has ever been threatened with an interdict in the Apennines? Who has ever been warned off the rocks of Tyrol? Who has ever been prosecuted for trespassing among Norwegian mountains?'

He went on to say that

the dingy unattractive town of Sheffield has at its very gates a great moor district, which was the proper recreation ground of the people. In the old days it was open to them and there the poet, Ebenezer Elliott,* found inspiration. Now, the workmen who came after him were not allowed to walk on the hills. They might go and look at Kinder Scout through glasses, but they could not go up without the chance of being chased by gamekeepers.'

In the long run they could not defend to the unprejudiced mind a claim to exclude a large and increasing number of men and women

---

*Ebenezer Elliot (1781–1849) was born in Rotherham, son of an iron-founder, and became a bar-iron merchant. He published several volumes of poetry in which he denounced the social evils of his day. He became known as 'The Corn-Law Rhymer'.

who were seeking health and recreation in the beautiful wild places of the country on the grounds that another set of people, much less numerous, but with more opportunities, wanted it for their exclusive recreation.[20]

The rejection of the Bill was moved by the member for Windsor who believed that its object would be better obtained by the preservation of existing rights of way and the creation of new ones. He was prepared to base his argument on the possibility of damage to sport. A tourist on a hill top, without the least intention of doing harm, could clear the whole valley of deer to which they would not return for several days. The three and a half million acres of deer forest brought in a rental of £165,000 a year. He knew a deer forest let at a rental of £3,100 which as a sheep run was let for £400 a year with a rental of £600 for grouse shooting. If the deer forests were returned to grazing there would be a loss of £80,000 a year, and a loss in rates of £12,000 to £15,000.[21]

Annan Bryce, on the other hand, 'held that the whole population of Scotland would be very much better off if there were a diminution in the number of deer forests'. He did not think it was sufficient to provide rights of way from hamlet to hamlet or house to house across a mountain as 'the ancestors of these very inhabitants originally had an equal right with the landlord'. Why should they be compelled to keep to a footpath when the lands originally belonged to their clan who had a free right to roam over them? On their behalf as well as that of the people generally he said that no regulation, by which more rights of way were safeguarded, would satisfy the demand which existed for the free enjoyment of the mountains and the moors.[22]

Ramsay MacDonald, future Labour Prime Minister, agreed that the extension of deer forests was not in the interests of inhabitants of the Scottish Highlands. He had listened with pleasure to the fair words about the desire of shooting tenants to allow the outsider to enjoy the beauties of Scotland. But when he walked over the Larig Ghru pass in the Cairngorms, which was kept open by litigation, he found that every signpost which had been erected by the Scottish Rights of Way Committee had been destroyed by the gillies of interested parties. He had been in many deer forests without permission and he would go again without permission. He believed that the more the working classes in the towns took an intelligent interest in their own lives, the more would this Bill, if it became an Act of Parliament, mean to them.

They were trying more and more, by organising clubs – walking clubs and clubs of all kinds – to take the people out of towns on to the moors . . . and that would do them an immense amount of good, but it could not be done unless the law were laid down on the broad and generous principles and ideas contained in this Bill.[23]

The Lord Advocate, Thomas Shaw, member for Hawick Burghs, gave the government's blessing to the Bill, commenting that it had been received favourably on both sides of the house and reminded those on the Tory side that their party were deeply committed to it. Just before the General Election of 1892 James Bryce's Bill had caught the public imagination and the government had brought in a bill 'conceived in many portions in identical language with that of Mr Bryce'.[24] At the division there were 190 in favour and 61 against. The 'Ayes' list contained some notable names, including Winston Churchill, J. R. Clynes, Arthur Henderson, David Lloyd George, Herbert Samuel and Philip Snowden.

The Bill then went on to the committee stage. The frequently expressed sympathy of the sportsmen with the idea that the public should be able to enjoy the scenery of their native land was seen for what it was worth in the six meetings of the Standing Committee. After five meetings they had only considered fifteen lines of the Bill. After the sixth meeting on 13 July the Committee reported that it was impossible in that session to complete the Bill and the House resolved not to proceed further. So what had appeared to be a glimpse of the promised land turned out to be a mirage.[25]

Annan Bryce tried again in 1909 and in the next thirty years nine access bills were presented, all basically the same as Bryce's and all with the vital clauses stating that the owner of uncultivated land could not exclude any person walking for the purposes of recreation or scientific or artistic study, and that on alleged trespass it should be sufficient defence to say the lands were uncultivated mountains or moorland. A few of them gained a short debate but all of them had the blessing, usually in a leader, of the *Manchester Guardian*. Commenting on P. Gilchrist Thompson's Bill in 1924, it said, 'the Bill is a matter of high importance to those of us who have to live half hidden in our own smoke, in any of the Lancashire and Yorkshire towns that lie couched in two long rows below the Pennine ridge of hills'. Once anyone who wished could roam anywhere on the Pennine moors but hardly anyone wished to. As a consequence of the Industrial Revolution the towns below the moorland slopes became places to flee from.

When you look down on Oldham or Rochdale from the top of the Pennines, you feel that nobody ought to stay down in that witches' cauldron on Saturday afternoon – everybody ought to be out where you are, on the moors, to get back a little of that vitality that the week has stewed out of him . . . But . . . there came a rapid increase of the vogue of grouse shooting and therefore a steep rise in the commercial value of the peaty Pennine wastes of bog-grass, bilberry and heather. The result had been the wholesale expulsion of Saturday afternoon walkers from what had for centuries been the free playground of all who cared to use it.[26]

The paper returned to the attack on 15 May, in a leader which in scathing terms refuted a *Times* leader of the previous day. This had declared there was no need for access legislation. Under the headline 'Mountains and Molehills' *The Times* said the lack of access was a bogey.[27] The *Manchester Guardian* said it feared innocent people might assume that this was an accurate statement. It continued:

after some sneers at the Bill as expressing (this is really a wonderful touch) the state of mind of urban football crowds who do not even want to see country places, *The Times* writer goes on to say that the whole of the present trouble is a 'bogey' and that 'as a general rule the man or woman or child who wishes to explore the waste places of this island can do so without let or hindrance from anyone'. Of Scotland, as every mountaineer or walker knows, this statement is quite untrue. Of the English Pennine moorlands it was almost true some fifty years ago, and it has definitely ceased to be so since. The case of the higher parts of the Derbyshire Peak, over which anyone could ramble at will in 1890, and which now are strictly preserved, to the exclusion of walkers and climbers, is only typical of what has been taken at almost every part of the Pennine range, from the inhabitants of East Lancashire and the West Riding.

More than sixty years ago, the writer of this leader demolished a type still, unfortunately, with us: 'the fanatical assertor of overstrained "rights" of property, who cannot yet see that there is a difference between asking for freedom to cross a man's barren mountain and asking for freedom to trample on another man's suburban garden of geraniums'.[28]

The next day the Duke of Atholl, that indefatigable defender of the deer forests, whose forbears had acquired thousands of acres in the Highlands, had a column-length letter in *The Times*, fully endorsing the 'Mountains and Molehills' leader. At the same time he took a swipe of an old opponent of his, Ernest Baker, who had frequently denounced the closing-off of the Highlands. He, the Duke said, was the explosive force behind the Bill and Mr Gilchrist Thompson was merely the finger on the trigger.[29]

The parliamentary struggle continued. Graham White, member for Birkenhead and one-time president of the Liverpool Ramblers' Federation, presented a Bill in 1930 and recalled that the Prime Minister, Ramsay MacDonald, had spoken in support of Trevelyan's Bill.[30] This observation did not assist his case, any more than did Ellen Wilkinson's request to MacDonald to provide facilities for the passage of the Access Bill she introduced in 1931. She got the barren reply that the pressure of business made it difficult to give a promise.[31] Unsurprisingly, many members well-disposed to the idea of an access bill grew disheartened. At the Winnats Pass rally in June 1931, P. M. Oliver, president of the Manchester Ramblers' Federation and a Manchester MP, said that he felt there was no hope of such a bill being passed in the near future.[32]

Geoffrey Mander, MP for Wolverhampton, presented a bill which was ordered to be printed on 8 July 1937.[33] Fortunately it got no further. Mander, it appears, proposed to withdraw it and introduce an amended version which would limit access to nine months of the year. The incident was the first intimation that the RA might have to go it alone without the wholehearted support of the Commons Society and other amenity societies.* Edwin Royce wrote to Mander:

The entry of the Commons and Footpaths Society is regarded with misgiving by northern ramblers and one Federation (West Riding) has already made a protest. The reasons are the propensity of the Society to make compromises with landowners, as it did in the case of the Rights of Way Act 1932 and the known antagonism of the Secretary, Sir Lawrence Chubb.

Mander replied to Royce saying that the action taken was a wise one. It gave an opportunity to see how far it was possible to secure by agreement a measure which could be passed at once. The Bill in its present form had no chance of passing into law as it was highly controversial. He thought Sir Lawrence Chubb was genuinely anxious to co-operate.[34]

The Access to Mountains Act 1939 and the National Parks and Access to the Countryside Act 1949 are dealt with in succeeding chapters, but to bring the story nearer to our own times we can leapfrog to 1978 when Arthur Blenkinsop, member for South Shields, a good friend of the open-air movement and one-time president of the

---

*This remark relates to the part Chubb played in the negotiations over the 1939 Access to Mountains Act, described the chapters devoted to that Act.

RA, introduced a simple but far-reaching bill.[35] It was scheduled for a second reading in January 1979, but objection was made and it was not debated. However, David Clark, Blenkinsop's successor in the South Shields seat and chairman of the Open Spaces Society, brought forward the same Bill in February 1980. The aim of the Bill was threefold; to allow legal access to all commons; to amend in minor fashion the Commons Registration Act 1965 and to grant right of access for air and exercise to all open land. From James Bryce in 1884, David Clark observed, there was a long tradition of such bills. Men only wanted the same rights as their Lordships' grouse, to wander on the moors, except that they did not want to be shot at. By giving access to uncultivated land they would bring this country into line with the more advanced countries in Europe. 'I have been told,' he said, 'to get off moors even though I have been on a statutorally registered public footpath. That has been said to me at gunpoint on two occasions by people who have told me that they do not recognise the law as applied to the Queen's Highway.' Once again the Bill failed to get a second reading.[36]

Andrew Bennett, member for Stockport North, was equally luckless when he introduced a Walkers (Access to Countryside) Bill in 1982. Among its provisions was one to establish a public right of access on foot to all open country and common land. Had the Bill been passed it would have required local planning authorities to publish within five years a draft access map showing open country; after a period for representations and objections a definitive map would have been published showing areas to which the public would have the right of access on foot.[37]

The Hobhouse Committee on Footpaths and Access to the Countryside,[38] discussed elsewhere, recommended in 1947 the production of a definitive map of open country, i.e. access land. That was a unanimous recommendation of a committee including farmers and landowners, representatives of the Ministry of Agriculture, John Dower of the famous report on National Parks,[39] and Francis Ritchie and me as ramblers' representatives. However, when the 1949 National Parks and Access to the Countryside Act was going through Parliament, Lewis Silkin, as Minister responsible, stubbornly resisted all arguments for what he called "blanket access". He preferred to let sleeping dogs lie. The result has been that very little has been achieved and as far as the access provisions of the 1949 Act are concerned, the planning authorities have long been sleeping soundly.

References

1   Access to Mountains (Scotland), Bill 122, 28 February 1884.
2   *Times*, 25 March 1884.
3   Access to Mountains (Scotland), Bill 103, 13 February 1888.
4   *Hansard*, 3rd Ser., Vol. 324, Col. 1463, 17 April 1888.
5   *Hansard*, 4th Ser., Vol. 2, Col. 104, 4 March 1892.
6   Mountains, Rivers and Pathways (Wales), Bill 129, 17 February 1888.
7   *Hansard*, 3rd Ser. Vol. 324, Col. 1286, 13 April 1888.
8   *Hansard*, 4th Ser., Vol. 2, Cols. 92–101, 4 March 1892.
9   *Rucksack*, Vol. 10, No. 5, June 1981, p. 9.
10 *Rucksack*, vol. 10, No. 6, October 1981, p. 11.
11 *Hansard*, 4th Ser., Vol. 2, Col. 101, 4 March 1892.
12 *Ibid.*, Col. 102.
13 *Ibid.*, Cols. 121–3.
14 *Ibid.*, Col. 125.
15 *Ibid.*, Col. 127.
16 Access to Mountains (Scotland) (No 2), Bill 379, 26 May 1892.
17 Access to Mountains (Scotland), Bill 71, 14 February 1898.
18 Access to Mountains (Scotland), Bill 39, 2 February 1900; Access to Mountains (Scotland), Bill 321, 23 July 1906; Access to Mountains (Scotland), Bill 30, 3 February 1908.
19 Access to Mountains, Bill 21, 3 February 1908.
20 *Hansard*, 4th Ser., Vol. 188, Cols. 1439–46, 15 May 1908.
21 *Ibid.*, Cols. 1449–50.
22 *Ibid.*, Col. 1464.
23 *Ibid.*, Col. 1477.
24 *Ibid.*, Col. 1483.
25 *Parliamentary Papers*, Session 1908, Vol. 6, p. 1.
26 *Manchester Guardian*, 9 May 1924.
27 *Times*, 14 May 1924.
28 *Manchester Guardian*, 15 May 1924.
29 *Times*, 16 May 1924.
30 Access to Mountains, Bill 124, *Hansard* (House of Commons), 5th Ser., Vol. 235, Cols. 419–21, 12 February 1930.
31 Access to Mountains, Bill 152, 13 May 1931; *Hansard* (House of Commons), 5th Ser., Vol. 252, Cols. 1357–8 14 May 1931.
32 *Manchester Guardian*, 29 June 1931.
33 Access to Mountains, Bill 193, 8 July 1937.
34 It has proved impossible to trace this correspondence – editor.
35 Access to Commons and Open Country, Bill 32, 1978.
36 Access to Commons and Open Country, Bill 153, *Hansard* (House of Commons), 5th Ser., Vol. 979, Cols. 1374–6, 27 February 1980.
37 Walkers (Access to the Countryside), Bill 111, *Hansard* (House of

Commons), 6th Ser., Vol. 22, Cols. 283–5, 21 April 1982.

38 *Report of Special Committee on Footpath and Access to the Countryside*, Cmd 7207, 1947.

39 John Dower, *National Parks in England Wales*, Cmd 6628, 1945.

1 P. M. Oliver MP, speaking at the 1931 Access rally at Winnats Pass

2 G. H. B. Ward at Winnats

4 C. E. M. Joad at Winnats

3 A. J. Brown at Winnats

5 Gamekeepers and police marching to intercept the Abbey Brook mass trespass. A photograph taken by Phil Barnes

6 Protest Rally at Winnats to protest against the severe sentences imposed after the Kinder Scout mass trespass, 1932

7 The conference held at Hope, Derbyshire, in 1930, which decided to found the National Council of Ramblers' Federations. *Standing, left to right:* Frank Turton, J. A. Southern, G. R. Mitchell, H. H. Everard, Arthur Roberts, J. Irving and Alf Embleton. *Seated, left to right*, Phil Barnes, Nora Willington, G. H. B. Ward, Stephen Morton, Molly Lower and John Francey

8 Executive Committee meeting at Matlock in 1934. *Left to right:* Eric Lodge, Stephen Morton, J. A. Southern, Alf Embleton, G. R. Mitchell, T. A. Leonard, unknown, A. W. Hewitt, Edwin Royce, and a Scottish representative

9 Access demonstration at Whatstandwell, Nottinghamshire, 1938. *Left to right*, Stephen Morton, an incongruously dressed representative of the county, Tom Saxton and George Mitchell

10 Tom's companions on his famous Pennine Way walk in 1948. *Left to right:* George Chetwynd, Geoffrey de Freitas, Hugh Dalton, Ted Castle, Fred Willey, Barbara Castle, Julian Snow; *seated*, Arthur Blenkinsop (*Daily Herald photograph*)

11 Rally to protest against a hydro-electricity scheme planned for North Wales, 1949. *Standing:* the Bishop of St Asaph; *seated*, H. H. Symonds

12 Lord Winster speaking at a rally to protest against the West Riding's decision that no action was necessary to provide access to open country in the county, 1958

13 Tom Stephenson addressing a rally to press for the creation of the Wolds Way in East Yorkshire, 1968

Chapter 7

The Kinder Scout mass trespass

The Kinder Scout mass trespass of 24 April 1932, which led to a brief scrap between some gamekeepers and ramblers and the imprisonment of five young demonstrators, was the most dramatic incident in the access to mountains campaign. Yet it contributed little, if anything, to it. Once the indignation roused by the severe prison sentences had subsided, the public interest soon faded. Edwin Royce,* foremost champion of access, wrote soon afterwards, 'The year 1932 will not be remembered as a red letter year for the rambler. It has been a period of more than the usual froth and bubble.'[1]

The truth is that there never was a mass trespass.† No-one reached the summit of Kinder Scout and the so-called victory meeting was held on a public path at Ashop Head. In saying this I do not wish to belittle the intentions or the enthusiasm of the demonstrators, but only to keep the record straight and, if possible, prevent the canonisation of myth as history.

*Edwin Royce was not opposed to trespass in itself, or even of using it as a weapon in the struggle for access. Tom Stephenson wrote on the occasion of Royce's death in 1947 of a letter he had received from him in 1945, expressing his pessimism about the prospects for access to mountains legislation.

He went on to explain that he was about to retire from business; that he had saved a small sum of money, and had no relations or dependants to worry about. He, therefore, proposed that he should trespass persistently on Kinder Scout until an injunction was obtained against him, and that he should then continue trespassing, with the inevitable consequence of being sent to gaol. His imprisonment, he thought, might give some publicity to the 'access' position and help forward the demand for new legislation. (*Out of Doors*, spring 1947, p. 27)

†Alternative views of the Kinder Scout mass trespass are contained in Benny Rothman's own book *The 1932 Kinder Trespass* (Altrincham, 1982) and Howard Hill, *Freedom to Roam, The struggle for access to Britain's Moors and Mountains* (Ashbourne, 1980). There is also a brief account in Stephen Humphries's *Hooligans or Rebels? An Oral History of Working-Class Childhood and Youth 1889–1939* (Oxford, 1981), pp. 206–7.

The demonstration was organised by an ephemeral body, the British Workers' Sports Federation (BWSF), an appendage of the Communist Party; by men not known to have evinced any previous interest in the access problem, and who did not, in fact, play any part in the subsequent campaign. Doubts as to the practical value of the exercise, as much as concern over the political colour of the BWSF, may have led the Manchester and Sheffield Ramblers' Federations and the National Council of Ramblers' Federations to stand aloof. Some of the ramblers' leaders may have feared to find Reds in the heather or to hear Marxism preached at the annual Winnats Pass access demonstrations. Whatever their reasoning, the Manchester and District Ramblers' Federation made the following declaration:

Mass trespass; – the Manchester and District Federation wishes to state as definitely as possible, that it had no part in the events which took place in Hayfield and on Kinder Scout on April 24, and that it had no connection whatsoever with the organisation responsible for the happenings on that day. As a result of the trespass, six men have been charged, one for grievous bodily harm, and all six with unlawful assembly and breach of the peace.[2]

In 1970 BBC2 Television broadcast a film entitled *The Battle of Kinder Scout*, in which Bernard Rothman, who led the demonstration, two of his fellow prison-mates and one of the gamekeepers involved, appeared. To help the producer Rothman supplied a tape-recording of his recollections of the mass trespass and the conditions from which it arose. He kindly lent me the tape to have a transcript made and I have made extensive use of it in the rest this chapter. On it he says that the British Workers' Sports Federation, of which he was the Lancashire secretary, considered that the policy of the 'official' rambling bodies to be futile, actually preventing ramblers from obtaining access to mountains. The BWSF had organised a camp for young people at the village of Rowarth some weeks before the mass trespass. Some of the campers were turned off the moors by gamekeepers and returned to camp smarting and very indignant. 'It was decided then and there that we would do something about it, and we decided to organise a mass trespass over Kinder Scout.'[3]

On 18 April Rothman gave an interview to a *Manchester Evening News* reporter, who was to appear later as a prosecution witness. The paper splashed the story that night under the following headlines.

CLAIMS TO
FREE ACCESS

CAMPAIGN TO FORCE
LANDOWNERS

CALL TO RALLY

SUNDAY'S ATTACK ON
KINDER

Tired of unproductive protest
and pleas, working-class rambling
clubs in Lancashire have decided
upon direct action to enforce their
claims for access to beauty spots[4]

Other papers took up the story and 'then, unfortunately', commented Rothman,

the Ramblers' Federation, the official body which had led all the normal agitation for access to mountains, made it their business to condemn it and urged all its members not to take part . . . In fact a number of their officials and ramblers came to the mass trespass, but they did nothing in any way to interfere with the trespass.[5]

The BWSF's preliminary arrangements included the distribution of leaflets to ramblers at railway stations, and the chalking of pavement notices urging attendance at a meeting at Hayfield Recreation Ground on 24 April.[6] As usually happens at open-air gatherings, there were widely varying estimates of the number of those taking part. The *Manchester Guardian*[7] said 400 to 500. Rothman claimed 600 to 800, perhaps 1,000.[8] At Derby Assizes, when some of the trespassers were tried, the prosecution spoke of a crowd of 150 to 200.[9]

When the organisers got to the recreation ground they found it was ringed with policemen. They also found that the Parish Council had a by-law prohibiting meetings in the recreation ground, and the Deputy Chief Constable of Derbyshire and two police superintendents, together with the Clerk and several members of the Council, were there to see the law upheld. According to Rothman's account, some of his supporters mingled with the crowd, telling them to get on the move outside the recreation ground and along the footpath towards William Clough. Soon a massive march had started and the police ran, trying to intercept them, but it was too late and all they could do was fall in at the rear.[10]

A different version was given at the trial when, according to the prosecution, Rothman made some remarks in the way of marching orders, 'one whistle will be sounded for "Advance", two for "Retreat", and three for "Advance in open formation".' 'The crowd moved off', continued counsel, 'with "General" Rothman at the head.'[11] The police, says Rothman, had obtained an injunction restraining him from taking part in the demonstration, and were on the look-out for him to Manchester and Hayfield.[12] The march 'was really a dense crowd of young people. All looked picturesque in rambling gear, khaki jackets, khaki shirts, abbreviated shorts, colourful jerseys. Away we went in jubliant mood, determined to carry out the assault on Kinder Scout which was planned, and determined that no authority would stop it.' Rothman addressed the crowd in a disused quarry, where he told them that the organisers wanted an orderly, disciplined march. They were not out to hurt anybody, but they were determined to make a demonstration in spite of any opposition they might meet.[13]

The *Manchester Guardian* correspondent, who accompanied the marchers, tells how from Nab Brow they saw the first gamekeepers dotted about on the slopes below Sandy Heys on the other side of William Clough.

In a few moments the advance guard – men only, the women were kept behind – dropped down to the stream and started to climb the other side. I followed. As soon as we came to the top of the first steep bit we met the keepers. There followed a very brief parley, after which a fight started – nobody quite knew how. It was not even a struggle. There were only eight keepers, while from first to last, 40 or more ramblers took part in the scuffle. The keepers had sticks, while the ramblers fought mostly with their hands, though two keepers were disarmed and their sticks turned against them. Other ramblers took belts off and used them, while one spectator was hit by a stone. There will be plenty of bruises carefully nursed in Gorton and other parts of Manchester tonight, though no one was seriously hurt except one keeper, Mr E. Beever, who was knocked unconscious and damaged his ankle.

He was helped back to the road and taken to Stockport Infirmary, but was able to return home that night.[14]

Rothman did not see the clash with gamekeepers. He says, 'I was on a section of the front myself that met no opposition and no resistance whatever.' 'One keeper', he says, 'made himself conspicuous by launching an attack on the ramblers, which, of course, was just asking for disaster for him.' 'That', he adds, was about the only bit of violence which took place, and I just didn't see it in detail, I could only hear the confused shouting on my right as I personally went towards the great goal, the top of Kinder Scout; and away we went, and when we were reaching the top we could see quite a dense crowd who later turned out to be a body of our boys from Sheffield who had come the other way from Edale and we stopped.[15]

Here Rothman's version differs from the account of the *Manchester Guardian* correspondent, who wrote that after the fight they continued uphill and

soon we turned to the left and continued along the hillside towards Ashop Head, the summit of the public path from Hayfield to the Snake Inn on the Glossop–Sheffield road. Before we regained the footpath a halt was made for tea, and the Manchester contingent was joined by a party of about thirty from Sheffield who had marched from Hope over Jacob's Ladder.[16]

Rothman evidently was not familiar with the land, for he said, 'We were then on the top of Kinder Scout, which is a large plateau. It isn't a little peak sticking on top of a hill or anything like that – we were on this sacred ground from which ramblers had hitherto been prevented from reaching – officially prevented from reaching.'[17] They were not, in fact, on the top of Kinder Scout but at the highest point of the Snake path, a good two miles to the north-west about 400 feet lower than the highest point of Kinder Scout. On 25 May 1970, during the filming of *The Battle of Kinder Scout*, I discussed this question with Rothman and Ewan MacColl, who had been in the demonstration and later became well-known as a folk singer. Both agreed that the *Manchester Guardian* report had been correct, and the so-called victory meeting was held near Ashop Head.

In 1982 there was a celebration of the jubilee of the demonstration and a spate of press publicity, much of it misinformed and contrary to authentic available records. Rothman continued to claim that the demonstrators held their victory meeting on the summit of Kinder. When reminded of his and Ewan MacColl's agreement that the meeting was at Ashop Head he has replied that the *Manchester Guardian* was the only paper to mention Ashop Head. There his memory was at fault. The *Daily Worker*, now the *Morning Star*, reporting the trial in the local magistrates' court of Comrade B. Rothman and five others, mentioned the encounter with the keepers and went on, 'meanwhile, the ramblers had streamed towards Ashop Head, at the top of William Clough . . . A victory meeting was held at Ashop Head undisturbed.'[18] In the introduction to his jubilee book[19] Rothman says, 'a whole mythology has grown around the trespass', and in the opening words of Chapter 1 he writes, 'they scrambled up the steep bank of William Clough and on to Kinder Scout. Hundreds of ramblers of the Mass Trespass shook hands and congratulated each other. They had overcome their first hurdle. They were standing on forbidden land'.[20] That is the greatest myth of all.

Writing in the *Guardian* a week before the jubilee celebration, Rothman still relied on his imagination. After referring to the clash with the keepers, he wrote, 'The rest of us, meanwhile, had gone to the top of Kinder, where we met a group of about 30 from Sheffield who had come over by way of Edale'.[21] Immediately below Rothman's story the *Guardian* printed a contradictory account of 75-year-old John Watson, one of the seventeen keepers and watchers who confronted the demonstrators.

Watson wrote, 'we could hear them cheering and yelling as if they had achieved something, when they had achieved nothing at all. They had only trespassed about 100 yards – never got half way up the clough.' As to the meeting on the summit, he wrote, 'they are supposed to have met another party coming from Sheffield, but we never saw them. Definitely nobody came near the Downfall.'[22] (Kinder Downfall is a waterfall on the western edge of the plateau.)

(Probably few of the ramblers there that day knew that they were on historic ground. That path from Hayfield to the Snake Inn was long disputed by the landowners and only legalised after prolonged negotiations by the Hayfield and Kinder Scout Ancient Footpaths Association, founded in 1894. The path was formally opened on 29 May 1897 by members of the Society walking from the Snake Inn to Hayfield, where they were welcomed by the village brass band.[23])

At the short victory meeting, Rothman congratulated the demonstrators on having trespassed so successfully. He warned them that some ramblers might be unfortunate enough to be fined and for their future benefit a hat was passed round.[24] On the way back to Hayfield the demonstrators kept religiously to the footpath. At the edge of the village the ramblers were met by a police inspector in a 'baby car'. 'At his suggesion,' said the *Manchester Guardian* reporter,

ramblers formed up into a column and marched into Hayfield still over 200 strong, singing triumphantly, the police car leading their procession. It was their last happy moment. When they got properly into the village they were halted by the police. Still they suspected no ill, and it was not until police officers, accompanied by a keeper, began to walk through their ranks, that they realised that they had been caught. Five men were taken to the police station and detained. The rest of the now doleful procession was carefully shepherded through Hayfield while, as the church bells rang for evensong, the jubilant villagers crowded every door and window to watch the police triumph.[25]

Rothman says that they were taken to a lock-up in Hayfield, 'but because of the efforts of the ramblers to release us, hammering on the door and threatening to break the police station down, we were taken later to New Mills, where we were kept overnight'.[26]

Next day, 25 April, the six detained men (one more had been arrested on Sunday afternoon) appeared at New Mills Police Court on charges arising out of the mass trespass. John Thomas Anderson, twenty-one, of Droylsden, was charged with causing grievous bodily harm to Edward Beever, Special Gamekeeper. He was also charged, together with Julius Clyne, 23, Harry Mendel, 22, Bernard Rothman, 20, and David Nussbaum, 19, all of Cheetham, and Arthur Walter Gillett, 19, a student of Manchester University, with unlawful assembly and a breach of the peace. They were remanded on bail and, after appearances at the local court, were committed to the Derby Assizes, where they were tried on 7 and 8 July.

All six were charged with riotous assembly and assault. Rothman, Clyne and Nussbaum were also charged with incitement and Anderson was charged with causing grievous bodily harm to Edward Beever. Only Gillett and Anderson were represented by counsel. Rothman decided to defend himself. 'I had never been in court', he said, 'let along conducted my own defence, but I was quite game.' 'I looked up a few books in the Reference Library – became a "legal expert".' He would conduct his defence from a historical and political point of view, not as a barrister would do, on legal and technical grounds. Rothman also says that the father of one of the defendants, a wealthy banker, was anxious to have all the defendants legally represented.[27]

Counsel for the prosecution said that a crowd of 150 to 200 assembled on Hayfield Recreation Ground and was addressed by Rothman, who gave military orders. The crowd then moved off, with Rothman at its head, and surrounded the keepers, one of whom was badly injured by Anderson.

Returning from the encounter, 'the hikers sang "The Red Flag" and shouted "down with the landowners and ruling classes and up with the workers" and "down with the bobbies".' One of the defendants, said counsel, had in his possession documents headed 'Friends of the Soviet Union'! The prosecution also drew the attention of the court to a notice in which the BWSF had called upon ramblers to take action to secure access to mountains. 'It is a crime', it said, 'for working-class feet to tread on sacred ground on which Lord Big Bug and Lady Little Flea do their shooting.'[28]

Rothman cross-examined some of the witnesses. He asked a special constable to justify his description of the crowd as undisciplined. The policeman replied, 'It must be undisciplined when a man is laid out unconscious by a howling mob.' Another policeman agreed that Rothman urged the crowd to behave in a quiet and orderly manner. Other witnesses said that only the keepers were armed with sticks. Edward Beever, the Stockport Corporation Waterworks keeper, said that Anderson grabbed his stick and in the struggle he was kicked in the groin and rendered unconscious.[29]

With the exception of Gillett, the defendants were ten minutes late in returning to court after the luncheon interval. Rothman said they spent most of their time looking for a café. The Judge, he said, 'stopped all proceedings, gave us a fearful lecture, and decided then and there that we would be kept in custody till the end of the trial for our contempt of court'.[30] Gillett was allowed out, but the others spent the night in Leicester Gaol.

On the second day Gillett and Anderson, who were legally represented, were the only two defendants to go into the witness box. Anderson said he neither hit nor struggled with Beever. In the notes Rothman prepared for the BBC in 1970 he said Anderson was not a member of the BWSF. 'He and some of the chaps who were actually hostile to us had been arrested at the site of one of the scuffles.' Anderson, he believed, 'came with the intention of trying to stop it (the demonstration), became isolated, left on his own, and the police, wanting someone for that particular incident, decided to pick on him'.[31] Gillett said that he approved of the aims of the BWSF but did not favour violence, and he did not hear it advocated by the other defendants. His admission of being a Quaker inspired a brilliant outburst of legal wit. 'Did you quake on this occasion?', asked prosecuting counsel.[32]

According to Rothman, the Judge, before passing sentences,

expressed surprise at seeing a young university student like Gillett involved with such associates. He asked Gillett if he were not ashamed of his behaviour. 'No sir', he replied, 'I would do it again tomorrow.' 'That finished him', said Rothman, 'and he went down with the rest of us.' Rothman added that when they were taken below after the sentencing, Mr and Mrs Gillett visited their son and Mrs Gillett said to him: 'I am proud of you, Tony, I wouldn't have had you do anything different.'[33]

Rothman read a long written statement from the dock. Some 300 or more ramblers, he said, had gathered to protest against the enclosure of moorland in Derbyshire. Ramblers, after a hard week's work, and life in smoky towns and cities, went rambling at weekends for relaxation, for a breath of fresh air and a little sunshine. They found that the finest rambling country was closed to them because certain individuals wished to shoot for about ten days in the year, and ramblers were forced to walk on muddy, crowded paths and denied the pleasures of enjoying to the utmost the countryside.

The BWSF thought the policy of the main ramblers' organisations was futile. The mass trespass demonstration was the commencement of a campaign amongst ramblers for action to obtain access to mountains. The demonstration was peaceful. Had the ramblers been unruly or hooligans it would have fared very badly for the keepers. It was obvious that Beever had started the scuffle with a rambler, and the crowd of ramblers gathered round and watched the scuffle in which Beever received his injuries. The ramblers had no hesitation in returning to Hayfield. Would this have been done, he asked, by a gang of hooligans who had just been engaged in a general riot? Would they have returned to a small village which they knew was filled with police?[34]

The Judge ruled that there was no evidence against Mendel, who was found not guilty and discharged. Rothman he described as a young man of no small ability. In a summing-up lasting two hours the Judge said he was sure the jury would not be prejudiced by the foreign-sounding names of two or three of the defendants.* It was the pride of the country to give a man even-handed justice, whatever his name, race, nationality or religion.[35] 'There was no country in the world', the Judge continued,

in which expression of opinion, however, extreme, was so free or in which

---

*The account of the Kinder Scout mass trespass given in Humphries, *op. cit.*, directly accuses the police, at least, of anti-semitism.

demonstrations of every kind were so little interfered with. No one would wish to see these liberties in any way restricted, but they could not be exercised in such a way as to amount to riot or unlawful assembly, or to disturb the public peace, and strike terror and alarm into the hearts of the King's subjects.[36]

Anderson, found guilty of occasioning bodily harm, was sentenced to six months. The rest were found guilty of incitement to cause a riotous assembly. Rothman was sentenced to four months, Nussbaum to three months, Clyne and Gillett to two months' imprisonment.

While the men were awaiting trial at the Assizes the BWSF sent some of its members to that year's Winnats Access Rally on the last Sunday in June. There they made their presence felt by heckling the speakers, C. E. M. Joad,* and P. M. Oliver, MP.[37] This did not deter the Manchester Federation a few weeks later from writing to the Home Secretary pleading for a remission of the sentences, especially as the men were first offenders.[38] The Home Secretary, Sir Herbert Samuel, replied 'that he had carefully considered all the circumstances and could find no ground for recommending any remission of the sentences'.[39]

Sir Lawrence Chubb, writing to George Mitchell, Secretary of the National Council of Ramblers' Federations, on the day after the demonstration, thought it had been a peculiarly stupid and mischievous business and those arrested should rightly face the consequences of their foolhardiness.[40] Edwin Royce took a more philosophical view. 'It would have been interesting', he said, 'to observe how the "powers" would have dealt with a large scale technical trespass. The trespass was, in fact, nominal, the demonstrators going a short distance on forbidden ground.' He added:

Public opinion expected the men to be punished, but was not prepared for the harsh sentences actually inflicted. There was at once a revulsion of feeling. Only one expression of opinion found its way through the press, a writer to the *Manchester Guardian* comparing the affair to a University rag, when arrested persons are not usually sent to prison.[41]

Some ramblers, including such luminaries of the access movement

---

*C. E. M. Joad (1891–1953) was a reader in philosophy at Birkbeck College, University of London, and a popular writer and broadcaster. He wrote and spoke frequently about rambling and was a public supporter of the campaign for access to uncultivated land, and was closely associated with the RA, particularly during the 1939–45 war when he was a member of the Reorganisation Committee which shaped the RA's post-war development.

as Harold Wild of Manchester, Stephen Morton of Sheffield, and Fred Heardman of Edale, thought the mass trespass had put back any hopes of access for twenty years. To my mind that was nonsense. The story, told elsewhere in this book, of the way in which Arthur Creech Jones's Access to Mountains Bill of 1939 was butchered in Parliament is sufficient indication of how little hope of access legislation there was at that time.

As to the effect of the demonstration on the access campaign, there can be no-one better qualified as a witness than Philip Daley. As a young man Phil joined the Manchester and District Ramblers' Federation. He succeeded Edwin Royce as access secretary to the Federation. For many years he was on the RA National Executive and served as national chairman from 1966 to 1969. He was a ministerial nominee on the Peak District National Park Board from 1950 until 1970 and for nineteen years was chairman of the Board's Access and Footpaths Committee. In the negotiations which secured access agreements covering seventy-six square miles, he found the 'mass trespass' was always used as an argument against public access. 'Such access as we have gained', he wrote on the occasion of the mass trespass jubilee, 'owes nothing whatever to the mass trespass organised by the British Workers Federation, and I can say quite categorically and without fear of contradiction, that the "mass trespass" was a positive hindrance and deterrent to the discussion and negotiations to secure the freedom of the hills'.[42]

Perhaps the best thing to stem from the episode was Ewan Mac-Coll's song, 'The Manchester Rambler'. Only a bog-trotting trespasser acquainted with Peak gamekeepers could have written that lilting, true-to-life ballad. Although only seventeen at the time, Mac-Coll joined the demonstration and was a most effective public relations officer for the BWSF.

References

1 'Federation notes', Manchester and District Ramblers' Federation *Handbook*, p. 85.

2 *The Signpost* (Bulletin of the Manchester and District Ramblers' Federation), Supplement, May 1932.

3 Transcript of tape made by Benny Rothman (hereafter referred to as Trans.), copy in Tom Stephenson Collection, RAA.

4 *Manchester Evening News*, 18 April 1932.

5 Trans.

6 *Ibid.*

7 *Manchester Guardian*, 25 April 1932.

8 Trans.

9 *Manchester Guardian*, 7 July 1932.

10 Trans.

11 *Manchester Guardian*, 7 July 1932.

12 Trans.

13 *Ibid.*

14 *Manchester Guardian*, 25 April 1932.

15 Trans.

16 *Manchester Guardian*, 25 April 1932.

17 Trans.

18 *Daily Worker*, 26 April 1932.

19 Benny Rothman, *The 1932 Kinder Trespass* (Altrincham, 1982), p. 7.

20 *Ibid.*, p. 11.

21 *Guardian*, 16 April 1982.

22 *Ibid.*

23 Peak and Northern Counties Footpath Society, *Kinder Footpath Opened*, (1897), pamphlet.

24 Trans.

25 *Manchester Guardian*, 25 April 1932.

26 Trans.

27 *Ibid.*

28 *Manchester Guardian*, 7 July 1932.

29 *Ibid.*

30 Trans.

31 *Ibid.*

32 *Manchester Guardian*, 8 July 1932.

33 Trans.

34 *Ibid.*

35 *Manchester Guardian*, 8 July 1932.

36 *Ibid.*

37 'Federation notes', Manchester and District Ramblers' Federation *Handbook*, 1933, p. 87.

38 *Ibid;* also Manchester and District Ramblers' Federation Minutes, 14 July 1932.

39 Manchester and District Ramblers' Federation Minutes, 8 September 1932.

40 RAA, Access File.

41 *Manchester Guardian*, 11 July 1932; Manchester and District Ramblers' Federation *Handbook*, 1933, p. 133.

42 *Rucksack*, Vol. 10, No. 8, June 1982.

Chapter 8

The 1939 Access to Mountains Act

There was great joy and jubilation and an inexplicable optimism in the RA in November 1938 when it was learned that Arthur Creech Jones, the Labour MP for Shipley, was to introduce an Access to Mountains Bill. For some unaccountable reason it was assumed that the Bill which had been repeatedly rejected by Parliament for the past fifty years would on this occasion reach the statute book. That it did, but in a form no longer acceptable to the RA.

Fundamentally the Bill, as initially presented, was the same as that presented by James Bryce half a century earlier. The preamble in both Bills declared that it was 'desirable to secure to the public the right of free access to uncultivated mountain and moorland, subject to proper provisions for preventing any abuse of such rights'. Clause 1 of both Bills provided, 'subject to the provision of this Act, no owner or occupier of uncultivated mountain, heath, moorland or uncultivated downland shall be entitled to exclude any person from walking or being on such land for the purposes of recreation or scientific or artistic study, or to molest him in so walking or being'.[1]

But that simple little Bill of five clauses was so mauled, mangled and amended by Parliament as to become a monstrous, unrecognisable changeling, not an access to mountains bill, but a landowners' protection bill. To the RA leaders this was a great betrayal, and it was hurriedly decided that the best course was to turn all possible pressure on Parliament to scrap the legislation for which they had campaigned for so long.

I too joined in the first burst of enthusiasm, publicising the issue in the *Daily Herald* and elsewhere. At a meeting of the National Executive Committee of the YHA in November 1938, I moved the following motion:

that the National Executive Committee of the YHA of England and Wales, representing 80,000 members, is of the opinion that the uncultivated mountains and moorlands of Britain should be open to the public for air and exercise. The Committee belives that it is not in the best interests of the nation that large tracts of hilly country, and especially those in the neighbourhood of urban populations, should be closed to young and active people seeking harmless recreation. The Committee therefore welcomes the re-introduction of the Access to Mountains Bill.

I was authorised to publicise the resolution through the press.[2] That decision, incidentally, was a notable event in the annuals of the YHA. Although its purpose was to encourage greater knowledge, love and care of the countryside, it has previously taken little interest in amenity issues, being more concerned with bricks and mortar – the provision of hostels. In later years the YHA was to become the greatest and numerically strongest ally of the RA.

By the part I played in that publicity campaign I unwittingly did the RA a great disservice. In December 1938, three days after the second reading of his bill, Creech Jones wrote to me, 'My dear Tom, our success on Friday was largely a tribute to your work and your endeavour in this opportunity. You made the contacts and got a move on. What might have happened without you I dread to think.'[3] By way of amends I can only plead that a few months later I was equally energetic in the campaign for the scrapping of the Bill.

Some prominent members of the RA, including H. H. Symonds, Edwin Royce, and G. H. B. Ward, doubted if the Bill would succeed where it had so often failed before. The *Observer* referred to the debate in a short paragraph which concluded, 'The sequel, we trust, will not be another intimation to the population of the north of England that "the great open spaces" are not for them but for their betters.'[4]

At the second reading,[5] Creech Jones pleaded eloquently and ably for a measure designed to extend to the general public freedom to enjoy open spaces and air on some of the wildest and most attractive moors and mountains in these Isles. There had, he said, been a remarkable development in recent years in the interest in open-air activities. He had been inundated with letters from various parts of the country setting out the grievances which ordinary people suffered in the matter of alleged trespass. He sometimes felt a little bitter when he remembered how the deer forests in Scotland were made, and how the enclosure of moors and mountains in England was achieved. Where men once freely walked they could no longer do so. He appealed to the gentlemen of Britain and to their sporting spirit, on behalf of those who were debarred from that loveliness which they themselves could enjoy. He asked that, after fifty years of agitation, in place of uncertainty and uneasy tolerance there should be the assured right of all to access to mountain and moorland.

The member for Nuneaton, Reginald Fletcher, seconded the motion, and said that when he was five years old he had been taken on his first walking tour in the Lake District. Since then he had walked and climbed over every fell and every rock face there. He remembered his father scrambling over the fells wearing a bowler hat and clasping an umbrella. He based his appeal on the national right to enjoy national scenery, on the simple enjoyment of those natural rights, the natural claim to health and happiness.[6] Twenty years later, as Lord Winster, he spoke at an RA rally on Ilkley Moor protesting at the decision of West Riding County Council that no action was required to provide for public access in the county. He said the only way ramblers could get access in some areas was to break the law. 'Break the law', he said. 'Break it with a good heart and a cheerful face. If you get prosecuted it will be the grandest publicity for this cause.'[7]

The rejection of the Bill was moved by the Conservative member for Bury St Edmunds, Captain Frank Heilgers, and his colleague Colonel R. S. Clarke, who sat for East Grinstead. Captain Heilgers thought the Bill attacked the whole principle of owning land. It would mean that an owner no longer had the right to enjoy his property. Furthermore, grouse moors provided employment worth about £3,500,000 a year. He believed there were between 20,000 and 30,000 gamekeepers as well as a large number of other workers, including cartridge and gun-makers.[8] Colonel Clarke also saw the Bill as a direct attack on the rights of private property. The individual who owned lands designated in the Bill would lose the protection the law gave him against trespass. He did, he said, have considerable sympathy with hiking; he could look back on many happy days spent with nothing more lethal than a map and a walking stick in his hands.[9] The Colonel must have been surprised when he received a letter signed by twenty-five members of a rambling club in his constituency expressing regret at his opposition to the Bill.[10]

The government view was given by the Under-Secretary at the Home Office. He was, he said, not ashamed to say that he was a hiker himself. He reinforced the appeal to landowners to consider whether they could not give reasonable facilities for this very healthy recreation to the working lads of this country. He revealed that negotiations were going on between the landowners' representatives and the Commons, Open Spaces and Footpaths Preservation Society, who had been in touch with the Ramblers' Association.[11] That was the first intimation the RA leaders had of those negotiations.

The alternatives before the House, he said, were whether it would be better to allow this Bill to lapse and to enable the negotiations to proceed with a view to a bill coming forward on the basis of an agreement reached in the future, or in the event of a second reading to defer slightly the consideration of the Bill in committee with a view to allowing the negotiations to come to a point. The government would leave the matter to a free decision of the House.[12]

At the close of the debate Captain Heilgers said that, in view of the assurance of the promoters of the Bill that their sole purpose was to promote national fitness, and their promise of reasonable amendments in the committee stage, he asked leave to withdraw the amendment for the rejection of the Bill. This was granted, the Bill was given a second reading and proceeded to the committee stage.[13]

Some RA leaders feared that the debate had been a charade and that drastic modification of the Bill had already been agreed. Some passages in *Hansard* support that conclusion. Thus Creech Jones said, 'I suggest that the bill can be amended in Committee to meet any conclusions which may be reached, in any negotiations designed to ensure acceptance of the principle of the extension of public rights.[14] 'The mover of the bill was good enough last night to tell me that he intended as far as possible to meet any reasonable objections at the committee stage', claimed Captain Heilgers.[15] Similarly, R. S. Clarke said Creech Jones had 'expressed willingness to allow almost unlimited modification to the bill in committee and for that we are very grateful'.[16]

However those quotations may be interpreted, the relevant Ministerial and Cabinet papers now available at the Public Record Office reveal many behind-the-scenes activities of which, in 1939, the RA knew nothing. For instance, there is a long and revealing letter from Sir Lawrence Chubb of the Commons Society to Mr L. N. Blake Odgers at the Home Office. Chubb writes, 'as promised', 'to let you know the present position of the negotiations which have been taking place between this Society and the Land Union and Central Landowners Association'. At the annual conference of the Society's branches and affiliated organisations in October 1937 he had pointed out what the Society regarded as inherent flaws in the Access to Mountains Bill. He had suggested that the Commons Society should find out how far the bodies representing landowners would be willing to co-operate with an alternative bill. This new bill should provide for

access to certain types of land where and when well-behaved members of a community could not conceivably cause any harm. I had in mind mountains, uncultivated hills, heaths, moors, downs, beaches and large areas of rough grazing. There would have to be definite exceptions for the protection of private interests. It would be necessary to make it an offence for anyone without lawful authority to light fires, drive vehicles, camp, leave litter, disturb stock or game, take an unleashed dog, injure flowers, trees, shrubs and so forth. Moreover, for the protection of sporting rights, I suggested that the Ministry of Agriculture in England and the appropriate department in Scotland might, on application of any owner, impose limitations and conditions as to when and how public access should be regulated or prohibited.

Both and Land Union and the Central Landowners' Association had been sympathetic and had agreed to confer with the Commons Society.

Such a measure I think would be wider and more satisfactory in its scope than the Access to Mountains Bill, and if, as I hope and expect, we can reach agreement with the Land Union and Central Landowners' Association, it would obviously be advisable to afford us an opportunity to do so. I ought to add that the decision of the Central Landowners' Association was only taken late last week so that there has been as yet no time to hold the intended conference.[17]

The outcome of these negotiations was reported to a conference convened by the Commons Society on 13 January 1939 and held in fulfilment of a pledge that the ramblers would be consulted before any agreement was entered into in their name by the Commons Society. The draft Bill presented to the conference gave public access to all uncultivated land, subject to the right of landowners to appeal to the Minister of Agriculture for orders restricting access and imposing special conditions governing the access. There appeared for the first time in these negotiations what became known as the trespass clause. This made it an offence, punishable by a fine of up to 40s (£2), for anyone to disregard any condition or restriction in a minister's order. On a grouse moor the restrictions might include prohibition of access during lambing time, the nesting season and the shooting season. The ramblers' delegates strongly opposed this clause, which made trespass a criminal offence, and made it quite clear they would not agree to any bill which made such an incursion in the common law of trespass.[18]

A second conference was convened on 10 February, but at such short notice that some of the northern federations were not represented.[19] A revised draft bill was submitted. This abandoned the idea of general access to all uncultivated land, and proposed an elaborate procedure for obtaining limited access to specific areas. The trespass clause had been dropped and, by a small majority, the draft was accepted. There would probably have been a different decision if the RA had been fully represented. Chubb lost no time in conveying the decision of the conference. L. N. Blake Odgers, writing to an official at the Ministry of Agriculture on 17 February, said that Sir Lawrence had succeeded in persuading both the RA and the landowners' organisations to agree in principle to a revised bill.

This accompanied a report of a meeting held in the Home Office in January 1939, attended by representatives of various ministries and Sir Lawrence Chubb. He said that the landowners were still considering the alternative draft Bill, which, they thought, conceded too much to the public and they would not accept it without drastic amendments. The extreme views to be considered were

(1) Those members of the public (e.g. in the Peak District) who insisted upon complete liberty of access, and (2) those landowners who objected to any public access because of possible interference with their stock or their grouse or deer, the risk of fires, and the question of compensation if their land were worsened in value.

The meeting agreed that Chubb, in his next discussion with the landowners, should suggest that rights of access should only come into operation when the responsible authority had approved (with such additional restrictions as might be needed) an application made with respect to specified land. It was also agreed that Chubb would inform Creech Jones of the course the discussion had taken, and ascertain his reaction to the suggestion that the present Bill should be withdrawn.[20]

A change of attitude on the part of the Cabinet is revealed in a memorandum by the Minister of Agriculture (Sir R. H. Dorman Smith) to the Home Secretary (Sir Samuel Hoare). The Bill, which, it claimed, was introduced by Creech Jones on behalf of English rambling associations, 'was considered by the Cabinet on 30 November 1938 when it was agreed that it should be blocked, but it received

Second Reading on 2nd December and is to be taken in Standing Committee on Tuesday 7th March'. Negotiations had resulted 'in an agreement accepted by the great majority of the English rambling associations, and this has been embodied in amendments which will result in a very different and much longer bill. Only a few words of the original bill are retained and the scope has been enlarged.'

The memorandum recommended an about-turn by the Cabinet. It said:

As a large measure of agreement on this contentious subject seems somewhat unexpectedly to have been reached, we feel that it would be a pity to let the opportunity slip of enabling the general public to have increased rights of air and exercise subject to reasonable restrictions for preventing damage being done to the interest of those who own the land in which the rights are to be granted. We recommend therefore that the Cabinet should give general approval to the new terms.[21]

Early in March the Commons Society produced yet another draft bill and it was on this that the amendments considered by Standing Committee B of the House of Commons were based. To the surprise and anger of RA leaders the unacceptable trespass clause had been reinserted, with a proviso that it should not apply to unintentional trespass. In those days northern ramblers were out every weekend ignoring prohibitive notices and risking encounters with aggressive gamekeepers. As the law then stood they could only be treated as trespassers, that is, required to withdraw or possibly be sued for damage. By this clause, unless one could prove the trespass was unintentional, one could in certain circumstances be fined for merely being on the land.

Creech Jones, supported by Fred Marshall, a Labour MP for a Sheffield constituency, addressed an open session of the RA's National Council in March. Creech Jones appealed for understanding and goodwill and said he was conscious of the feeling of disappointment with which the Bill had been received. He spoke of the difficulties an MP had to contend with in introducing a private member's bill. He thought it meant a considerable advance and gain, and he appealed to ramblers to attempt to work the Bill when it became law. Fred Marshall added that each side had the right of amendment in the committee stage. At the time there was a great deal of interest in the physical fitness of the population and he thought this made conditions favourable for getting an access bill through Parliament. Creech Jones was asked numerous questions, particularly about the trespass clause, and there was considerable criticism of the Bill from other speakers.

The next day Council unanimously carried a motion proposed by Stephen Morton and seconded by Edwin Royce. It reiterated the RA's claim to unrestricted access to mountain and moorland and, while fully appreciating the efforts of Creech Jones and the Commons Society in trying to reach an agreed bill, it offered vigorous protests against and opposed the trespass clause. It also stressed the importance of access to water-catchment areas – otherwise nearly the whole of the Pennines and other large areas would be outside the scope of the Bill, and profoundly regretted the exclusion of Scotland from it.[22] Similar motions were carried by meetings convened by various of the northern ramblers' federations.

The trespass clause was debated at the fourth meeting of the Standing Committee. As it stood the clause 'provided that a person shall not be guilty of an offence under this section by reason only of any *unintentional* trespass constituting a contravention of a condition specified in an order so made'. Fred Marshall moved an amendment to leave out the word 'unintentional'.[23] This would have taken simple trespass, either intentional or unintentional, out of the penalty clause and allowed it to be dealt with by the provisions of the law of trespass.

Creech Jones admitted that quite a number of the open-air fraternities would prefer to have no bill at all rather than a bill which carried a provision of this kind. He concluded:

I feel that, as this is very largely a compromise bill, I must stand by the arrangement which has been entered into, but I would put to the Committee the very real apprehension and the very great disturbance that there is in the minds of the rambling fraternity as to how this clause is likely in their judgement to operate.[24]

As another member put it later in the debate, 'the speech of the Hon Member was really in favour of the amendment, although he was bound to say in the end that he could not support it'.[25] Marshall's amendment was lost and that decision led to increased activity in the RA and a further bombardment of MPs and ministers by letters and resolutions, though the gunning seems to have come mostly from the federations. There are some criticism of the lack of activity at the London end, where Chubb had more influence.

The RA had a sub-committee to deal with access matters, and it met at Bradford on 16 April. It agreed unanimously to oppose the Bill as it stood, and to circularise MPs with a letter stating their case against the Bill over the signatures of well-known access campaigners. Phil Barnes, who was a member of the sub-committee, sent a letter to Tom Fairclough, secretary of Merseyside YHA, who was then acting as organising secretary of the RA nationally.[26] He replied to Barnes with a telegram saying he could not circulate it without the authority of the Executive Committee. In a follow-up letter he said he had received from George Mitchell, RA secretary, a letter which presented a different point of view from that of the access sub-committee, and also said that inadvertent trespass would not be an offence.[27]

Faced with this discouragement, Barnes then single-handedly made a supreme effort. Within two days, by letters and telegrams, he obtained the signatures of a dozen well-known access campaigners to a letter which, on the third day, he circulated to the press and more than 600 MPs. The letter said that the trespass clause had been vehemently opposed by the ramblers' organisations since it was first mooted by the Commons Society in a draft bill. If the Bill went through in its present state it would be a retrograde step and ramblers would be in a worse position than they were. The House of Commons had been assured on 2 December that efforts would be made to produce an agreed bill, but this was not an agreed bill, and they urged members to oppose it unless the objectionable features were withdrawn.

The letter was signed by Ernest Baker, veteran mountaineer and author of such books as *Crags and Caves of the High Peak* and *With Rope and Rucksack in the Highlands*; Phil Barnes himself, author of *Trespassers Will be Prosecuted*, which included many photographs obtained by trespassing; Alfred J. Brown, another outdoor writer whose books included *Striding through Yorkshire*; C. E. M. Joad, the popular philosopher, who had written *A Charter for Ramblers*; Stephen Morton, secretary of the Sheffield and District Federation; Lilian Robinson, secretary of the West Riding Federation, Edwin Royce, RA vice-president, secretary of its Access Sub-committee and author of innumerable articles on access to mountains; Alfred Sclater, chairman of the West Riding Federation; Kenneth Spence, RA vice-president; W. S. Tysoe, secretary of the Liverpool and District Federation; G. H. B. Ward, veteran rambler and writer on the outdoors, especially the Peak moorlands, chairman of Sheffield and District Federation, and me.[28]

During the third reading of the Bill on 21 April, several members referred to this letter and to other letters and telegrams they had received. Fred Marshall once again tried to nullify the trespass clause by omitting the word 'unintentional'.[29] Once again Creech Jones confessed his sympathy for the amendment but felt he must keep to the agreement he had entered into.[30] Geoffrey Mander thought too high a price had been paid to the landowners. For forty or fifty years ramblers had been urging that the matter should be dealt with and their views should receive special consideration.[31]

The most damning (though equally ineffectual) speech of the day came from J. Chuter Ede. He was later to become Home Secretary in the Labour Government of 1945–51 and was for many years president of the Southern Area of the RA, also serving as national president. He said that he was one of the backers of the Bill but, had he known that it would appear in this form, he would have moved its rejection at the second reading. 'By this so-called compromise', he said, 'the landowning classes are getting with respect to their land a thing that the old "landlords' Parliaments" would never have given them in the eighteenth century.' Of the trespass clause he said:

surely so fundamental an alteration in the law of England as this ought not to be slipped in as a final amendment into a Private Members' bill as a result of some compromise arrived at, not upstairs, but mainly between the various landowners' associations and the Commons and Footpaths Preservation Society. This is an amendment which we ought not to pass. Compromises arrive at outside the House are not binding on the House. No one will deny that my Honourable Friend the Member for Shipley has loyally stood by the agreement into which he has entered, and I do not think the landowning classes can complain that he has done other than manfully for a bargain which they struck with him. I do not know what they struck, but they managed to secure his consent to it. I appeal to the House not to be party to what is not a compromise but is just the complete surrender of one of the most cherished possessions of an Englishman who likes to wander about the face of his country and behaves himself reasonably when he does so.[32]

Marshall's amendment was defeated by eighty-six votes to seventy. It is notable that the minority included Clement Attlee and seventeen MPs who became ministers in his 1945 Government.

The day after the third reading, Barnes wrote to Mitchell:

I am very disappointed at the extremely slow way in which the Ramblers' Association, officially, have moved in connection with the Access to Mountains Bill during the last fortnight, and I would like to place on record my protest that steps were not taken to call the Committee together immediately it was known that the trespass clause had been inserted. If stronger action had been taken, particularly in bringing pressure to bear on Sir Lawrence Chubb, Marshall's amendment yesterday might easily have been carried, and the worst feature of the bill removed.

In a postscript, Barnes said he had written to Royce suggesting an intensified campaign directed at the House of Lords, and circularising them with the RA's arguments against the Bill. There should be a demand to Chubb to convene a further conference and northern federations should hold emergency rallies.[33]

Barnes also enclosed a copy of a long letter he had written to Chubb on 20 April. He reminded Chubb that ramblers' representatives had always been most strongly opposed to the trespass clause. At the January conference Joad, Ede and other speakers made it abundantly clear that the ramblers would not accept the clause as part of any agreement. 'Later', he said,

the clause appeared again in another draft issued by your Society with the saving paragraph as to unintentional trespass, but accompanying this draft was a confidential sheet of notes, one of which stated that the word 'unintentional' had been inserted in error and steps would have to be taken to have it removed.

Since the February conference the ramblers had not had the opportunity of discussing this or any further amendment so no-one could claim that this bill went forward with the ramblers' support as an agreed measure. He concluded, 'The bill in my opinion is such a weak compromise that I hope it will be defeated tomorrow, rather than it should go forward to the Lords for further amendment as a measure approved by the hill lovers and ramblers of England.'[34]

The RA Executive Committee meeting in May decided the Bill was unacceptable in its present form and asked for an explanation of the introduction of the trespass clause. It also accepted a recommendation of the Access Sub-committee that a memorandum by Barnes should be revised and printed and circulated to the House of Lords.[35] It also decided to ask the Minister of Agriculture to receive a deputation. The deputation was received, by Lord Feversham, parliamentary secretary to the Ministry of Agriculture, on 15 May. It was led by Fred Marshall and consisted of A. J. Brown, Phil Barnes, G. H. B. Ward and C. E. M. Joad. Creech Jones was also present, as was Lord Radnor, representing the landowners. Creech Jones does not appear to have spoken. A. J. Brown denied that the Bill as it stood was an agreed measure. It was unlikely that the landowners or the local authorities would apply the Act and it would be left to ramblers' organisations to apply for orders. Those associations had not the money or the facilities for going through the legal process of applying for numerous orders. They objected to the trespass clause, to the clause under which persons suspected of trespassing had to give their names and addresses and that which allowed expulsion by force.

Phil Barnes said that they had sought a bill which legalised the harmless trespasser over the wild moorland areas. The present Bill was not applicable to wild country of this kind but was based on public path legislation. Under the Bill there was no prospect of getting complete access and in fact there would be severe restrictions. Everything depended on the goodwill of the Minister. They did not appreciate why the ordinary law of trespass, which had been sufficient up to the present, would not be adequate in the future. G. H. B. Ward spoke of his long experience with the problems which they had hoped the Bill would solve. Since the war a great deal of bitterness between keepers and ramblers in certain areas had arisen, and it had been found impossible to negotiate with some of the landowners, for instance in Derbyshire.

C. E. M. Joad summed up the main points of complaint which were that the Bill was not an agreed measure and ramblers felt they had not had a square deal, the Bill would not help them attain access and the law of trespass had been altered. Lord Feversham, himself an owner of grouse moors in North Yorkshire, spoke of his personal interest in preservation of the countryside and granting public access within reasonable limits. He regretted the ramblers could not agree to the measure and thought there was some misunderstanding of its provisions. He thought owners and local authorities would apply for access orders, but was not in a position to give an undertaking that the public would not be excluded from the grouse moors during nesting and shooting.

Fred Marshall suggested that the Bill should be given a trial without the penalty clause relating to trespass, or that its operation should be postponed for five years. Lord Radnor objected that the Bill had been the subject of long negotiations with landowners as well as ramblers and that any material change would upset the agreement obtained. The deputation then made clear that they would rather not have the Bill if the trespass clause were to remain, but Lord Feversham persisted in hoping that when the Bill had passed the ramblers would review their present attitude of antagonism.[36] The deputation was not without outcome at all. The trespass clause was amended in the House of Lords so that it would not apply automatically, only if it were stipulated in an access order or a subsequent amendment to an order.

The day before that deputation, some 2,000 ramblers gathered near Leith Hill, Surrey, at the greatest ramblers' rally ever held in the south of England. The large attendance was mainly due to the vigour and organising ability of Philip Poole, the young secretary of the London-based Progressive Rambling Club, who filled fifty 32-seater coaches with ramblers.[37] Alex McIntosh, RA chairman, presided, and the speakers were Lewis Silkin MP, J. E. Holdsworth, who was cycling organiser for the National Fitness Campaign being run at the time, and me. I concluded my speech with words to the effect that Creech Jones had told me that his bill was the most we could hope for short of a minor social revolution. Why then, I asked, were we wasting time on this piffling legislation instead of getting on with the minor revolution? Six years passed before I met Silkin again. He was then Minister of Town and Country Planning, and I was his Press Officer. 'How is the revolution progressing?', he asked.

Barnes's memorandum, authorised by the RA Executive Committee, duly appeared as a pamphlet, setting out the RA's objections to the Bill. It was Phil Barnes at his best, with no punches pulled, and was sent out to MPs and the press. Barnes told how representations made by the RA at the meeting convened by Chubb had been ignored, and new, unacceptable clauses had not been discussed or even seen by RA delegates, who had never, in all the negotiations, met the landowners' representatives. On access, the Bill was nebulous and indefinite and ramblers had to rely upon the goodwill of the Minister. For moorland owners, the Bill was definite to an amazing degree. All possible and some impossible threats to the landowners' or the sporting tenants' interests were most minutely covered. The change from a simple measure giving general access to one merely providing machinery for gaining access to a specified area was a disastrous step. The ramblers' organisations were the only ones likely to apply for orders, but they had neither the money nor the personnel to fight wealthy landowners at numerous public inquiries.

That anyone should be liable for prosecution for being on access land was a blow to the freedom of the individual and should be opposed as punitive and anti-social legislation.

To enforce these socially unjust provisions the gamekeepers are to be given certain powers hitherto employed by the police. Presumably they will have to decide just how much violence is necessary to remove the offender. They will be entitled to demand names and addresses if they have reason to think any offence, including trespass, has been committed, and refusal to comply will itself constitute an offence.

During the second reading debate the House of Commons had been assured that efforts would be made to bring forward an agreed bill, but this Bill had never been agreed by those directly concerned and ramblers now asked that the bill should be opposed.[38]

On June 25 the Manchester and Sheffield Federations held their annual access demonstration in the Winnats Pass. A resolution, 'Ramblers strongly disapprove of those provisions of the Access to Mountains Bill whereby the financial liability of obtaining access is made a burden on the ramblers, and of the trespass penalty fine, and demand the removal of those provisions.'[39] was carried and forwarded to the Minister of Agriculture.

But all the campaigning was to no avail. The memoranda, demonstrations and resolutions, the innumerable letters to MPs and the persistent lobbying had failed to move Parliament. The Bill came into law on 1 January 1940. It allowed for access orders to be applied for by county, borough and urban district councils or bodies representative of people likely to benefit, such as the RA. It also listed fifteen punishable offences such as lighting fires, leaving litter, damaging land, plants and animals, hindering or obstructing the owner or occupier.

Miserably inadequate as the Bill was, the Statutory Rules and Orders, the details of its administration, made it even more useless for a body like the RA. If it, or one of the federations, applied for an order, the following procedure would be required. The application for an order would be made on a prescribed form to the Minister of Agriculture and would be accompanied by a payment of £10. This payment would be exclusive of the cost of any maps and advertisements and of any local inquiry which the minister might consider necessary. With the order would be a map on the scale of six inches to the mile showing the area, access points and any excepted land. Notices would be sent by registered post to every landowner and occupier and others having an interest in the land, for example, shooting tenants and local authorities. The notice would be advertised for two successive weeks in one or more local papers, the application displayed and copies supplied at a charge of 1s. Objections would be received and if it were impossible to resolve them, they would be forwarded to the Minister.

If a public inquiry were necessary, the Minister might require the applicant to deposit a sum of money to meet the costs of the inquiry and of any other expenses or fees incurred by or payable to the Minister. Should there by an inquiry the applicant would, of course, have to be represented; the RA probably by a layman who would have to stand up to highly qualified lawyers acting for the other side.

Even then the Minister might decide not to grant the order. If an order were made, the applicant would be required to erect and maintain noticeboards giving details of the order and the offences listed in the Act. Imagine the cost of covering the thirty-seven square miles of Bleaklow with such notices, and maintaining them against the ravages of the weather. If the order were revoked, the cost of removing the notices would fall on the applicant. If the Minister decided to close the land for a specified period because of the danger of fire, the applicant would have to post notices on the boards, publish the order in two or more local newspapers and send copies of the order to the local authorities and to the county police.[40] If after all this the Minister made an order, say for Kinder Scout, it might specify conditions and limitations. These might include the lambing, nesting and grouse shooting seasons, with rambling restricted to the more inclement months. If the public persistently disregarded the limitations, the Minister could issue an order making any breach of them an offence. If was also an offence in itself to refuse to give one's name to an owner, tenant or gamekeeper, if suspected of having committed an offence.

One outcome of all this taradiddle was that under an access order a boggy moorland such as Bleaklow, or a soggy morass like Black Hill, could be better protected than good agricultural land.

References

1   Access to Mountains, Bill 7, 11 November 1938.

2   Youth Hostels Association Executive Committee Minute 244, 26 November 1939, copy Tom Stephenson collection, RA History file, RAA.

3   RAA, letter to author from A. Creech Jones, 5 December 1938, in 1939 Access Bill file, folder marked correspondence.

4   *Observer*, 4 December 1938.

5   *Hansard* (House of Commons), 5th Ser., Vol. 342, Cols. 747–55, 2 December 1938.

6   *Ibid.*, Cols. 755–65.

7 *Ramblers News*, No. 30, Autumn 1958, p. 5.

8 *Hansard, op. cit.*, Cols. 764–6.

9 *Ibid.*, Cols. 772–7.

10 *Daily Herald*, 3 February 1939.

11 *Hansard, op. cit.*, Col. 819.

12 *Ibid.*, Col. 820.

13 *Ibid.*, Col. 829.

14 *Ibid.*, Col. 755.

15 *Ibid.*, Col. 764.

16 *Ibid.*, Col. 771.

17 Public Record Office (PRO), file MAF 48 724, Sir Lawrence Chubb to L. N. B. Odgers (Home Office), 23 November 1938; Copy 1939 Access Bill file, Public Records, Ministerial Documents folder, RAA.

18 RAA, various papers in 1939 Access Bill file, envelope marked Comons Society and Draft Bills.

19 RAA, undated report by Alfred J. Brown, president of West Riding Ramblers' Federation, 1939 Access Bill file, correspondence folder.

20 PRO, file MAF 48 724.

21 PRO, file CAB 24 248.

22 RAA, National Council Minutes, 1939, Minute Book from February 1939.

23 *Hansard* (Standing Committee), Session 1938–39, Vol. 2, Access to Mountains Bill, Col. 1572.

24 *Ibid.*, Col. 1576.

25 *Ibid.*, Col. 1578.

26 RAA, Phil Barnes to author and G. R. Mitchell, 17 April 1938, 1939 Access Bill file, correspondence folder.

27 RAA, T. Fairclough to G. R. Mitchell, 18 April 1939, 1939 Access Bill file, correspondence folder.

28 Ramblers' Association, *Access to Mountains*, A Memorandum on the Amended Bill, Liverpool [1939], pamphlet.

29 *Hansard* (House of Commons), 5th Ser., Vol. 346, Cols. 729–32.

30 *Ibid.*, Cols. 734–5.

31 *Ibid.*, Cols. 740–1.

32 *Ibid.*, Cols. 737–8.

33 RAA, Phil Barnes to G. R. Mitchell, 22 April 1939, 1939 Access Bill file, correspondence folder.

34 Copy appended to *ibid.*

35 RAA, Executive Committee Minutes, minute 41/39, May 1939.

36 PRO, file MAF 48 724; Copy, RAA 1939 Access Bill file, Public Records and Ministerial Documents folder.

37 *Daily Herald*, 6 May 1939.

38 Ramblers' Association, *Access to Mountains* (1939), pamphlet.

39 PRO, file MAF 48 728; Copy, RAA, 1939 Access Bill file, Public

Records and Ministerial Documents folder.

40 *Access to Mountains, England and Wales, Regulations,* Statutory Rules and Orders, No. 746, 1940.

Chapter 9

The aftermath of the 1939 Act

For four years RA leaders dithered, bickered and sometimes wrangled as to whether or not the RA should, after the war, apply for access orders under the Act. Wide divisions separated the realist from the impossiblist, those terms being reversible according to one's point of view. One side thought they should try to work what was admittedly a bad act with the intention of proving its deficiences, and then campaigning for amending legislation. Those on the other side said the Act could not be made to work and they should waste no time on it, but start agitation for the fundamental principle of access to all uncultivated land.

These different ideas had been voiced from press and platform while the Bill was still before Parliament. The controversy continued with increasing bitterness.

In May 1939 Creech Jones told the *Manchester Guardian*[1] that from letters he had received it was obvious that there was a lack of understanding of the principles of the Bill. The trespass clause disappointed a large number of ramblers as it did himself, but the Bill extended access and offered a reasonably fair solution in existing circumstances to a difficult subject. The owners had made concessions and it would be a pity if the merits of the measure were denied because certain hopes had not been altogether realised. A short leader in the same issue suggested that 'the best that can be said for the bill is that at last it makes legislative admission of the principle that "it is desirable to secure to the public access to mountain and moorland" '. Its method will still have to be the subject of a campaign for amendment.'[2]

Two days later a letter appeared, again in the *Manchester Guardian*, written by Edwin Royce.[3] He considered that the trespass clause had almost overshadowed a very serious departure from an elementary principle of English law, the innocence of the defendant until he has been proved guilty. A person who was suspected of an offence under the Act committed another offence if he refused to give his name and address on demand. The keeper was above the magistrate. However, in the same issue, Harold Wild, former secretary of Manchester Ramblers' Federation, expressed appreciation of the efforts of Creech Jones. He thought some real freedom of access to mountains and moors was now within grasp.[4] Unsurprisingly, a letter from Sir Lawrence Chubb the next day defended the Bill, stating that the whole object of which was to extend and not to limit public rights, and it was likely that amendments to be moved in the House of Lords would make that point abundantly clear.[5]

A differing viewpoint was expressed in a letter immediately following Chubb's and headed 'Not acceptable to ramblers'. This was from Walter Tysoe, who said that the Bill was not workable from the ramblers' point of view. Ramblers' organisations were composed for the most part of working-class members and had neither the time, personnel nor money to make numerous applications nor even to fight those made by landowners. The Bill was worse than useless to the rambler; its value to the landowner was proved by the way in which it was passing through the House of Lords and a Tory House of Commons.[6]

In the *New Statesman* a similar correspondence was taking place at about the same time. On 6 May, Creech Jones,[7] replying to editorial criticism in the previous issue,[8] said he took full responsibility for the Bill. He had received invaluable help from Sir Lawrence Chubb and his Society but neither he nor his Society had made any attempt to make him their docile medium. Chubb had a letter in the same issue, stating that his Society was satisfied that if the Bill were utilised, the results would be to give the public access on reasonable conditions to very large tracts of land from which they were then excluded.[9] The following week Cyril Joad reminded Chubb and Creech Jones that the Bill was not an agreed measure. As to its being a compromise, it reminded him of the young married couple who agreed to adjust all differences by compromise. In the first weeks of married life they differed as to the colour of the dining-room wallpaper; A wanted it to be blue, and B green. Compromise, B reminded A, was the basis of marriage, so compromise they did and it was green.[10]

In the 27 May issue Phil Barnes reiterated the objectives to the Bill. He also reminded Chubb, who had said the original Bill was ill-conceived, that it had, in fact, been conceived by James Bryce, a former chairman of the Commons Society.[11]

So, with the battle lines marked out before the Bill passed into law, hostilities continued.

The RA National Council in March 1940,[12] thanks largely to the persuasive oratory of Cyril Joad, decided to try out the Act. According to the sketchy minutes of the meeting Joad said he shared the general disappointment of ramblers, but suggested they should try to make the best they could of it. If the Act proved unworkable in practice they could then try to get it amended or replaced. He suggested that friendly landowners should be approached and that pressure should be brought to bear on the government to see that the existing freedom was not filched from them. In reply, Phil Barnes pressed for all action to be localised and the working of the Act to be left until the war was over.

After some debate Joad moved

That this meeting of the Council of the RA instructs its Executive Committee to press for the early establishment of the machinery described by the Access to Mountains Act for the making of applications for access, and further wishes to place on record its view that the relevant Federation or Federations should, at their discretion, at the earliest practicable moment after the establishment of the machinery, take the initiative in making application for orders for access for areas falling within the territory of the Federation.

Stephen Morton then moved 'That the Council of the RA recommends that all applications for access under the Act in accordance with the principle laid down in the foregoing resolution shall be made by and in the name of the local Federations concerned, in collaboration of the Access Committee of the Association.' After discussion these motions were carried.

It is worth noting that the ramblers attending National Council were obviously convinced of Creech Jones's sincerity and desire to serve the rambling movement, much as they disliked the Act, for they made him a vice-president.

Joad's standing at Council and the validity of his motion was later questioned though never challenged. 'Bowland', described as a well-known official in the RA, wrote an article in *Progressive Rambler*,[13] a cyclostyled, left-wing journal edited by Philip Poole of the Progressive Rambling Club, for March 1941. In it he said that Joad was neither an official nor an appointed delegate to the Council. Royce wrote to

Mitchell on the subject and commented, 'Some of us, too, consider that Joad's resolution at the AGM was out of order, primarily because no prior notice was given.'[14]

At the December 1939 meeting of the RA Executive Committee it was decided that T. A. Leonard and Kenneth Spence should be authorised to approach Sir Charles Trevelyan with a view to a friendly agreement for access to his moors.[15] There is no evidence that such an approach was made, but the decision was enough to rouse the ire of Phil Barnes. The Access Sub-committee meeting in May 1940 adopted a motion moved by Barnes which said

that the Access Sub-committee regret the fact that the EC came to an important decision on December 2nd and 3rd 1939 in regard to the policy of the RA towards the Access to Mountains Act, without prior consultation with the Access Sub-committee. If this Sub-committee is to continue in being as an advisory body we ask that some assurance be given to us by the EC that they will await our advice before making any further decision which may or may not be in accordance with our views.[16]

Barnes annoyed some of his colleagues with an article he wrote under the pen name of 'Kinder' in the September 1940 issue of *Progressive Rambler*.[17] After listing the deficiencies of the Act. Barnes gave what he considered to be the reasons for this wretched outcome. In the first place the ramblers had not got a national organisation sufficiently strong and wealthy to put forward their own case and were induced to allow the Commons Society to do so. Indeed, the original Bill had been lost when the RA had agreed in 1937 (at the conference mentioned in Sir Lawrence Chubb's letter quoted in the last chapter) to the modifications proposed by the Open Spaces Society. Other mistakes followed but this was the prime one. The second reason was the lack of mass support and a clear knowledge of the issues involved amongst the public and MPs, including certain members of the Labour Party.

The third reason, said Barnes,

was the lack of virile leadership and consistent policy on the part of the Ramblers' Association. We suffered from a lack of drive from the top. Our leaders were too ready to accept defeat and the necessity to compromise. What little spirit and determination there was in our midst came from a woefully small band, and it was not until the 11th hour that their advice was taken and some show of determination made apparent. The bill went through its final stages opposed by all but one of the district Federations and by the Ramblers' Association itself. This last-minute stand did at least result in the worst features of the bill – the so-called 'trespass clause' being substantially modified. As soon as the Parliamentary stage was passed and the country saddled with this Act which no-one wants, our representatives in the conference switched over hastily and decided to endeavour to work the Act. They were in such a hurry they could not even wait for the issue of the statutory regulations to ascertain exactly what they were committing themselves to do. The moral of this is that the ramblers who really want access must demand more virile leadership and above all a consistent policy carried through with courage and determination. The lesson to be learnt was that we cannot hope for any real progress towards access to mountains until we have a people's Government prepared to place the aspirations of the people before the claims of any vested interests by the rich and powerful. The inescapable conclusion was that the access to mountains was a political issue, and ramblers should not shrink from accepting this unpalatable fact.

This article sparked off a series of replies. In the November issue Stephen Morton said Kinder was generally correct in his deductions. The Access to Mountains Act was obviously unworkable and was revealed as simply window-dressing legislation. But Kinder was not fair to his colleagues in his criticisms. There was a wealth of virile, tenacious leadership in the RA. 'Recrimination', he said, 'is dangerous – cut it out – planning is the real need.'[18]

In the same issue Walter Tysoe, as a member of, though not speaking for, the RA Executive Committee also replied to Kinder. He said that members of the Committee had not changed their views but it was no use them shutting their eyes to the fact that there was a so-called Access to Mountains Act on the statute book. If they tried to work the act and the results were as bad as they feared they would have some magnificent propaganda material and good grounds for agitating for a new and better one. It was no part of the RA's function to wait for a people's government; like all similar non-party bodies, it was their job to stimulate and achieve as much progress as the circumstances of the time permitted.

Tysoe concluded:

I personally agree wholeheartedly with Kinder that a genuine Access Act cannot be expected under the present regime. Disappointing as the Act is, it remains no mean achievement that a Tory administration should have paid even lip service to the principle of access. When a people's government does control this country, when the aspirations of the people do count for something, then we shall be so much the nearer access, for having the experience of the present feeble measure, so much the nearer for having tried and probably failed to work it.[19]

In March 1941 Edwin Royce contributed in playful style.[20] He described himself as a 'has-been, cynic and pessimist', and said that knowing the actions, character and composition of the government, Kinder could not really and truly expect it to pass his good old bill. It would be spendid to have a people's government. But how and when? It was a Liberal Government which threw out Bryce's bill time after time and they had seen Labour MPs voting to make trespass a criminal offence.

He referred to Kinder's claim that they had been fobbed off with a worthless Act because they had neither a strong national organisation nor mass support of the public. Before they could ask for that support, he said, they would have to show unity in their own ranks. Early in 1938, one Federation (which enjoyed practically 100 per cent access on its local hills) objected to access propaganda on the lines then followed, apparently out of deference to the opinions of its president. (Royce was probably referring to the Lake District Federation.)

'No wealthy Ramblers' Association', he went on, 'would arise out of twenty cigarettes per annum. Put no hope in a people's government until the 21st or 22nd centuries (if then). Put it in your own selves; fork out at least one shilling a year. Thousands of you do not do that.'

For another three years the bickering continued, G. H. B. Ward leading those in favour of trying to work the Act and Barnes and I leading those in favour of ignoring it. For much of that time Royce kept a low profile. He wrote to Mitchell in May 1940, 'my own personal view now is that I cannot recommend any Federation to incur the trouble, expense and responsibility of working this act'.[21] Strangely enough, though, the first suggestion of working with it came from Royce's own bailiwick, the Manchester Federation. At the Federation's Executive Committee meeting in May 1939, that is before the Bill had become law, it was decided by six votes to four that it should be given a trial and that after it had become law they should seek amendment at the earliest opportunity. Royce was not present at the meeting.[22] However, five days later the motion was put to Council, the Federation's governing body.[23] It was lost by a large majority. Among those supporting the Bill was Phil Daley, who in later years became the chairman and driving force of the Access Sub-committee of the Peak Park Planning Board.

At the July 1942 meeting of the Executive Committee Arthur Roberts, secretary of the Liverpool Federation, said that evidence must be obtained that the Access Bill was unworkable in order to get it amended. Stephen Morton proposed that the Access Sub-committee should meet and concentrate on finding ways and means to secure an act which would be satisfactory.[24] At a meeting of the Sub-committee in October members concurred in the opinion that, short of a revolution in the attitude and outlook of those in control of the nation's social and political destinies, there was no hope of securing year-round access to mountain and moorland, certainly where sporting interests were concerned. Two methods of approach were open: (a) advocacies of complete access on the lines of Bryce's old bill; and (b) proposals for limited access which would be acceptable for a period and form a reasonable compromise.

They based their recommendations on course (b) which they thought practicable, although not the most desirable. They suggested a bill on the lines of the section of the Law of Property Act 1925, which gave public access to all urban common land. They had not changed their opinions about the trespass clause in the 1939 Act. Limitations of access should apply only during the grouse breeding and shooting seasons, with control of dogs during the lambing season. Such limitations should be confined to the beginning of March to the end of May with a further period from 10 August to 10 September for sporting estates.[25] The January 1943 meeting of the Executive Committee approved a memorandum on these lines for circulation to National Council.[26]

At a short meeting of the Executive Committee before National Council in April, Ward reported on an emergency meeting of the Access Sub-committee, at which it was decided to ask for a comprehensive resolution on access to be placed on the agenda. The committee refused to do this. Instead it decided to recommend to Council that consideration of access motions, including three already on the agenda, should be deferred for consideration at a special Council to be convened in September. This was agreed to.[27] Although no-one realised it at the time, that decision was to lead to a complete reversal of the majority opinion on the 1939 Act. Council appointed Barnes and me to the Executive Committee, which in turn appointed us to serve on the Access sub-committee together with Ward, Morton and Royce, who was to continue as secretary and convenor.

At their first meeting in May the sub-committee appointed me chairman and there followed the stormiest meeting I have ever known. Ward flailed his arms and thumped the table as he thundered denunciations of Barnes, who replied with quiet, rapier jabs. Points of order and threats to adjourn the meeting were useless. After three hours of wrangling Barnes, Morton and I outvoted Ward and Royce and decided to recommend an all-out campaign for new access to mountains legislation.[28] At a second meeting in July the Sub-committee considered a draft access to mountains policy based on the decisions of the previous meeting.[29] It produced the following policy statement.

1. The war had profoundly improved the prospects of achieving access to mountains, along with many other socially desirable aims, provided that in the case of access full advantage was taken of this opportunity by the RA. Council should adopt a policy based on a bold uncompromising declaration that lack to access to uncultivated land for harmless air and exercise was a social injustice which could no longer be tolerated. The RA should insist that the freedom to roam on moors and mountains was an elementary right of citizenship which a properly planned society should recognise.

2. The Scott Report[30] had declared that the principle that the countryside was the heritage of all involved the corollary that there must be facility of access for all. That should be the text of the RA. It should demand a government bill which would give general freedom of access to wild uncultivated land throughout the Island subject to adequate safeguards against damage or misuse.

3. If the RA failed to assert itself on these lines it would not only fail to secure any solution of the problem, but it would also seriously weaken the strength and influence of the Association in future.

4. The 1939 Act was unsatisfactory and unworkable except in districts where there was no real difficulty in regard to access at present. It would be a mistake to expand time and money in attempting to apply the act and efforts in that direction would fail to secure access in a district hitherto strictly preserved.[31]

The policy statement was submitted to the Executive Committee meeting in August. The meeting also had before it a memorandum signed by Royce and Ward. Royce argued that the policy outlined by Barnes, Morton and me was impracticable until the RA became a much stronger and more cohesive body. Ward and he recommended working the existing measure with a view to securing maximum benefits now and demonstrating the need for improved legislation later. Barnes moved and I seconded the adoption of the majority report. This was then discussed at length and a number of amendments made mostly of a minor textual nature. The only one of any

substance was to paragraph 4, which was altered to allow an application for an order to be made with the consent of Council where it
might be necessary to prove the inherent weakness of the Act.

When the memorandum was submitted to the special Council
meeting in October 1943 one of the strongest opponents was Arthur
Roberts of the Liverpool Federation. He argued that Council was
deceiving itself in thinking there was any chance of success. The
memorandum had no relation to practical politics. He thought two-
thirds of access was possible under the present Act and proposed, but
later withdrew, a motion asking for applications to be made under it.
Ward pressed for the Act to be tried, to convince the public that it
would not work and suggested it might be necessary at some time to
apply it to a difficult area to see how far they could get. No party would
sponsor an amending bill as a government measure until an attempt
had been made to work with the existing legislation.

However, the resolution finally carried nailed the Scott Report's
acceptance of the principle of access firmly to the mast and declared
that the government should, at the earliest possible date, initiate
legislation to replace the Access to Mountains Act 1939. Such an act
would have to provide a general freedom of access to all wild uncultivated land and to other suitable land, subject to proper safeguards
against damage and misuse, and subject also to the right of appeal.
With the trespass clause in mind, the National Council stipulated that
if after an appeal access was restricted or withheld, the law related to
trespass should not be made more onerous than under the common
law. A second part to the resolution, proposed by G. H. B. Ward, had
been added which allowed local negotiations for access to be pursued
in conjunction with the national Executive Committee and that the
machinery of the 1939 Act should only be used with its consent,
backed by a postal ballot of the National Council if necessary.[32]

That resolution shaped the policy and the future access activities of
the RA. There was still a hankering to try the 1939 Act. Ward in
Sheffield, Harold Wild in Manchester and Roberts in Liverpool,
among others, still maintained that unless it were proved wanting
there was no hope of new legislation. Those of us who said that it was
the duty of the RA to create precedents and not to be hidebound by
tradition had to wait six years for confirmation of our views. Although
Creech Jones's Act had never been applied, Section 84 of the National
Parks and Access to the Countryside Act 1949 said, 'The Access to

Mountains Act 1939 is hereby repealed'.

References

1　*Manchester Guardian*, 10 May 1939.
2　*Ibid.*
3　*Manchester Guardian*, 12 May 1939.
4　*Ibid.*
5　*Manchester Guardian*, 13 May 1939.
6　*Ibid.*
7　*New Statesman*, Vol. 17, No. 428, New Series, 6 May 1939, p. 684.
8　*New Statesman*, Vol. 17, No. 427, New Series, 29 April 1939, p. 635.
9　*New Statesman*, Vol. 17, No. 428, New Series, 6 May 1939.
10　*New Statesman*, Vol. 17, No. 429, New Series, 13 May 1939, p. 739.
11　*New Statesman*, Vol. 17, No. 431, New Series, 27 May 1939, p. 824.
12　RAA, National Council Minutes, March 1940.
13　Bowland [pseud], 'The act which somebody wants', *Progressive Rambler*, Vol. 1, No. 71, March 1941, pp. 20–1.
14　RAA, letter from Royce to Mitchell, 25 April 1940, in 1939 Access Act file, correspondence folder.
15　RAA, Executive Committee Minutes, minute 74/39, December 1939.
16　RAA, Access Sub-committee report, 1940, copy 1939 Access Act file, RA Minutes folder.
17　Kinder [Phil Barnes], 'The act which nobody wants', *Progressive Rambler*, Vol. 1, No. 69, September 1940, pp. 9–12.
18　Stephen Morton, 'A shabby act', *Progressive Rambler*, Vol. 1, No. 70, November 1940, p. 10.
19　Walter Tysoe 'Access Act must be tried', *Progressive Rambler*, Vol. 1, No. 70, pp. 17–18.
20　Edwin Royce, 'Who killed the good old Bill', *Progressive Rambler*, Vol. 1, No. 71, March 1941, pp. 16–19.
21　RAA, letter from Royce to Mitchell, 5 May 1940, 1939 Access Act file, correspondence folder.
22　Manchester and District Federation of Rambling Clubs, Executive Committee Minutes, 11 May 1939.
23　Manchester and District Federation of Rambling Clubs, Council Minutes, 16 May 1939.
24　RAA, Executive Committee Minutes, minute 205–42, July 1942.
25　RAA, Access Sub-committee Minutes, 10 October 1942, copy in 1939 Access Act file, RA Minutes folder.
26　RAA, Executive Committee Minutes, minute 249/43, January 1943.
27　RAA, National Council Minutes, minute 260/43, April 1943.

28   RAA, letter and memorandum, 1939 Access Act file, RA Minutes folder.

29   RAA, draft memorandum of Access Sub-committee, 29 May 1943, copy 1939 Access Act file, RA Minutes folder.

30   Report of Committee on Land Utilisation in Rural Areas, Cmd 6378, 1942.

31   RAA, Access memorandum, 10 August 1943, copy in 1939 Access Act file, RA Minutes folder.

32   RAA, National Council Minutes, October 1943.

Chapter 10

Stepping-stones

From a very early stage ramblers' leaders saw the importance of influencing government and public opinion. In the past fifty years any government committee or commission concerned with the countryside has been plied with written and oral evidence from organised ramblers. Even before they had any national structure, several ramblers' federations gave evidence in 1931 to the National Parks Committee.[1] A series of reports, beginning in 1931 and culminating in a flurry of interest in the outdoors during and after the 1939–45 war, show ramblers becoming increasingly successful at putting their views.

The National Parks Committee, 1931

Ramsay MacDonald, who became Labour Prime Minister in 1929, was a great walker. In September 1929 he appointed a committee under the chairmanship of Christopher Addison, MP,

to consider and report if it is desirable and feasible to establish one or more national parks in Great Britain with a view to the preservation of the natural characteristics, including flora and fauna, and to the improvement of recreational facilities for the people; and to advise generally and in particular as to the areas, if any, that are most suitable for the purpose.[2]

Ramblers were not conspicuous on the Committee and its report shows little evidence of consideration having been given to 'the improvement of recreational facilities for the people'.

Written and oral evidence was submitted to the Committee by many individuals and representatives of organisations including the Commons Society, the CPRE and CPRW, and the Ramblers'

Federations of Glasgow, Huddersfield, Liverpool, London, Manchester, and Sheffield. The ramblers' representatives argued that a national park should be large enough to furnish at least the greater part of a day's walking – say, twenty miles. This need not be continuous open space but the average rambler wanted to feel sure of a day's walk in natural surroundings without the necessity of going through towns or covering long distances on metalled roads. In the development of a national park nothing should be done to make the rambler worse off in relation to access to and passage over the country than he was before. Whenever possible, new footpaths should be opened up, especially as connecting links and to avoid roads – such paths were in no way inconsistent with allowing land to remain in agricultural occupation. Access to uncultivated land should be allowed as it already was on urban commons.

In the Peak District, the deputation said, seven million people were packed round a large area of private moorland which, apart from a few rights of way, was then almost inaccessible. The areas comprising Kinder Scout, Bleaklow and the Derwent Moors included 205 square miles, 85 per cent of which was said to be uncultivated. The national park need not interfere with farming and grazing, but they considered that it would be essential to purchase the shooting rights. In Scotland, they said, national parks were necessary in view of the encroachment of industrialisation on the countryside, and of restrictions imposed on public access in certain areas. In the selection of sites precedence should be given to a mountain district within easy reach of Glasgow and neighbouring towns; the Cairngorms and the Trossachs were second and third priorities.[3]

The views of other organisations on the question of public access are worth looking at as a way of sketching in the various strands of thought current at the time. The National Trust said preservation was a primary need; access, however important, only came second. If necessary or desired, access should be arranged when the places to which all attached value had been made safe.[4] On the other hand, Patrick Abercrombie, speaking for the CPRE, said, 'The recreational use of national parks should be the primary consideration.'[5]

The Central Landowners' Association and their satellites, the Surveyors' Institution and Land Agents' Society, said that where access to the public was given it would probably be useless to attempt to confine it to the use of specified tracks. On open land trespass could not be prevented without a large number of wardens. The value of grazing rights might depreciate if access were allowed, and the value of sporting rights would be destroyed or seriously reduced.[6] The British Waterworks Association said there would be serious objection to the inclusion of gathering grounds in national parks. The protection of the water supply must be the paramount consideration.[7]

The Commons Society was mainly concerned, naturally, with common land. They suggested a national body to arbitrate and conciliate in cases of dispute – conciliatory negotiations would be required if the goodwill of all classes was to be obtained and the fear of confiscation of private rights avoided.[8]

Some Scottish witnesses seemed strangely misinformed about prevailing conditions in Scotland. The Scottish Forest Reserve Committee and Association for the Preservation of Rural Scotland said, 'with regard to access, the people of Scotland are accustomed to liberty of range, and landed proprietors have not usually exercised a jealous exclusion'.[9] The Association of County Councils in Scotland and the Convention of Royal Burghers were not aware of any demand in Scotland for national parks. Visitors were incompatible, they said, with shooting rights in sporting areas. They did admit, however, that a demand for free access existed all over Scotland.[10]

The Committee's report, published in April 1931, had little to say of any value on the subject of access to uncultivated land. The Committee noted the growth of the open-air habit and referred to the ramblers' federations and the recently formed YHA. They thought that these tendencies should be encouraged but they did not, however, accept that the improvement of recreational facilities necessarily involved the acquisition on an extensive scale of areas over which the public would have the right to roam at large, though they did not rule out completely the possibility of acquisition of land.[11] A system of national reserves and nature sanctuaries would have among their objects the improvement of public access to areas of natural beauty.[12] The most positive paragraph in the report said, 'We desire to record our conviction that such measures as we have advocated are necessary if the present generation is to escape the charge that in a short-sighted pursuit of its immediate ends it had squandered a noble heritage.'[13]

The Scott Report, 1942

That time could be found in the middle of the greatest war in our history to appoint a Committee to consider the preservation of rural amenities was an inspired act of remarkable foresight. In October 1941 Lord Reith, as Minister of Works and Buildings, appointed a Committee under the Chairmanship of Lord Justice Scott, a good friend of the RA and the amenity movement generally.[14] The Committee was 'to consider the conditions which governed building and other constructional development in country areas consistently with the maintenance of agriculture and in particular the factors affecting the location of industry, having regard to economic operation, part-time and seasonal employment, the well-being of rural communities and the preservation of rural amenities'.[15]

The RA submitted to the Committee a lengthy memorandum which they afterwards published as a pamphlet[16] and was well-represented on a deputation which gave oral evidence. It supported the creation of a Ministry of Town and Country Planning with several regional planning committees. National parks should be established with a special central committee under the Ministry. This would appoint local committees for the detailed management of each park. There should, argued the RA, be a new access act giving real access to all uncultivated areas including water-gathering grounds, the fore-shore and the coast. All coast not yet built on should be acquired for the public and wild flowers should be protected nationally. In addition there should be numerous new footpaths and long-distance routes such as the Pennine Way.

The Scott Committee's voluminous report made many far-reaching recommendations, some of them obviously inspired by the proposals of the RA. They considered the growth of open-air organisations of various kinds one of the most praiseworthy developments of this century. 'Such excellent movements as the Youth Hostels Association and the Ramblers' Assocation, which have bought the young town dweller into the countryside, have afforded him many delights and benefits that his prototype of so recent a date as thirty or forty years ago rarely enjoyed.' The opening of the countryside to the townsman, though, had not been without its difficulties.

When people have for a long time been cut off from the enjoyment of an amenity they have to learn again how to use it for their own sakes and for the sake of others. And this the townsman had had to learn to do with the country. In the first jubilance of his reintroduction in the 1920s and the 1930s his conduct there was often regrettable – especially the townsman who is not a member of one of the open air organisations, for these have themselves done much to educate their members in country habits.[17]

On the preservation of amenities the Committee said, 'we regard the countryside as the heritage of the whole nation, and furthermore, we consider that the citizens of this country are the custodians of a heritage they share with all those of British descent and that it is the duty incumbent upon the nation to take proper care of that which it thus holds in trust'.[18] It did not, however, see a conflict between the nation caring for the countryside and the population being able to go into it, rather the reverse. 'The principle that the countryside is the heritage of all involves the corollary that there must be facility of access for all.' They qualified this up to a point – facilities for access should not interfere with the proper use of land in the national interest. The Committee recognised both the resentment which was caused by trespass notices and closing of access to the fields and footpaths and that damage was caused by visitors. They saw education as the answer to the latter problem, not exclusion. 'We consider that it is essential to extend definite instructions in the schools, urban and rural alike, and to carry on the vigorous wireless, press and poster campaign to educate the public.'[19] They did, however, note the efforts of open-air organisations to maintain a good standard of conduct – and wished there could be similar efforts by motoring organisations, as motorists were often the worst offenders.

The Committee made useful suggestions on footpaths, but from the ramblers' point of view there was a serious omission from this otherwise excellent report. It made no specific proposals to implement their declaration that there should be access for all to the countryside provided that it did not interfere with the use of the land in the national interest. Here, as in other quarters, there seemed to be an assumption that a footpath over uncultivated land was sufficient to meet the needs of ramblers.

The Dower Report, 1945

John Dower's Report on *National Parks in England and Wales* was the first government document to make specific, positive recommendations for national parks and access to the countryside. However, the foreward stated that it was published for information and as a basis for discussions. It went on, 'As is indicated in the Report further preliminary work is necessary on this subject. This is being undertaken and in the meantime, the Government are not committed to acceptance of the recommendations and the conclusions of this

Report.'[20]

The Report echoed many statements made by the RA over the years. This was not surprising, since Dower had many friends in the Association, including H. H. Symonds, Kenneth Spence, Cyril Joad, and Francis Ritchie* all of whom held RA office, as did Dower later on. I first met him at a meeting of the Friends of the Lake District at Keswick in 1938. Between then and the outbreak of war I met him several times and we met again in 1943, when I was press officer at the newly created Ministry of Town and Country Planning and he was there drafting his report. We had many discussions and I remember we disagreed about the Howgill Fells. I regarded them as among the finest hill country in England, but Dower gave them a very lowly rating in his 'Division B' – reserve for possible future national parks.[21] Some years later, after his death, I was able to persuade the National Parks Commission to include the Howgills in the Yorkshire Dales National Park.

Of Dower's masterly and eloquent statement of the case for national parks we deal here only with those paragraphs concerning access to uncultivated mountain and moorland. If the insistent claims of the ramblers' organisations were to be at all satisfied, he said, there must be a right to wander at will over the whole extent of uncultivated land such as mountains, moors, hill-grazing, and heath. Such freedom could be subject only to a minimum of regulation to prevent abuse, and to a minimum of excepted areas where such wandering would clearly be incompatible with some other publicly necessary use of the land.[22]

In his famous and widely-accepted definition of national parks he stipulated that access and facilities for public open-air enjoyment should be amply provided. Full rambling access, freedom of the hills, was a national park requirement, and every national park must contain a substantial element of relatively wild uncultivated land suitable for such access.[23] He referred to the Lake District, some 500 square miles where, by long-established custom, the fell lands were freely open to all comers. On the other hand, practically the whole of the enclosed moorland of the Peak District – most consistently claimed as

---

*Francis Ritchie became a member of the RA's National Executive in his teens and his involvement with the organisation continued until his death in 1988. He was an influential figure in the outdoor movement, sitting on many committees, particularly the Standing Committee on National Parks and, for seventeen years, the National Parks Commission.

a lung and a recreation space for the many millions who lived in the surrounding ring of cities and towns, the most urgently needed of all access areas – was kept emphatically, if not entirely successfully, closed to the public by their owners on the grounds either of protecting the grouse shooting or of ensuring the purity of the water supplies.[24]

Between rambling and farming he saw no major conflict of interest, nor any serious amount of trouble in practice. Farmers in most parts of the country did from time to time have just complaint about the small proportion of visitors from the town, few of them genuine walkers, who made a nuisance of themselves. Damage and interference would best be checked and reduced, and farmers' interests protected, not by hopeless efforts to keep all walkers off their land but by encouraging full access over all uncultivated land, so tending to discourage wandering in cultivated areas. Farmers should support measures to make such access a legal right – by and large they would gain more than they could possibly lose from access. Grouse shooting, he said, although it had produced more conflict and controversy, probably presented a less difficult problem than water-catchment areas. He went on to make a ringing declaration which ramblers have quoted ever since. 'When the issue is seen as a broad question of principle – whether the recreation needs of the many should or should not outweigh the sporting pleasures of the few – there can be little doubt of the answer; that walkers should, and sooner or later will, be given freedom of access over grouse moors.'[25]

On the question of access to gathering-grounds he said there were instances where access was severely restricted although there was full treatment for purification. 'One may suspect', he said, 'that grouse shooting and the rent and rates derived therefrom are often the main incentive in such cases.'[26]

After summarising the deficiencies of the Access to Mountains Act 1939, Dower went on to say:

if the popular claim to walk freely over mountains, moors and other uncultivated land and the popular need for a full measure of such health-giving recreation are admitted (and the Act clearly implies such an admission) then there is a strong case for the early introduction of new legislation to start, like the original Bill, from the other end – to confer public rights of access over *all* uncultivated land (suitably defined) by direct and immediately operative provision; to subject it to appropriate general regulations with penalties for abuse; and to establish a case-by-case procedure for determining any particular areas of uncultivated land for which special conditions are desirable, or even complete exemption from the general right of access.[27]

The RA welcomed the report as a valuable statement of their case. Here was a Daniel come to judgement. Here was a White Paper which might have been written in the RA office. At National Council in March 1946 Dower was appointed president.[28] When Council next met in 1947 Dower was a very sick man, but he might have attended had snow not prevented him from leaving his Northumberland home. He died at the age of forty-six in October of the same year after a life devoted to the very end to the amenity and open-air movement.

Report of the National Parks (England and Wales) Committee, 1947

Shortly before the 1945 General Election a Committee was appointed under the chairmanship of Sir Arthur Hobhouse* in effect to consider the recommendations of the Dower Report.[29] Dower himself was a member of the Committee.

The RA, of course, submitted a statement of its views.[30] On the subject of access to open country it said that the RA

can justly claim to be the only organisation which has ever made the winning of access to the uncultivated mountains, moors, heaths and downs of Britain a cardinal point of its policy. For many years we were alone in fighting the battle for access, and even those who might have been expected to be our friends were indifferent. But we have, through our long campaigns, succeeded in winning general support for our views and it has been a great encouragement to us to know that the Minister of Town and Country Planning shares our opinions both of the need for access and the complete inadequacy of the present Access Act.

This last sentence referred to the sympathetic hearing Lewis Silkin had given an RA deputation in December 1945.

The statement went on to urge the Committee to add its voice to the call for a completely new access act to replace the abortive measure passed in 1939, and that any new act should *provide access* – not set up

---

*Arthur Hobhouse began his career as a solicitor in London but took up farming in 1919. He was MP for Wells 1923–24. At the time to which Tom Stephenson refers he was chairman of Somerset County Council and president of the County Councils Association (England and Wales) and was on the Ministry of Health's Rural Housing Committee.

another cumbersome and expensive way of obtaining it by application.

The Footpaths and Access to the Countryside Committee Report, 1947

Originally appointed as a sub-committee of the National Parks Committee, the Footpaths and Access to the Countryside Committee was later asked to report directly to the Minister.[31]

In mid-May 1946, while I was still working at the Ministry of Town and Country Planning, Lewis Silkin sent for me, told me he was setting up the Sub-committee and asked me to be its secretary. This I agreed to do. John Dower, as a member of the National Parks Committee, heard of my appointment and asked me to spend a weekend with him at his home in Northumberland. He was then a dying man, but only the persistence of his wife, Pauline, prevented us from spending Sunday having a non-stop discussion of his ideas for the Footpath and Access Committee.

A few days later Sir Arthur Hobhouse bustled, with characteristic haste, into my room at the Ministry and said, 'You are the secretary of this new committee, aren't you?' I replied that I was, and he went on, 'Draft terms of reference and come and have tea with me at the Athenaeum Club at 4 o'clock and we will discuss your draft.' I did so and the draft was later accepted with some minor amendments.

After that meeting I had some misgivings about acting as secretary. It would mean that I would be muzzled and would much rather be a member, free to express my own ideas. Lewis Silkin agreed to this change, which meant that I would have to resign from my post at the Ministry, but I would have had to have done so a little later in any case, as I was under contract to take on the editorship of a magazine.

The RA's witness was Phil Barnes, who bludgeoned the committee with seventeen closely-typed foolscap pages of evidence. It included a general statement, a draft access to mountains bill and a memorandum which had been previously submitted to the Ministry of Town and Country Planning. The draft Bill may not have had the word-binding precision of a Parliamentary draftsman, but it set out in terms understandable by the layman the policy of the RA on the question of access to uncultivated land. Subject to a right of appeal, it stated, access must be general over all uncultivated mountain and moorland. No public authority or voluntary association should be put to expense in gaining suitable land. New legislation should apply to Scotland as well as England and Wales. The 1939 Access to Mountains Act, which satisfied no-one, should be repealed. The only limitations on access should be a period not exceeding twelve days in the shooting season for grouse moors and deer forests, or the withdrawal of certain limited access if there were a risk of pollution of water supplies. Access must be for the full twenty-four hours a day, not sunrise to sunset, and the so-called trespass clause of the 1939 Act should be omitted altogether.[32]

The Committee's report, when published, bore the distinct marks of the RA's hobnailed boots all over it.

In an introductory chapter the committee said

Over 80% of the 40 million people of this country live in towns and cities. Indeed, nine-tenths of the population occupy, with their dwellings, less than one-tenth of the land surface. But these town dwellers only make regular contact with the world of nature and clean fresh air with difficulty and expense. To reach open country at all is not easy for most of them. Moreover, in many of the wilder parts of Britain it is often the experience of visitors to be met with repellent notices 'Private', 'Trespassers will be Prosecuted' or W.D. Danger Keep Out'. There are to many areas where visitors run the risk of being turned off open moorland by owners or their agents, by water gathering ground authorities or by service departments.

'Where then can these people roam?', asked the committee.

The demands of the services for manoeuvre and training space, the anxiety to protect water supplies and the reseeding or cultivation of many thousands of acres of downland and rough pasture have cut severely into the wild open country that was free to the rambler in former years. As the urban dweller fought in the past for his urban commons and open spaces, so he and the countryman need today to agree together how best to achieve fuller public use of the countryside through footpaths and access to uncultivated land.[33]

The second half of the Report opened with a resumé of the history and law relating to access to uncultivated land to the Access to Mountains Act of 1939. The Committee thought that a new government measure was required which would be simple and comprehensive in its application, and at the same time bring the machinery for providing access to the wilder parts of the countryside into line with the planning machinery of the country as a whole.[34]

Land designated as access land should include all uncultivated land, whether mountain, moor, heath, down, cliff, beach, or shore. They recommended that it should be obligatory on the planning authority to designate as access land, subject to mechanisms for reconciling access and agricultural use, all such land and uncultivated land generally.[35]

It should be noted that this recommendation was unanimous, and by a committee which included, not only members of the RA, but also a landowner, a farmer, a county clerk and an officer of the Ministry of Agriculture.

There was a difference of opinion on the Committee on the question of providing for withdrawal of land from the access provisions in exceptional cases on the grounds of serious or wanton damage by sections of the public. Dower, Ritchie (also a member), and I opposed such a provision as we thought any damage would be caused by a few irresponsible people who were not likely to be deterred by withdrawal of access designations. Such withdrawals would not lead to effective exclusion of the public, and it would be unfair to penalise the public generally for the misdeeds of a few. The majority, however, held that such a provision would reassure owners and occupiers.[36]

With an exuberance unexpected in a White Paper the Committee summed up after their detailed recommendations,

If our proposals are accepted, and pass into law, they will confer upon the public a precious gift of greater rights and privileges. They will protect and preserve more simply and yet more adequately than in the past, the footpath engraved on the face of the land by the footsteps of our ancestors. They will provide long distance footpaths which may be followed for many miles away from the din and danger of busy motor roads. In the wilder parts of the country our recommendations will provide for the greatest freedom of rambling access consistent with other claims in the land. They will enable active people of all ages to wander harmlessly over moor and mountain, over heath and down, and along cliffs and shores, and to discover for themselves the wild and lonely places, and the solace and inspiration they can give to men who have been 'long in city pent'.[37]

Step by step

Such high aspirations were not, in the event, to be realised in the 1949 National Parks and Access to the Countryside Act, the end product of all this lobbying and deliberation. But the 1949 Act was not the end of the story and the RA has continued to make strong representations to such committees since. The results of all these efforts has frequently been disappointing. However, by these and similar stepping-stones, the RA has sought to cross the Slough of Despond in the search for Mr Legality, hoping that when found he would belie his reputation for being a cheat.

References

1   *Report of National Parks Committee 1930–31*, Cmd 3851, 1931.
2   *Ibid.*, p. 4.
3   *Ibid.*, pp. 72–3.
4   *Ibid.*, pp. 52–5.
5   *Ibid.*, pp. 55–6.
6   *Ibid.*, pp. 59–61.
7   *Ibid.*, pp. 62–4.
8   *Ibid.*, pp. 97–101.
9   *Ibid.*, p. 67.
10 *Ibid.*, pp. 90–1.
11 *Ibid.*, pp. 10–11.
12 *Ibid.*, pp. 18–19.
13 *Ibid.*, p. 43.
14 *Report of Committee on Land Utilisation in Rural Areas*, Cmd 6378, 1942.
15 *Ibid.*, p. iv.
16 Ramblers' Association *Proposed Post-war Country and Town Planning* [1942], pamphlet.
17 *Report of Committee on Land Utilisation in Rural Areas*, *op. cit.*, pp. 26–7.
18 *Ibid.*, p. 47.
19 *Ibid.*, p. 57.
20 John Dower, *National Parks in England and Wales*, Cmd 6628, 1945, p. 4.
21 *Ibid.*, p. 10.
22 *Ibid.*, p. 28.
23 *Ibid.*, p. 6.
24 *Ibid.*, pp. 30–1.
25 *Ibid.*, p. 32.
26 *Ibid.*, p. 33.
27 *Ibid.*, p. 36.
28 RAA, National Council Minutes, 1946.
29 *National Parks, England and Wales*, Cmd 7121, 1947.
30 RAA, National Parks, A Statement by the Ramblers' Association to the Hobhouse Committee, Tom Stephenson collection, file marked Memoranda etc.
31 *Report of Special Committee on Footpaths and Access to the Countryside,*

Cmd 7207, 1947.

32 RAA, Memorandum accompanying the Association's Draft Access to Mountains Bill; Draft of a new Access to Mountains Bill; Access to Mountains, Copy of a Memorandum submitted to the Minister of Town and Country Planning, Tom Stephenson collection, file marked Memoranda etc.

33 *Report of Special Committee and Footpaths and Access to the Countryside*, *op. cit.*, pp. 1–2.

34 *Ibid.*, p. 31.

35 *Ibid.*, pp. 31–2.

36 *Ibid.*, p. 34.

37 *Ibid.*, p. 44.

The National Parks and
Access to the Countryside Act 1949

In March 1949, Lewis Silkin, Minister of Town and Country Planning, received a large deputation from the Standing Committee on National Parks and the RA to discuss the prospective National Parks Bill. There was a lengthy discussion at the end of which the deputation realised that the Bill fell short of their expectations and there was little hope of improvement.

The Bill was published on 18 March and that morning a member of the RA staff was waiting for the Stationery Office to open in order to purchase twenty copies. That weekend the RA Executive Committee went through it line by line. At the end of their deliberations they had very mixed feelings; they welcomed the general intentions but were disappointed that the Bill departed in many important aspects from the recommendations of the Hobhouse Reports. Once again it was a piecemeal approach, this time leaving the necessary action to local planning authorities. The Standing Committee on National Parks appointed H. H. Symonds, Francis Ritchie, and me to brief sympathetic MPs and, where necessary, consult parliamentary agents on the drafting of amendments to the Bill. We decided among ourselves that Symonds should concentrate mainly on national parks, Ritchie on rights of way, and that I should deal with access to open country.

There was an amusing incident during our first consultation with a parliamentary agent. Symonds and Ritchie had had their say when I asked him to draft an amendment to embody the recommendation of the Hobhouse Committee that access should be given to all uncultivated land. The poor man was horrified and spluttered, 'Have the landowners no rights? This is not Russia, you know.' I pointed out to him that all we were asking him to do was to put into parliamentary language the unanimous recommendations of a government-appointed committee, which included not only ramblers but also landowners and farmers.

In the fortnight between publication of the Bill and the second reading, there was intensive lobbying at Westminster by the amenity societies. In one week I spent three afternoons at the House of Commons talking to various members. One of them was H. D. Hughes who was to prove at the second reading and later in the standing committee to be one of our most effective advocates. He lost his seat (for Wolverhampton West) in 1951 and later became principal of Ruskin College, Oxford.

The second reading spread over two days and during it, except for occasional visits to a cafeteria, Francis Ritchie and I sat through the debates. We often wished there was a free-for-all in which we could correct or refute some of the statements made. My discussion of the Bill here is restricted to those aspects of it which concern access to open country.

Lewis Silkin was not normally an impressive speaker, but he gave of his best in moving the second reading of the National Parks Bill and made what was probably the finest speech of his ministerial career. In a speech lasting one and half hours Silkin referred to the lack of access in the High Peak which was within reach of millions of people living in conditions of great congestion. The objects of the Bill were broadly to preserve and enhance the beauty of the countryside; and to enable people to see it, get to it and enjoy it. He mentioned Bryce's Access to Mountains Bill and the Access to Mountains Act 1939 which, he said, 'passed into law in a very attentuated form – in such a form that it was regarded by the amenity societies as entirely unsatisfactory and unworkable. Indeed, one of the main planks in their programme in recent years has been the repeal of this measure.'[1]

The most difficult part of the Bill to prepare, and possibly the most controversial, had been Part V relating to access to the countryside. 'I have not be able,', he said,

to accept the rather sweeping recommendations of the Special Committee under which the right of public access is afforded automatically on all uncultivated land, mountains, moor, heath, downs, cliff or foreshore, whether privately owned or not, and apparently unconditionally. I have come to the conclusion that where public access is in fact provided today – and I must in fairness say that applies to large areas all over the country – there is no reason why the machinery of this bill should be applied.[2]

He thought it worth considering representations made to him that local planning authorities should, within a certain period, make a survey of their access requirements, and enter into access agreements or orders, or acquire land to give the public access to open country. By this means 'ramblers will not be trespassers as long as they confine themselves to the land which is subject to the agreement or order, so long as they comply with the not very serious rules of conduct set out in the Second Schedule to the bill'. Those rules of conduct would have to be rigorously obeyed if the measure was to succeed. 'The public are being put on their honour not to do anything which would create wilful damage to the farming interest. For the first time in the history of this country there will be a legal right on the part of the public to wander over other people's land.'[3]

In his closing remarks Silkin said:

The enjoyment of our leisure in the open air and the ability to leave our towns and walk on the moors and in the dales without fear of interruption are, with all respect to my Rt Hon Friends the Ministers of Health and National Insurance, just as much a part of positive health and well-being as our building of hospitals or insurance against sickness. I am particularly proud to introduce this bill because it represents something which men and women have wanted for a long time and have struggled for, often with little hope of success.'

Then came the often quoted peroration:

Now at last we shall be able to see that the mountains of Snowdonia, the lakes and waters of the Broads, the moors and dales of the Peak, the South Downs and the tors of the West Country belong to the people as a right and not as a concession. This is not just a bill. It is a people's charter – a people's charter for the open air, for the hikers and the ramblers, for everyone who loves to get out into the open air and enjoy the countryside. Without it they are fettered, deprived of their powers of access and facilities needed to make holidays enjoyable. With it the countryside is theirs to preserve, to cherish, to enjoy and to make their own.'[4]

Had it been allowed, Francis Ritchie and I would probably have applauded such great aspirations, even though we had doubts about their fulfilment.

There was more than the traditional formality in the opening remarks of his predecessor at the Ministry of Town and Country Planning, W. S. Morrison. He said:

I am sure the whole House will wish to congratulate the Minister on having

survived a considerable mental and physical ordeal in the careful and
exhaustive survey which he has given in presenting this Bill today. That
Honourable Gentleman took us fully into past history and voiced in the
concluding passages of his speech so many of the aspirations which are
common to all of us.[5]

In the ensuing debate there were many references to access. The
following selection will give an idea of the flavour of the proceedings.
The first specific criticism of the provisions for it in the Bill came from
H. D. Hughes. He congratulated the Minister on the footpath section
of the Bill, then went on, 'I must say that I regard the access provisions
as the weakest part of the bill. I want to see that part strengthened in
order to put an end to the present uncertainties and anomalies.' This
Bill fell very short of the recommendations of the Footpath and Access
Committee.

He referred to Bryce's bill, which contained the 'simple principle,
that a human being should have the right to stand on his native heath
as long as he does no damage and that is the simple principle which I
would like to see embodied in this bill'. He quoted the Dower Report,
which had said there was a strong case for new legislation comprising
public rights of access over all uncultivated land and went on to say,
'that is the principle which the Ramblers' Association would like to
see embodied in this bill. I cannot see why it should not be done'.[6]

Hugh Dalton* also referred to Bryce on the second day of the
debate, and said that when he introduced an access to mountains bill
he was regarded as a hopeless crank, as was Sir Charles Trevelyan,
who tried to introduce bills from time to time. He went on, 'largely as
a result of the activities of the voluntary societies and in particular the
open air societies, as they are called – the Ramblers' Association, the
Youth Hostels Association and the National Trust . . . there has been
a great ripening of opinion'. Of differences between the general body
of ramblers and landowners in the Peak District he thought the
solution was only to be found in a very large measure of public
acquisition. The powers of acquisition in the Bill, he said, were very
strong and could be used if it should seem fit to the Minister and the
park authorities.[7]

However, in his speech Dalton also gave an illustration of the

---

*Hugh Dalton, Labour-MP for Bishop Auckland, was Chancellor of the Exchequer
1945–47. He was one of a group of MPs who accompanied Tom Stephenson on a walk
along the proposed route of the Pennine Way in 1948.

different views held as to what exactly was appropriate in a National Park. He said,

I do not believe that hydro-electric development in the long run damages the landscape . . . I remember, in particular, how very much impressed I was when I went to the Tennessee Valley some years ago at the way in which these artificial lakes have been created behind the dam, and how, although in the first year or two the whole thing was rather rough and around the edges of the lake nothing had grown up, with the passage of time around some of the older and more established ones there were both additional facilities for holiday making, fishing, bathing and so on, and an improved effect on the land-scapes.[8]

At the time the Central Electricity Generating Board was pushing a monstrous hydro-electric scheme for North Wales, most of it in the proposed Snowdownia National Park. The scheme provided for seventeen new power stations, 22 dams, 23 reservoirs, 80 miles of tunnel, 40 miles of hillside canals or leats, and 4½ miles of exposed steel pipelines. Among the enormities there would be the rocks burrowed from a tunnel under the Devil's Kitchen in Cwm Idwal; a power station at the foot of Ogwen Falls and the Nant Ffancon drowned under a reservoir 2½ miles long.

A week after the second reading the RA held their National Council and a public meeting addressed by Dalton, Silkin and me. I referred to Dalton's remarks on hydro-electricity and said I would like to take him to Snowdonia, up the North Ridge of Tryfan and up the Bristly Ridge on to Glyder Fach and over Glyder Fawr to the top of the Devil's Kitchen. If, after that, he still believed that there was anything man could do to improve that magnificent landscape, then the Devil's Kitchen was a suitable place to end the argument. The editor of *Ramblers' News* was perhaps only stating more definitely what I might have implied when he reported me as saying I would have thrown Dalton over the precipice.[9]

However, the debate in Parliament continued. Osbert Peake, Conservative member for North Leeds, who said his home was in the North Yorkshire Moors, had some strange idea about the 1939 Access to Mountains Act. 'The reason that the Act has been valueless', he said, 'is because it was emasculated in committee by its own promoters in order to try to meet completely the views of the Ramblers' Association.' After this curious reversal of history he went on to be supportive of the Bill. They had not heard, he continued, as much as he had expected in the debate about the attitude, sometimes offensive, towards hikers by farmers and gamekeepers. This was not altogether surprising in view of the damage and desecration which had occurred in the past. Public manners were improving, but he had known fires started carelessly, gates left open, dry-stone walls pushed over, roadside turf made smooth by rabbits and sheep cut out in squares and carted away; he had seen holly bushes slashed for Christmas decorations.

Considerable education would be needed to avoid this in future, but the only real conflict was between sport and agriculture on one hand and public enjoyment on the other.

As the result of long experience, I believe that this conflict is almost entirely imaginary, and I am quite sure it can be reconciled by wise planning and mutual accommodation. I know of excellent moors, Ilkley Moor is one, where Yorkshire men and others resort in great numbers both with and without hats. Ilkley Moor carries a wonderful stock of grouse although people are continually crossing and recrossing it on footpaths.[10]

The RA had, of course, often quoted Ilkley Moor as a place where ramblers and grouse appeared to mingle amicably.

Mr Fred Willey, who, as head of the short-lived Ministry of Land and Natural Resources, was sixteen years later to open formally the Pennine Way, declared himself a fell-walker or scrambler. As such he had committed an inordinate amount of trespass. He was one of those who had trudged behind Mr Dalton the previous May on the Pennine Way, a journey described by Mrs Barbara Castle as 'blazing a trail'. Personally he had found it more of a forced route march.

He would add his voice to the many who had sung the praises of general access and would always be a very strong advocate of this right being given to the public in the case of uncultivated land. As far as the owners of shooting rights were concerned, 'if it came to the striking of a balance I would say that the interest of the public generally should override the sectional interests of people who enjoy that sport'.[11]

A. L. Symonds, Labour member for the Borough of Cambridge, criticised the access provisions of the Bill – he would have all unculti-vated land designated as access land, unless there were good reasons to the contrary.[12] Hugh Molson, Unionist MP fo the High Peak in Derbyshire and therefore MP for Kinder Scout, on the other hand, was glad the Minister had not adopted the drastic proposals of the Footpaths and Access Committee. He believed that if a sufficient number of new footpaths were created, it would not be so necessary to make use of the access provisions, or to give a large amount of access to what was technically uncultivated land but which was in fact used for pasturing sheep and cattle.[13] Summing up for the government, Evelyn King, Parliamentary Secretary at the Ministry of Town and Country Planning, said the government thought it right, in contrast to the blanket provisions of automatic access, that they should obtain access first by agreement, then by order, and, if all else failed, by compulsory purchase. He agreed there was an attractive simplicity about the idea of automatic access, but he was convinced they would thereby provoke the hostility of agriculture, and that would be a grievous thing.[14]

As was anticipated, the Bill was given an unopposed second reading and proceeded to the committee stage. Standing Committee A, which dealt with the bill, met on thirteen occasions, starting at 10.30 a.m. and finishing a few minutes before 1 p.m. I had the task of sitting through the meetings, and I know of nothing more tedious or frustrating than to sit as a member of the public through interminable debates, unable to applaud a good point, or, on the other hand, to cry 'nonsense!'. One was not allowed to write notes, so the only way one could help an MP was to withdraw with him to the corridor. This meant that any briefing of sympathetic members had to be done mainly in the afternoon or evening of the previous day.

At the eighth sitting the Committee began to discuss the provisions for public access to open country. Silkin said the government had not been able to accept the Hobhouse Report's conception of making what he described as a 'blanket order' that all land which fitted the definition of open country should become subject to access by the public, and that owners should seek to get out of it by representations to the local authority and satisfying it that their land ought not to be access land.

'After all', he said, 'in the existing state of society and the law a person's land is his land. I think it is wrong to give the public an automatic right to go over all private land of a certain character.' He went on to say:

that where we are providing for access on private land the onus should be on those who seek that access to show that they need it, and that it is right that they should have it, rather than on the owner of the land to establish that there ought not to be access. That is the difference between the Hobhouse approach and the approach in this bill.[15]

At the next sitting, on 24 May, a clash occurred between Silkin and some of his Party colleagues. H. D. Hughes expressed himself deeply sorry that the Minister had not found it possible to accept the Hobhouse recommendations on access. 'I am', he said, 'even more alarmed and despondent at his reasons for rejecting it. I am afraid that the Minister's ideology as put forward at the end of the late sitting is over a century out of date.' He went on to quote John Stuart Mill who, in his principles of political economy in 1848 had said, 'The exclusive right to the land for purposes of cultivation does not imply an exclusive right to it for purposes of access.' 'Personally', continued Hughes, 'I prefer the ideological views of John Stuart Mill and of many socialist and progressive people who have struggled for the right of English people to walk on their own country.'[16]

A. L. Symonds spoke along the same lines.

I very much regret that the Minister has gone back to ideas which were discarded a hundred or more years ago. I wonder why he is so suspicious of the so-called blanket approach outlined by the Hobhouse Committee. After all, the Hobhouse Committee were not a collection of dangerous revolutionaries. There were members of the Committee representing the National Farmers' Union and the Ministry of Agriculture, and they saw no great dangers in the blanket approach.[17]

He thought that the provisions which the Minister proposed might result for a considerable time in there being less access than there had been.[18] Another Labour member, Anthony Greenwood, took very definite exception to Silkin's tendency to concentrate far too much on the privileges which the public were to have made available to them. 'I think', he said, 'that is the wrong attitude for this party to adopt because it has, in my opinion, been the traditional policy of the Labour Party that the public had certain rights in these matters, and that it would be wrong for the Government to regard what we believe to be a right as a privilege.'[19]

He remembered that the Liberal Party used to say 'God gave the land to the people.' He went on,

I want the people to enjoy that land as a right. I do not want the women in my constituency who work in weaving sheds, and the men who work hard, to be allowed to go on somebody else's open country as an act of grace or a privilege conferred by the landowner. I certainly do not like the Minister's principle that it is expedient to let sleeping dogs lie, and not worry about this because, perhaps, if we go quietly about it there will be more access land than there otherwise would be. I hope that we shall abide by the principle, so that the working people of this country can enjoy fresh air and quiet as a right and not as a privilege.[20]

Replying to these critics on his own side, Silkin defended his refusal to adopt what he called 'blanket access'; where the public already enjoyed access it was better to let sleeping dogs lie. He said, 'I explained, following the words of the sacred Hobhouse himself, that there is, in fact, no access problem anywhere in the proposed national park areas except in the Peak District.'[21] H. D. Hughes retorted that the access problem was not confined to the Peak District and there had been difficulties in recent years in Durham, Yorkshire, Lancashire, Denbighshire, Suffolk, and Hampshire, and he could give details of all these cases.[22] After this passage of open disagreement, the remaining sittings were concerned with less dramatic minutiae and details of administration.

During the third reading debate in July Anthony Greenwood moved an amendment which would provide that, unless there were exceptional circumstances, the public would not be excluded from access land on any public holiday, or Saturday or Sunday immediately following or preceeding a public holiday, or for more than twelve consecutive days, or for a total period of more than twenty days during the twelve months.[23] Rejecting the amendment, Silkin said that every single access agreement would have to satisfy the Minister that it was a reasonable agreement and that in all the circumstances it was giving the public a reasonable amount of access. Grouse shooting, he said, had been referred to as if it were an evil and that no facilities ought to be provided for it. 'I do not know whether it is or not, but it is certainly no part of the business of this bill to determine that subject and I am not in a position to do so.'[24]

The debate in the House of Lords covered similar ground. Lord MacDonald of Gwaenysgor, who moved the second reading, commented that it would be futile to tell the house that 90 per cent of the recommendations made by the Hobhouse Committee had been implemented in the Bill. Their Lordships would at once say 'Yes, but are you aware that the other 10% consists of major recommendations and, therefore, the percentage calculation is utterly useless.' Much as many were disappointed, he thought there was sufficient of the Hobhouse Report in the Bill to make it acceptable by the house.[25] The part of the Bill relating to access to open country would for the first time make it possible for the public to walk on private land without being trespassers.[26]

For the Conservatives, Earl De La Warr said there was virtually universal acceptance of the objects of the Bill. 'The objectives, he said,

are the preservation of the countryside, the diminution of spoliation, the opening up of greater access to the enjoyment of the countryside. When one thinks of that great body of 150,000 or 200,000 young ramblers organised throughout the country, who are today finding immense enjoyment, and who in future may get more, I think we must all be pleased. Looking at it from the point of view of agriculture, one must feel that anything which builds up a greater feeling of understanding of friendliness between town and country is all to the good.[27]

Viscount Samuel also welcomed the Bill but sounded a warning note. Might not this Act of Parliament be evaded, as they often were? 'It all depends upon the constitution and the powers of the various authorities that are set up to carry out these tasks.'[28] The Earl of Radnor said that if he were not quite so welcoming as other speakers, it was because he was apprehensive of the effect of creating national parks upon the area and the life of the people who lived in them.[29] As far as access was concerned, he hoped a piecemeal approach would be avoided. 'There is likely to be a certain amount of controversy over any access order as between town and country. If these access orders come forward one by one it will focus attention on each one individually, and one side or the other, according to the result of the inquiry, will claim a victory or feel defeated.' He was also concerned on the grounds of the cost of implementation, and concluded, 'I hope, therefore, that His Majesty's Government will seriously consider whether they can postpone the active operation of those parts of the bill which deal with the National Parks and Access Land.'[30]

The Duke of Rutland made a curious contribution. As an owner of property in the Peak District, he claimed to know that area fairly well, and, he said, 'I know of no farmer, or landowner for that matter, who is not prepared to permit ramblers over his land in those areas where it is unlikely that they can do any harm, and provided that they behave themselves.' Sheffield ramblers of the day would have had no difficulty in listing numerous areas where no such liberty existed. He went on,

I would like to ask the noble Lord who will be replying what sort of people he envisages will be asked to serve on the National Parks Commission. It is important that the National Parks Commission should be impartial and should be representative of all interests concerned. I sincerely hope that it will not consist only of members of the TUC and the Workers Rambling Association.[31]

As in the Commons, the Bill was given an unopposed second reading and went on to be a considered by a committee of the whole house, during which there was another fruitless attempt to bring in the amendment moved in the Commons by Anthony Greenwood. After the Lord's third reading, the Bill came into effect on 16 December 1949. On the same day the membership of the National Parks Commission was announced. It included Pauline, widow of John Dower, Francis Ritchie, and me.

References

1 *Hansard* (House of Commons), 5th Ser., Vol. 463, Col. 1463, 31 March 1949.
2 *Ibid.*, Col. 1478.
3 *Ibid.*, Col. 1479.
4 *Ibid.*, Cols. 1485–6.
5 *Ibid.*, Col. 1486.
6 *Ibid.*, Cols. 1562–7.
7 *Ibid.*, Cols. 1586–92. 1 April 1949.
8 *Ibid.*, Cols. 1597–8.
9 *Ramblers' Association News*, No. 28, Spring 1949, p. 2.
10 *Hansard, op. cit.*, Cols. 1599–1602.
11 *Ibid.*, Col. 1619.
12 *Ibid.*, Col. 1654.
13 *Ibid.*, Col. 1650.
14 *Ibid.*, Col. 1663.
15 *Hansard* (House of Commons Standing Committees), Session 1948–49, Vol. 2, National Parks and Access to the Countryside Act, Col. 834, 19 May 1949.
16 *Ibid.*, Cols. 840–1, 24 May 1949.
17 *Ibid.*, Col. 844.
18 *Ibid.*, Col. 846.
19 *Ibid.*, Col. 850.
20 *Ibid.*, Cols. 852–3.
21 *Ibid.*, Col. 854.
22 *Ibid.*
23 *Hansard* (House of Commons), 5th Ser., Vol. 467, Col. 1300, 19 July 1949.

24 *Ibid.*, Col. 1301.
25 *Hansard* (House of Lords), 5th Ser., Vol. 164, Col. 880, 18 October 1949.
26 *Ibid.*, Col. 887.
27 *Ibid.*, Col. 890.
28 *Ibid.*, Col. 899.
29 *Ibid.*, Col. 906.
30 *Ibid.*, Col. 914.
31 *Ibid.*, Col. 921.

1 Striding Edge, **1926**

2 The Cuillins, Isle of Skye

3   Above the clouds, Glydr Fawr, Snowdonia, 1949

4   View northwards from Scafell Pike

5 Used on the cover of a pamphlet 'The Right to Roam', published by the RA in 1964

6 The Trough of Bowland

7 The Howgill Fells

8 Wensleydale

9 Maize Beck near High Cup Plain on the Pennine Way

Chapter 12

Vindication

'You can't have ramblers and grouse', said an anonymous landowner in a broadcast in the thirties.[1] Ramblers disturb hill-grazing sheep, said many farmers. Ramblers traversing an upland gathering ground might pollute a reservoir and start a typhoid epidemic. Research has since discredited these and other fallacies regarding access to mountains and moorlands. The Duke of Devonshire, for instance, has said that since he allowed public access on his Bolton Abbey Moors the gamebags have not suffered. On Kinder Scout, despite the thousands walking the Pennine Way there are now three times as many sheep as in pre-access days. It is true the experts differ among themselves on points of detail, and some of them still regard the rambler as an intruder and an enemy of conservation.*

A three-year study by N. Picozzi on the Peak District Moors, reported in 1971, found that ramblers and grouse were not incompatible. It found that there was no difference between grouse breeding numbers on access-agreement moors and non-agreement moors; 'and there was no evidence that increased public access had led to a new sustained decrease in gamebags'.[2] The author thought that the

---

*Whether or not access by walkers to upland country is inimical to birds in general and grouse in particular is still a subject of controversy. The available evidence is, at the time of writing, being evaluated for The Ramblers' Association by Roger Sidaway, a former Head of the Countryside Commission's Recreation and Access Branch, now a freelance consultant. Early results of his work suggest that grouse numbers are largely dependent on the proper management of moorland vegetation and that the presence or absence of walkers is not significant. As far as other species are concerned, there is concern about a number of characteristic moorland birds, the merlin in particular. However, there is very little relevant research on the effects of human disturbance. Such evidence as there is suggests that public access changes the distribution rather than the overall numbers. That is, that species such as golden plover are less likely to nest in heavily used areas but that population totals overall do not suffer.

decrease in grouse bags in recent years had been partly due to poor heather management.

R. S. Gibbs,[3] of the University of Newcastle upon Tyne, interviewed thirty-five landowners, farmers, sportsmen, and representatives of gathering ground interests in the Peak District, Yorkshire Dales, and Dartmoor National Parks and the Forest of Bowland Area of Outstanding Natural Beauty. He endorsed Picozzi's findings and said that little disturbance was caused to grouse populations by public access. Research on an intensively visited area in Scotland had shown that grouse had become accustomed to and were to a large extent undisturbed by large numbers of people. It could be argued, said Gibbs, that public access during the nesting season could be beneficial as predators, particularly crows, would be scared off by visitors. His overall conclusion was that public access in general had not led to a decline in breeding performance and grouse populations.[3]

Gibbs also studied the impact of access on farming and dispelled some old notions about damage caused by ramblers. Worrying of sheep by dogs was feared by farmers. In the Peak District dogs had to be kept on a lead on access land, while in the Forest of Bowland and the Yorkshire Dales National Park dogs were prohibited by access agreements. Seven out of nineteen farmers in the Peak District had suffered from dogs worrying sheep but the proportion of damage attributable to dogs belonging to people visiting the area for recreation was likely to be low and stray dogs were often the major source of trouble. Even in the Peak District the cost of sheep worrying by visitors' dogs was not an important cost to the farmer.[4]

After surveying the cost of public access to farmers, grouse shooters and water authorities, Gibbs concluded that the impact of access was very small.[5]

I attended a conference convened by the Peak National Park Study Centre in 1979,[6] at which the Duke of Devonshire declared himself an unexpected ally of ramblers. The Duke owned the Bolton Abbey Estate which included one of the best grouse moors in the country. He declared a double interest as an owner of good grouse moors and as a keen walker. Arguments that had existed between the richer grouse-shoot owner and the poorer recreationist had gone as everyone had the same aim, to conserve the moorland.[7]

The Duke had spoken in a similar vein two years earlier at the annual meeting of the Sheffield and Peak District branch of the CPRE.[8] He then said:

we willingly gave access to moorland in Derbyshire. We have very good grouse moors in Yorkshire. It so happens that I do not shoot, not on any point of principle, but because I never hit anything. So when the Yorkshire Dales Park approached us about access (I am a very keen walker), my sympathies were very much for the access agreement. The keeper, the agent and my wife were not so keen on access to the moors, for people to be able to walk everywhere. But both from inclination and, at the risk of being priggish because I felt it was (one hesitates to use the word 'morally right') I felt it was right, as the fortunate owner of these country areas that one should share them and also to be perfectly honest, I knew right was on the other side and that I was going to lose the argument and if you are going to lose an argument you had better give way gracefully and as soon as possible. For a variety of reasons I said yes. My keeper did not think much of me for a bit. Anyway, that was some seven or eight years ago and now on our part of the Yorkshire Moors anyone can walk anywhere except on a limited number of days when they are closed for shooting. Well, it did pay. We got the goodwill of the people who like to walk and I proved my point rather triumphantly by 1971 with the best year's grouse shooting for over sixty years. Which goes to show that the old idea with the maddening and tiresome class overtones of the different interest of the grouse shooter and the rambler which I am happy to say is rapidly dying out, that both those who wish to walk on the moors and those who wish to shoot over them, their interests are not necessarily rival but perfectly compatible provided that there is just a bit of goodwill and a bit of give and take on both sides.

The views expressed at that Peak Park conference were as varied and almost as numerous as the interests represented. There were divergent views on the effect of public access on sheep farming. Paul Hutton, land agent at Blenheim Palace, said, 'if unrestricted, increased access were allowed throughout the North York Moors then the sheep farmers would be forced to leave'.[9] This sweeping statement prompted me to mention that tourism and sheep-farming had flourished in the Lake District and North Wales for a long time. The voice of experience came from Ken Wilson, the head keeper at Leadhill Estate, Lanarkshire. He said that this was a 23,000-acre estate of which 12,000 acres were heather moor and the rest white or grass moor. Sheep and grouse were the principal crops. The estate was in a popular area. Despite the large numbers who invaded the area at weekends and holidays, there was no evidence that sheep or grouse had suffered in the popular sites. Keepers whose policy it was to be pleasant directed parties of geologists to the high-quality sites on the estate.[10]

To ramblers familiar with the Peak District it was apparent in the 1970s that, far from increased access making sheep-farming impossible, there was an increase in the sheep population on Kinder Scout and Bleaklow. Thus if one sat down to open a lunch packet at the Downfall on Kinder Scout, several sheep would appear from nowhere waiting for scraps to be thrown to them. The increase in the sheep population was confirmed by Derek Yalden of Manchester University who spoke on recent research on sheep grazing on moorlands.[11] According to a census conducted by the Ministry of Agriculture, the number of sheep in the Peak District had trebled since 1930. This was so in the Kinder Scout/Bleaklow areas. In the period 1930–35, the mean number of sheep was 16,539 and in 1973–75 the number had risen to 48,224, nearly three times as many as in pre-access days. The density of sheep per hectare had risen in nearly the same ratio, i.e. 0.70 to 2.04. This was important in understanding the causes of erosion in the Peak. Dr Yalden reported that it had been found that sheep densities of only 1.8 per hectare could initiate erosion on grassland. There had been much discussion on the peat erosion in the Kinder Bleaklow area. Three likely causes were a drier phase leading to loss of vegetation cover; industrial pollution which killed the covering of sphagnum moss; and over-grazing by sheep.

In the ensuing discussion I said I was pleased to find that it was now accepted that ramblers had no effect on grouse nor was erosion always the result of recreation. The report of the conference says:

Dr Yalden confirmed this view by quoting Picozzi, who suggested that about 20% of the favoured grassland had been destroyed by sheep over-grazing. The areas people pass through, such as Grindsbrook in Edale were eroded on the path but this was not spreading. Even the spreading of paths on less tolerant vegetation, particularly that on peat; was minimal compared to erosion created by sheep.[12]

Neil Bayfield of the Institute of Terrestrial Ecology at Banchory said that the access given to walkers, horse-riders and vehicles had caused problems of erosion, but this erosion must be put in context. An area of 4,000 square kilometres in the Cairngorms had been surveyed recently. This included one of the largest wildernesses left in Britain. It also contained two of the main skiing areas in the country. In the survey the size, share and causes (where apparent) of any bare ground were recorded in several hundred random two metre square quadrats. On this scale, disturbance caused by humans was found to be negligible.[13]

Dr Bayfield returned to this subject later in the conference. He was concerned that too much education would encourage too many people to go into the countryside and we should examine ways of restricting use, especially where the carrying capacity was already exceeded. To this I at once responded saying that people could not be cooped up in towns like battery hens.[14]

There were several references to moorland fires at the conference. I have been interested in the origin of such fires for more than half a century.

On one occasion I had a brush with the Earl of Feversham who had previously been friendly with the RA. In the House of Lords on 19 April 1961, he said that in the previous year a fire started by a party of hikers on his land in the North York Moors National Park had covered six square miles of moorland and destroyed 3,700 acres of heather.[15] I thereupon wrote to *The Times*[16] asking what evidence he had for accusing ramblers.

I went on to mention that the Chief Fire Officer of the North Riding had been quoted in a local paper as saying that the fire was not discovered until 7.00 a.m. by estate workers, when, in a gale-force wind, it must have been burning for six or seven hours. He had also said that Lord Feversham was known to have had a permit to burn off forty-four acres of Bransdale moors on 28 April and that local farmers were astounded that such late burning had been allowed. It was more than likely that the 4,000-acre fire had been caused by the originally controlled fire.[17] Lord Feversham replied, accusing me of quoting an inaccurate statement by the Chief Fire Officer. The main fire, he said, broke out on 29 June about 11½ weeks after the controlled burning. He then referred to another fire where two local residents had separately given directions to a party of hikers; within an hour a fire broke out on the route they had taken.[18] This, I replied, was not evidence. As to the 11½ weeks between the two fires, there were records of moor fires smouldering underground longer than that and then bursting into flames.[19]

It is on such flimsy evidence that fires are often attributed to ramblers. A man with a rucksack is seen to pass. A farm worker or a gamekeeper may go the same way unnoticed, but if a fire breaks out it must have been started by the man with the rucksack – *post hoc, ergo propter hoc*.

With forest fires the rambler is again often the prime suspect. This was so in March 1938 when, during a spell of dry weather, there had been a large number of fires. The *Daily Herald* (then a national daily with a large circulation) ran a series of news stories with the caption: 'The Fool in the Forest'. I was given the task of feeding the news desk with daily paragraphs mostly gleaned from the Forestry Commission.

The campaign came to an abrupt end with this short story.[20]

TWO BOYS FACE FIRE CHARGE

Two boys, aged 9 and 12, are to be charged with having started a fire on private property near Forest Row, Sussex. Police and forest watchers patrolled Ashdown Forest yesterday on the lookout for fires which might be started by careless ramblers or troublemakers.

On the Sunday, the day before publication, I had spent several hours driving and walking round Ashdown Forest seeking a story. Never a rucksack nor picnic basket did I see. At the police station, I learned that two boys, boarders at a local private school, had started a fire with hopes of a holiday to fight the flames. Without making any definite accusations, the police also told me of a recent village dance. As the revellers were homeward bound in the small hours of the morning several bushwood fires lit up the night and no effort was made to extinguish them. That made a good story, I thought; not so the night editor. Hence the above abbreviated story, the spiking of the rest of the copy and no more 'Fool in the Forest'.

On the origin of moorland fires, there is more speculation than factual evidence. When the fire has burnt out, how can anyone possibly say how it was started and by whom? It might have been a match, a cigarette-end or a bottle left – of course – by a rambler, never by a local land-worker. I have tried to test these suspect fire starters. On a Buckinghamshire lawn on a hot summer day I have made repeated efforts to light a fire of dried grass and twigs of heather with lighted matches, smouldering cigarettes, a magnifying lens and broken bottles of various shapes. I have never created more than an instantaneous spark or a fleeting wisp of smoke. This may not prove anything but it increased my scepticism about fires being started by bottle glass. The existence of a piece of glass of the exact lens shape lying at the critical focal distance to ignite anything would seem to be a rare possibility.

At the 1979 Peak National Park conference, Ken Wilson of Leadhills Estate said, in reply to a question, there had never been a deliberate fire caused by a visitor, but two serious fires had been attributed to a careless gamekeeper, and to a shepherd burning a white moor.[21] John Lees said that in 1959, the shooting syndicate started a fire.[22] From the ramblers' point of view the most useful evidence came from Paul Hutton, but not in the way he intended. He said, 'in some instances, July fires can still be burning in November three feet down in the peat. Infra-red photography taken from the air is the only way of detecting these latent fires.[23] That being so, it could happen that a controlled burning of a moor in March, though seemingly dead, might only be dormant and liable to burst into flames in July or August.

Some of the subjects at the Losehill conference were also dealt with by the same speakers in a more technical document published by the Peak Park Board under the title *Moorland Erosion Study, Phase 1 Report*.[24] This was a scientific treatise with minute details such as the number of millimetres of peat on Kinder Scout eroded each year. After two years' study by experts, the Report sought to bring together existing information about the various facets of erosion, to assess their contribution to the present-day landscape, and to formulate suggestions for remedial measures.

There was evidence that the rate of erosion in the Peak District had increased in the last two centuries. A major cause was the disappearance of the big moss *sphagnum*. This and the loss of other mosses and lichens which protected the underlying peat and added to its growth. This loss was ascribed to soot from the smoke of factory chimneys in the surrounding industrial areas and pollutants including lead, zinc, sulphur dioxide, and acid rain. But this atmospheric pollution had decreased in recent years.[25] In the section on moorland vegetation, it is interesting to note that in the 1930s there were five gamekeepers along the northern edge of Bleaklow, where there are now two, and two keepers were responsible for the west face of Kinder.[26]

Derek Yalden again dealt with sheep densities and the result of over-grazing. He calculated that a sheep exerted more than twice the pressure on the ground that a man did. 'A sheep weighing 40 kg has a hoof area on the one side, one front and one hind (foot), of 43 cm^2 giving a notional pressure of 0.92 kg/cm^2 whereas one of us (DWY) weighing 84 kg and with a foot area (one foot) of 214 cm^2, exerts a notional pressure of 0.39 kg/cm^2. A sheep's hoof, being sharp-edged, is also a more potent cutting tool.[27] David Shimwell dealt with people pressure. He found that a number of visitors to Edale had trebled in the period 1968–79. It should be noted, though, that this figure is based partly on the number of visitors to Edale Information Centre, many of whom would go no further. More reliable were the results of monitoring at the entrance to Grindsbrook, which gave a figure for twenty-four hours on a Sunday of 2,331 persons (entry and exit). Fifty-two per cent of them were classified as serious walkers, that is those carrying a rucksack and/or wearing fell boots.[28]

Tables and diagrams were used to show the increase in width of the path on the Pennine Way between 1971 and 1980. At Kinder Downfall the minimum width had risen from 1·7 to 6·1 metres and the maximum width from 7 to 12·6 metres. The Downfall is the most frequented spot on Kinder and lower increases were found at other points.[29]

After dealing with footpath erosion at four points on the Pennine Way, Shimwell comments, 'it is from changes in these four sections that is derived the erroneous impression that recreation pressure is the major causative factor of moorland erosion in the Dark Peak in general. These four sections and the Mill Hill to Snake Pass section are simply those in which the greatest erosive effects of recreation pressure are to be seen.'[30]

This view was shared by Derek Yalden:

the scale of erosion caused by recreation is fairly modest; if there are 56 km of footpath with the bare width of 10 metres, which is an exaggerated width, there would be 56 hectares of bare ground attributable to this cause. Though locally significant, it is less important that the 648 hectares of bare and 2,202 hectares of half-eroded ground identified by the ground survey. Moreover, as its cause is obvious, and some remedies are already known, it is also less worrying from an academic viewpoint.[31]

At a seminar held at Losehill Hall in May 1981 to consider the report, Neil Bayfield said the eroded path amounted to only 0.4 per cent of the moorland area.[32] With such admissions of minimal footpath erosion, it is difficult to see how Derek Yalden could later write, 'the extent of erosion caused by moorland footpaths was one of our major concerns'.[33] In the concluding chapter of the Report he makes some suggestions for possible management to ameliorate erosion. He emphasises that they are only suggestions and not recommendations, and are put forward to stimulate discussion. Recreation pressures, he said, can certainly be managed and mitigated. This would include the provision of alternative routes rotated to allow damaged areas to rest;

re-routing of main paths away from 'sensitive' areas; and devices to limited the extent of use, to wit, seasonal closures, 'rationing', even charging for the use of particular paths. He recognises there could be practical as well as political and legal problems with such actions, but he evidently does not realise the full measure of difficulty or the volume of opposition they would create.

Can anyone visualise Kinder Scout ringed with an electric fence, entry limited to two points, each with a computerised gate displaying, as necessary, such notices as 'No Entry', 'House Full', 'Please join the queue'? Yalden also thinks the provision of harder walking surfaces would concentrate walking pressures, so minimising damage to the surrounding vegetation. Various materials have been used for this purpose, including heather, brushwood bundles, chestnut palings, and plastic matting. At Wessenden Head (incredible as it may seem), 'old road metal (waste from road repairs) has been used very effectively and has indeed concentrated the use and reduced the damage to vegetation.'[34] Secondhand tarmac on the Pennine Way! Could it not be classed as litter and appropriate action taken against the perpetrator?

The unforeseen volume of traffic on the Pennine Way has led to some ugly scars in a number of places. The amount of traffic shows that it has met a need. Instead of covering these scars with foreign material such as old tarmac, by periodic diversions and encouragement of re-vegetation it should be possible to make amends.

This minutely detailed research into erosion in the Peak District seems somewhat akin to counting the angels on a pinpoint when it is remembered that the Central Electricity Generating Board said in 1978 that it was considering a pump storage scheme in Longdendale and in July 1983 the Board said that 'there are no overriding environmental objections to the possible pump storage scheme'.[35] That scheme would require the construction of a new reservoir on open moorland covering forty-five hectares. This would mean the excavation of 1.5 million cubic metres of peat and depositing it on moorland lagoons covering another seventy hectares.[36]

Many have damned the course of the Pennine Way up Grindsbrook in Edale, seeing the sandy path as an eyesore, though to the artist it might make a useful and attractive line in his composition. To another that much maligned path might be a pleasant reminder of the thousands of pilgrims who have travelled it on their way to the Border and beyond. Some complain that the path can be seen from two miles away, presumably at Hollins Cross on the way to Castleton. They do not mention that from the same viewpoint one can see a road, a railway, an electricity line, a car park and two caravan sites.

The Sandford Report[37] has a photograph showing the erosion caused by human feet on this stretch of the path. Few people today know the history of this path. Before 1948 Grindsbrook was a secluded valley, its beauty unknown except to a few trespassers. In that year the landowner, Mrs Follick, opened a permissive path up the valley. A little later she wrote to me through her solicitors saying she would like the path to be the start of the Pennine Way. Since then tens of thousands of people have walked up the valley, some of them never getting beyond the first steep rise to the edge of Kinder. To me the broad path they have trodden in the lower part of the valley is no great eyesore, nothing that could not be put right by a temporary diversion of the path and some reseeding. The erosion is really negligible compared with the erosion due to natural causes. Walk up the bed of the river in its upper reaches and at every turn of the stream you will find a bank of bare earth. To a seeing eye, a far more dominent feature is a tumble of boulders beneath the edge of Nether Tor. Like the crags far above them, from which they have fallen, they should be the colour of the sandy beaches where they were deposited millions of years ago. Instead they are black with the grimes of two centuries of industrial pollution. Go to the summit of Bleaklow, something which the Sandford Commission never did. There a large hummock of peat rests on a plateau of sand speckled with pebbles of quartz. An interesting measure of denudation but by no means beautiful.

The idea of limited access is a vestige of the Wordsworthian fear of the Lake District being invaded by hordes of untutored Lancashire mill workers incapable of appreciating nature in her more majestic form. Like Wordsworth, some people think that artisans and labourers should not be tempted to such scenery. But others might agree with John Dower, 'there will have to be, from place to place, some sacrifices of those scenic delicacies which are only possible "among the untrodden ways", and of the completely peaceful seclusion which cannot be enjoyed by more than a very few at a time'.[38] The idea of protecting natural beauty and then prohibiting public enjoying of it is preposterous and impracticable. Even with the public enjoyment section deleted from the National Parks Act, and with each park policed by a host of wardens, great numbers of people would insist of enjoying what they considered to be their natural rights.

Willy-nilly, people will continue to visit the parks and money and means must be found to accommodate them without detriment to the landscape.

Let the last word on the subject be with H. H. Symonds, father of our national parks. In the preface to that superb book *Walking in the Lake District*, published in 1933, he wrote:

Many now preach the gospel 'preserve the countryside'. Let us then preserve it in the best possible way, by teaching as many as we can to use and value it; not by locking it up, or by making a museum of it, a kind of spectacle which a man looks at with his hat tipped well back on his head, as if it were a sacred picture, or some holy survival from a better past. 'Visitors are requested not to touch the countryside.' Nonetheless, born and confined as we now are, or at best among the sham gentilities of the 'Tudor Teashop' style, our problem is not easy; there is a risk, a certain crudeness in us. But we can only learn liberty from the use of liberty.[39]

The story of the conflict with the water authorities is told elsewhere. The Manchester Water Authority (now absorbed in the North West Water Authority) was content to supply its consumers with unfiltered water for 100 years. Now it takes water from Windermere, which, after all, is only a large marina with passenger boats, private boats, yachts, and other sources of pollution. The North West Authority, though, still only allows very limited access to Boulsworth near the north-east Lancashire towns. On the other hand the new Kielder Reservoir in Northumberland, said to be the biggest man-made lake in Western Europe, is regarded as a recreational area for fishing, Outward Bound courses, water sports, and nature reserves.

Finally, there is the question of the compatibility of ramblers and deer. Sportsmen have claimed that those timid, shy creatures are so far-sighted that a distant glimpse of a rambler may drive them out of a glen to which they may not return for several days. That has not been my experience, for on several occasions I have looked down on deer grazing contentedly. Nowadays, in some places in the Highlands, instead of stalking the deer they have domesticated them and are farming them for venison.

At a deer farm in Glen Etive a little boy climbed beneath a fence into a two-acre field occupied by three stags. One of the stags chased the boy and to rescue him, his 49-year-old grandmother climbed in after him. The stag turned on her and she had to be rescued by the farmer. She was taken to hospital with a punctured lung and body and head

The right to roam

wounds.[40]

So much for the timid deer.

References

1 See *Hansard* (House of Commons), 5th Ser., Vol. 342, Col. 800, 2 December 1938.
2 N. Picozzi, 'Breeding performance and shooting bags of red grouse in relation to public access in the Peak District National Park, England', *Biological Conservation*, Vol. 3, No. 3, 1971, pp. 211–15.
3 R. S. Gibbs, *The impact of recreation on upland access land*, Agricultural Adjustment Unit University of Newcastle upon Tyne, 1976, pp. 23–4.
4 *Ibid.*, pp. 13–14.
5 *Ibid.*, p. 34.
6 Peak National Park Study Centre, *Moorlands, Management and Access, report of conference* (Castleton, 1979).
7 Duke of Devonshire, 'Keynote talk' in *ibid.*, p. 10.
8 Sheffield and Peak District branch CPRE Annual General Meeting, 11 June 1977, RAA, Tom Stephenson Collection, Access 1 file, transcript supplied by Lt. Col. G. Haythornthwaite, Sheffield CPRE.
9 Peak National Park Study Centre, *op. cit.*, p. 17.
10 K. Wilson, 'Leadhills Estate, its management', in *ibid.*, p. 20.
11 D. Yalden 'Sheep-grazing on moorland, recent research', in Peak National Park, *op. cit.*, pp. 21–3.
12 *Ibid.*, p. 25.
13 Neil Bayfield, 'The Problem of erosion', in Peak National Park, *op. cit.*, p. 42.
14 'Concluding remarks', in Peak National Park, *op. cit.*, p. 48.
15 *Hansard* (House of Lords) 5th Ser., Vol. 230, Col. 620, 19 April 1961.
16 *Times*, 25 April 1961.
17 *Malton Gazette and Herald*, 15 July 1960.
18 *Times*, 5 May 1961.
19 *Times*, 11 May 1961.
20 *Daily Herald*, 28 March 1938.
21 Park National Park, *op. cit.*, p. 25–6.
22 *Ibid.*, p. 15.
23 *Ibid.*, p. 13.
24 J. Phillips, D. Yalden and J. Tallis (eds.), *Peak District Moorland Erosion Study Phase 1 Report* (Bakewell, 1981).
25 John Lee, 'Atmospheric pollution and the Peak District blanket bogs', in Phillips *et al.*, *op. cit.*, p. 107.
26 Penny Anderson and Derek Yalden, 'Former vegetation and vegetational Changes', in Phillips *et al.*, *op. cit.*, p. 43.

27 Derek Yalden, 'Sheep and moorland vegetation – a literature review', in Phillips *et al.*, *op. cit.*, p. 139.

28 David Shimwell, 'People pressure', in Phillips *et al.*, *op. cit.*, p. 148.

29 David Shimwell, 'Footpath erosion' in Phillips *et al.*, *op. cit.*, p. 163.

30 *Ibid.*, p. 164.

31 Derek Yalden, 'Practical interpretation', in Phillips *et al.*, *op cit.*, p. 240.

32 Frank Head, letter, *Peak Park News*, autumn 1981.

33 *Peak Park News*, summer 1981.

34 Derek Yalden, 'Remedies suggested', in Phillips *et al.*, *op. cit.*, p. 240.

35 *Guardian*, 29 July 1983.

36 CEGB, *A preliminary Environmental Study into a possible pump storage scheme at Tintwistle*, 1983.

37 *Report of National Park Policies Review Committee* (London, 1974).

38 *National Parks in England and Wales*, Cmd 6628, 1945, p. 15.

39 H. H. Symonds, *Walking in the Lake District* (London, 1933), p. vii.

40 *Observer*, 17 March 1985.

Index of names

General index